CATALOGUING OF INDIC NAMES IN AACR-2

A Study

D. K. Kaushik

O

ORIGINALS

AN IMPRINT OF LOW PRICE PUBLICATIONS

Distributed By:
D K Publishers Distributors P Ltd.
1, Ansari Road, Darya Ganj,
New Delhi-110002
Phones: 3278368, 3261465
Fax : 3264368
visit us at: www.dkpd.com
e-mail: dkpd@del3.vsnl.net.in

First Published 2000

ISBN 81-7536-187-5

Published By:
ORIGINALS
(an imprint of Low Price Publications)
B-2, Vardhaman Palace,
Nimri Commercial Centre,
Ashok Vihar Phase-IV,
Delhi-110052
Phone: 7401672, 7452453
visit us at: www.lppindia.com
e-mail: lpp@nde.vsnl.net.in

Printed At:
D K Fine Art Press P Ltd.
Delhi-110052

PRINTED IN INDIA

ACKNOWLEDGEMENTS

I wish to acknowledge with profound thanks the invaluable assistance extended to me by various persons and sources, in clarifying different aspects of the complexities associated with the names-of-persons from different linguistic parts of the country. In specific, I wish to express my sincere thanks to the following persons, for the help provided to me in the course of my research work.

Dr. D.B. Eswara Reddy, University Librarian, (Retd.) Acharya N.G. Ranga Agricultural University, Hyderabad for his unstinted attention, arduous and meticulous guidance and work in all its stages. Ineffable is my gratitude and sincere thanks to him for his transcendent suggestions and constructive criticism to embellish the study.

Dr. H.S. Rama Rao and Shri P.S. Sastry, both Director II (Retired), Defence Research and Development Laboratory, Hyderabad for discussing several aspects of naming, regularly. My colleagues Sri. K. Jayathiratha Rao, Dr. R.N. Biswas, Sri. G. Balu and Sri. A. Balavardhana Rao have helped me in several ways.

Dr. (Mrs.) S. K. Rait for sending her publications, from England. Shri A. Subba Rao, Scientist E1 in Insdoc, New Delhi- for getting me a few relevant publications from Bangladesh. Likewise, the Librarian, Karachi University in Pakistan also arranged to forward a few articles. The Director, Library of Congress Office, New Delhi presented me a set of the Accessions List - South Asia for 1995.

Prof P. Kamaiah from S.K. University, Anantapur (A.P.) and (Late) Prof. Kamleshwar Nath Gupta, University of Delhi - for suggesting specific line of action in the pursuit of the work.

Dr. Doris H. Clack, (Late) Professor, School of Library and Information Studies, Florida State University, Tallahassee (U.S.A.) for suggesting me the subject of this research. She had always been motivating me to continue working on this subject.

Dr. A.P.J. Abdul Kalam, Principal Scientific Advisor to the Government of India and my earlier Director at Hyderabad, Lt. Gen (Retd.) Dr. V.J. Sundaram, former Director, Research Centre Imarat, and Shri K.V.S.S. Prasad Rao, Director, Research Centre Imarat have always been supportive and encouraging.

My wife Dr. (Mrs.) Vandana Kaushik, Reader, University of Delhi had to bear a lot of difficulties, during the course of my research work.

D. K. KAUSHIK

PREFACE

It was during 1985-86, while I was a student of Master of Science in the School of Library and Information Studies at the Florida State University, Tallahassee (USA) that I came across a few serious inconsistencies in rendering the Indic names-of-persons in the catalogue of the University Library. These were brought to the notice of Dr. Doris H. Clack, then Professor and teaching cataloguing, in the School. She advised me of taking up the subject as a part of my Master's degree dissertation. As time at my disposal to investigate the problem, was merely less than 4 months, and sufficient interaction with all categories of persons from various linguistic belts was not there in a small city like Tallahassee, it was not possible to cover all aspects of the subject. Nevertheless, I was able to submit the dissertation, which was well appreciated by Dr. Clack and others. Unfortunately, she passed away several years before the present work has come in its final shape.

My experience of the dissertation made me fully confident that I could further go deep into the subject. After a few years time, I vigorously carried out my task of collecting the requisite material from different parts of the country, and including major minorities. I also located more research papers on the subject. My working in *DRDO* too helped me immensely in actively coming in direct contact with persons of different linguistic regions. In addition, my frequent travelling to different parts of the country, by train as well as by air enabled me in establishing good contacts with persons of various cultures. My visits to the offices of Sikkim, Andamam and Nicobar, Lakshwadeep, etc. in New Delhi brought further clarity on their naming systems. The collectived data was scientifically analysed and was given the final shape of this book. It is hoped that this work will be effectively useful to the cataloguers, bibliographers and indexers.

Importance of names of library catalogues has already been accepted. However, Indic names are quite unique as there is no fixed structure of their component parts and the stability of the words is less developed. In addition, usage of prefix titles and suffixes brings futher complications. Foreign influences exerted on the names-of-persons have added another dimension. The situation has become so much confusing that it can baffle even an Indian cataloguer. In this respect, it is stated that no catalogue code provides solutions to the complexities of the Indic Names-of-persons. The efforts made by individuals even with the full support of UNESCO, IFLA, IASLIC, and so on, have brought no relief to the cataloguing world. This work is being attempted to provide a comprehensive coverage of the subject.

Broadly, the work is divided into three parts. In the first part, sociological investigation on different aspects of naming has been carried out. Based on its outcome, rules in conformity with AACR 2 have been devised. In the third part, Accessions List-South Asia has been evaluated in the context of rendering the Indic names. It is found that about 6.1% mistake have occured in the List. Correct entries have been prescribed and proper explanation provided in defence of the correction. Finally, I wish to record here that I am alone responsible for any mistake which might have crept in inadvertently.

6th January, 2000

Devendra K. Kaushik
Joint Director,
Defence Scientific Information
and DocumentationCentre,
Metcalfe House, Delhi-110 054

CONTENTS

Chapter 1.	Introduction	1
Chapter 2.	Survey of Relevant Literature	11
Chapter 3.	Indic Names- Characteristics	49
Chapter 4.	North Indian Names	73
4.1	North India	73
4.2	Hindi Names	74
4.3	Punjabi Names	96
4.4	Jammu and Kashmiri Names	108
4.5	Muslims Names	120
4.6	North Indian Names in AACR-2	134
Chapter 5.	East Indian Names	141
5.1	East India	141
5.2	Bengali Names	142
5.3	Oriya Names	156
5.4	Sikkimi Names	167
5.5	Andaman And Nicobari Names	175
5.6	East Indian Names in AACR-2	179
Chapter 6.	South Indian Names	185
6.1	South India	185

6.2	Telugu Names	186
6.3	Tamil Names	200
6.4	Malayalam Names	213
6.5	Kannada Names	225
6.6	South Indian Names in AACR-2	237
Chapter 7.	West Indian Names	243
7.1	West India	243
7.2	Marathi Names	244
7.3	Gujarati Names	256
7.4	Konkani Names	266
7.5	Sindhi Names	274
7.6	Parsee Names	280
7.7	West Indian Names in AACR-2	285
Chapter 8.	Evaluation of the Accessions List	291
Chapter 9.	Conclusions and Findings	315
Appendices		
A. Glossary of Terms		325
B. Bibliography		331

Chapter-I

INTRODUCTION

1.1 GENERAL

India is a land of great diversity from the point of view of culture, with its society stratified into a large number of religious, ethnic and linguistic groups. These linguistic and religious groups settling down in different parts of the country had adopted different practices of naming their members. With the passage of time, due to several factors, further changes had occurred. In the present scenario, so many diverse practices of naming are in use that even within a given linguistic/ethnic area more than one practice is discernible. During the ancient and medieval times, names-of-persons belonging to these groups had largely consisted of single words derived from Sanskrit, and where they were made up of more than one word, the words were mutually qualifying, and complimenting each other with none of them standing intelligible or distinct on its own. Names so derived and considered as structurally unitary pose no major problems for the cataloguers and bibliographers.

1.1.1 Impact of Foreign rule

Seven or eight centuries of foreign rule, firstly by the Muslims and the British next, has despite its other devastating consequences, profoundly influenced the naming pattern in the country. For instance, the following changes have been witnessed after the establishment of the Muslim rule in the country.

1. Persian and Arabic words

As Persian was made the official language during the Muslim

rule in the country, certain Persian and Arabic words had come into common usage. In names also, quite a few of them found their place. In this way, names got corrupted. This phenomenon had been more prominent in those regions where the foundation of the Muslim rule had been firm. In the remaining areas the impact of the Islamic culture particularly in names, has been minimal. This change once brought about several centuries ago, is continuing.

2. Prefixes and Suffixes - usage

Several attachments to the Indic names-of-persons also came into regular usage. For instance, takhallus or the pen-name was suffixed by some poets and writers, in their names only after the establishment of the Muslim rule. Similarly, a variety of prefixes, denoting the caste or the profession, etc. were also employed in the names.

The contribution of the British rule has been many folds, in bringing changes in the pattern of the Indic names-of-persons. Important among them have been described as under :

1. Surnames or Family Names

The emergence of the British rule in the country, hadbrought in the usage of "surname" as the end part of the names. The most elite who had to interact with the Englishmen regularly, had started using surnames. As they were not in usage earlier, a majority of such Indians had started deriving the same from their caste, sub-caste or gotra. In addition, there have been other sources of obtaining the family names. Gradually, this strange practice of using the surnames in the rear portion of thenames was adopted by the other sections of the Indian society. Nevertheless, it had remained confined to the English educated people. Yet, the wide spread adoption of the surnames as the end part of the names has not come into the middle and lower classes of the country till the end of the British rule in India. As Western education has been given a priority by the Government, and more people are getting educated, employment of family names on Western pattern is taking place more widely during the recent decades. Still, it has not become universal in all parts of the country.

2. Anglicised words

Another discernible change among the English educated persons has been the occasional usage of anglicised words instead of their vernacular ones in the names-of-persons. Sometimes, both the formats are employed by one and the same person. In this process, it has been observed that many times, words have been so much distorted that it may be difficult to recognise them in their vernacular form.

3. Western transformation

Still, another major contribution of the British, has been that the majority of the educated persons have often shortened their names by representing all portions of the names by the initials, except the last word which is usually given in its full form. However, contracted names are not employed in the vernacular languages, as they make no sense.

In addition to the Muslim and the British influences on the names-of-persons, there have been Portuguese and French impacts, due to their continuous rule in some pockets in the country. As the geographic area under their control had remained very small, the changes are discernible only in those pockets. The specific transformation which has come about due to prominent Portuguese and French cultures, has been in the form or spellings in certain words used in the names-of-persons. Similarly, there are places in the country where Arabic settlements are existing. The pattern of their names-of-persons is quite different in these settlements. Likewise, there are regions located in the proximity to Tibet. Their naming pattern bear a Tibetan influence. This too has been included in the present research work.

The above practices have come from foreign cultures and in this way, Indic names have undergone changes practically in all the linguistic regions of the country. These non-standardized traditions have further complicated the subject of Indic names, particularly belonging to the educated and elite persons. To put in other words, more complexities in the names have crept in, on account of the enlargement of the modern educational facilities.

1.2 INDIC NAMES AND THEIR FEATURES

Indic names-of-persons are the personal names of the people of India and those of Indian origin. They appear in catalogue of the libraries where the publications contributed by the persons of Indian origin are stocked. In some books, they may also be present in series, title, etc. However, the wide variety of practices which are existing in different parts of the country makes the task of the cataloguer in deciding the entry elements, almost impossible. As various elements in the names-of-persons can occur in different ways, it is very much important to identify their structures correctly. If the structures of the names are not known to the cataloguer, the entry element chosen could be the father's name, in some instances, or an inseparable auxiliary in some others, or the village name of the author, etc. in yet some other cases, which may adversely be affecting the retrievability of the publications from the library catalogue. As author's name is and will remain a very important approach for locating publications, it becomes imperative that they are rendered logically and unequivocally.

1.3 PROBLEM

A modern Indic name-of-person seldom consists of a single word, and hence, it is essential to know which part of the name carries the greatest potency. Furthermore, it is also necessary to understand the selection as well as the relative succession of the parts or the elements in the name for the purpose of the main entry or filing words in the catalogue (Sengupta, 1958). As they vary from one region to another, it is desirable to study them from the linguistic point of view. In addition, there are names starting with prefix titles which are needed to be dropped in a cataloguing system as they may be denoting specific features such as caste, profession, religion, or social status, etc. On the other hand, there had been Indian titles conferred on a few natives, by the erstwhile British rulers, which have to be retained in an inverted order in AACR 2. Likewise, there are several attachments in the names used as suffixes. Some of them are impotent non-essential elements. They are dropped out in cataloguing. Similarly, there are essential but less-potent words which have to be retained in cataloguing, in subordination to the other parts.

Adding, dropping, or changing family names in the names have also been observed in rare instances by specific individuals in different phases of their life. These are causing headaches to the cataloguers, in bringing all the works of a single author together.

Splitting the personal names against the canons of the local grammar, is another major problem encountered by the cataloguers. If a name is so splitted that its essential elements are reduced into initials, except the last part, the results may be quite ridiculous, in many instances.

In some regions of the country, there are persons using the name of their village as the last part of their names. Yet, there are some other linguistic regions where the first part of the names represents the name of their place of origin.

Another variety of complexities can be observed as certain people do not adhere to the known standardized pattern of their names prevailing in their area. This may usually arise after the person comes in close contacts with different cultural groups. In this way, either additional features are added or deleted in some cases, or some rearrangement of different elements takes place.

Naming the persons whose fore-fathers immigrated to another linguistic region ages ago, has also been influenced by the prevailing practices, in some cases, of naming persons in the new area, and in this way, a new category of the names has come into existence. On the other hand, there are families with a similar background who have continued to adhere to their original practice of naming even after settling permanently in the new place, and living there for a very long period of time.

Some persons deviate in the matter of writing their names from the known prevailing practice of naming in the region. Similarly, there are some individuals who use academic degrees, and titles on the pattern of surnames in the Western sense.

Besides the major problems associated with Indic names described above, there have been many more instances in which a cataloguer gets easily confused. These have also been studied, and proper guidelines have been provided. These will help a cataloguer to deal Indic names, correctly.

1.4 OBJECTIVES

The objectives of the study are:

a) Studying the structures of modern names-of-persons from different parts of the country, in order to identify the most potent part for the purposes of cataloguing.

b) Framing and/or modifying cataloguing rules in AACR 2 for entering modern Indic names.

1.5 HYPOTHESIS

Despite continuous efforts by several scholars, the major problems of the Indic names-of-persons in cataloguing, could not be resolved mainly because of the absence or near absence of the sociological investigation, prior to the formulation of the cataloguing rules. This has resulted in prescribing inadequate treatment, or formulating vague rules of the cataloguing. Hence, in the present research work, the hypothesis has been framed, in the following words :

"A sociological frame-of-reference of the Indic names-of- persons has a direct bearing on the formulation of the rules of cataloguing for the personal name entries."

1.6 METHODOLOGY

It is evident from the above discussion that framing of cataloguing rules for rendering Indic names-of-persons can not be accomplished, logically and correctly without having a proper understanding of the sociological aspects of naming in all the regions of the country. The hypothesis framed for this research also directs investigation of the names-of-persons from the stand point of sociology. Ranganathan (1952), the doyen of Library Science, has also expressed a similar view which is reproduced as under :

"A knowledge of the sociology and the linguistics of personal names is necessary to design rules for the rendering of the names of personal authors in entries of catalogues and bibliographies. It is helpful not only to know the present practice in naming persons but also to know the evolution of the practice. While a knowledge of the findings on this subject is useful to the designers of catalogue codes, the research in the subject does not fall within their purview."

The present research work has been undertaken in order to bridge the existing gap between the cataloguers on one side, and sociologists on the other. In the first part of the work, names have been studied from the point of view of sociology. Relevant examples have been cited so as to bring more clarity. Linguistic aspects of naming, have been ignored. In the end of each chapter, discussion on the sociological investigation has been summarised, and major findings have been reported.

For the present study, names-of-persons have been chosen irrespective of the fact whether they denote real authors or not. For this purpose, India Who's Who was taken as a standard source of supplying the information. Three editions of the publication have been utilised (Infa, 1972; 1982; and 1992). The other sources providing biographical data have also been consumed. Also, a questionnaire was specifically designed for obtaining more detailed information from people of various states. In addition, personal collection of data was also done by meeting the persons of different areas of the country.

Data obtained in the manner described as above has become the basic input for analysis and further processing. It has been processed, by grouping them together according to the similarity in their structures. Theoretical explanations have been provided from a variety of existing sociological books. However, only a limited number of such publications were consulted. The experiences of professionals as reported in different library science journals, conference proceedings, etc. have been exhaustively studied and cited. Findings have been presented, and based on them, specific rules for their correct rendering in AACR 2 have been prescribed. In addition, guidelines have been provided to help a cataloguer to treat them properly.

After the above study on the structures of Indic names has been completed, "Accessions List : South Asia" for 1995 has been evaluated from the point of view of rendering Indic names. The outcome of this exercise has enabled to test the validity of the hypothesis.

1.7 SCOPE OF THE WORK

The work covers the entire country except the seven states situated in the North-East. The states excluded from the study are Arunachal Pradesh, Assam, Manipur, Meghalaya, Mizoram, Nagaland and Tripura. The reason for non-inclusion of the North East states, has been the fact that a doctorate has recently been awarded by Manipur University in consideration of the work in this area (Madhuri Devi, 1993). This thesis has discussed in detail, the problems of the names-of-persons from the North-Eastern parts in cataloguing and based on the study, solutions have been provided.

Names-of-persons of both the sexes, from the point of view of structure, have been studied and it has been investigated as to how the names of females change after marriage. However, names-of-persons belonging to major religions have been covered. A few minorities having an insignificant demographic proportion, have been included, if it was found that such groups are important from the cataloguing point of view. Based on these considerations, the linguistic regions along with different religious communities, have been studied. The presentation of the work has been done in the following chapters:

S.No.	Name of the chapter	Remarks if any
1.	Introduction	Statement of the problem, scope, methodology, and planning and presentation

2. Survey of relevant literature (including treatment by AACR 2)

3. Indic names - characteristics

S.No.	Name of the Chapter	Linguistic Regions	Religions
4.	North Indian Names	Hindi, Punjabi, Jammu and Kashmiri including Kashmiri, Ladakhi and Dogri. In addition, Muslims have been dealt with separately.	Hindus, Muslims, Sikhs, Buddhists, Jains
5.	East Indian Names	Bengali, Oriya, Sikkimi including Nepali, Bhutia and Lepcha, and Andaman and Nocobari including aborigines.	Hindus,Muslims Buddhists, Christians
6.	South Indian Names		Hindus, Muslims, Christian
7.	West Indian Names		Hindus, Muslims, Christians Parsees

8. Evaluation of the Accessions List.

9. Conclusion and findings.

Apart from the chapters described above, two appendices have been provided. Their details are given as under :

Appendix A - Glossary of terms.

Appendix B - Bibliography.

In the coverage of the work, phonetic variations in the names-of-persons have not been included. Thus, In the text of this thesis, spellings of the names have been retained as they are found to be in use. Hence, in some cases, variation in the spellings of one and the same name, has come into existence. Pseudonyms and nicknames have been kept out of the scope of this work. In this research work, only modern Indic names-of-persons have been covered. The period of time has been defined as modern if the bearer of the name has flourished in or after 1900. The reason for selecting the turn of the century as the cut-off year, has been the fact that the British rule in the country had stabilized by then, and because of it, naming pattern was getting settled in favour of the new order. After the study was over, distinct cataloguing rules were framed and proper guidelines were provided for the users of AACR 2.

In this context, it may be added that the latest edition of AACR 2, generally referred to as AACR 2R has been used. As there is no difference in the provisions for the Indic names in the two editions, and in view of the fact that AACR 2 continues to be used widely in the libraries in the country, the work takes into consideration AACR 2R. Therefore, in the text of this thesis wherever AACR 2 is appearing, it should be taken to denote AACR 2R.

1.8 SUMMARY

Indic names-of-persons, as can be seen from the above description, are a bewildering ambiguity to a cataloguer. It is because the names can be formed in any possible sequence. There are no set rules in AACR 2 for identifying the parts of Indic names. The problems are further accentuated because of the personal choice of many individuals, based on other considerations. Therefore, this study on Indic names will be useful to the cataloguers, bibliographers and indexers. It would provide a pragmatic approach in analysing different elements of Indic names so as to enable them to pick up the most potent part in the same, for entering in a cataloguing system. Earlier, there have been some efforts to deal with the problem. In almost in all these efforts, sociological aspects of naming were not considered. Hence, all the studies were proved inadequate. It is hoped that the findings of the present research work, would render help to the cataloguers, bibliographers and indexers in dealing Indic names logically and rationally.

Chapter II

SURVEY OF RELEVANT LITERATURE

2.1 GENERAL

The review of the relevant literature is presented in three parts. Part one dealing with the publications contributing to the cataloguing and indexing aspects of Indic names, are cited and discussed in a more or less chronological order. In the second part, popular publications of general nature are included which throw a light on the complexities associated with the names in each linguistic region of the country. Part three of this review critically examines all the provisions in AACR 2 in handling modern Indic names-of-persons. Collectively, the three parts reflect the author's efforts to put forth a comprehensive survey of the literature aimed at enlarging the understanding of the subject by the cataloguers and indexers.

2.2 EARLIER ATTEMPTS

Perhaps, Ernst Haas, the compiler of the 'Catalogue of Sanskrit and Pali Books' in the British Museum was one among the first few British bibliographers who had encountered difficulties in rendering the Indic names-of-persons. In the preface of the compilation, he (Haas, 1876) recorded that Indic names were in "direct contrast to the Euro-pean usage". His further observations were expressed in the following words :

"Family names in our sense of the word do not exist in India. The tendency to establish them here and there has become observable only in our own days, and is still far from being widely imitated; for our purpose this should accordingly be left out of account. The consequence is that each component part of a name is of equal importance in our eyes, and names have to be taken in their totality and in the same order in which they stand, with the exception of course, of titles of honour prefixed to a name.

...Although we recognize the subordinate position of one part or the other in Hindu names, in as much as they only serve to distinguish persons of the same common-birth name, it has been found impracticable to mark their position outwardly,... Clearly, the simplest rule for treating Hindu names is therefore to take them as they stand, without making any difference between nomen, praenomen, cognomen, or agnomen."

The result of the above prescription has been quite queer in respect of many names-of-persons. Yet, the decision to treat an Indic name in its natural sequence, was not disputed by any one. On the basis of the above simple rule of Dr. Haas, another publication entitled "Catalogue of the Bengali Books" was compiled by Blumhardt (1886). This however, had evoked a strong protest against this unusual native practice of the British Museum Library. The protest has been recorded in the following words (Book review, 1887) :

"....of the three names which generally constitute the full appellation of a native of India - the personal name, the father's name, and the caste title, original village name or other analogous designation, - he [Blumhardt] has given the precedence to the first, though the tendency is now amongst the English speaking Bengalis, as it is in fact all over India, especially amongst the Marathas, also to a great extent amongst the Parsis, to make hereditary and distinctive the third appellation, and, to all intents and purposes to convert it into a regular surname of European style. So, also, the natives of India are gradually introducing more and more, the custom of referring to each other, in the regular European style, by this surname in full, and only the initials of the two preceding names. Any one who has had personal and practical experience of India and all the surroundings of life in that country, knows how much easier it is to recall any particular Hindu to his recollection by, or at least chiefly with the help of, this third distinctive appellation. And it is much to be hoped that, in any revision of the present catalogue, and in the first preparation of any other on the same plan, the surnames, and not the personal names, will be made the basis of the arrangement. It would be difficult enough to turn up even English books, if one had to search for them through the 'Christian names' of the authors, and the difficulty is greater in the case of works by foreign writers, whose first names are perfectly strange and unfamiliar."

The reply to the above protest was given by Cecil Bendall (1887) of the British Museum who had opined that it was appropriate to render an Indic name-of-person under the given name and not under the family name. Perhaps, he was not aware that Indic names could not be handled with such a generalised sweeping prescription.

In the next supplement to the Catalogue of Sanskrit and Pali Books published in 1893, the same general principle of rendering Indic names, as was adopted by Dr. Haas, was continued, but with two exceptions, described as under (Bendall, 1893) :

1. The Bengali (and North Indian) addition of the word "Sharmaṇ" (Brahmin) after the personal name had been disregarded, as conveying no useful new information, the vast majority of Sanskrit writers then being of the highest caste.

2. In the South Indian names, Dr. Haas's plan of cataloguing such names under initials had been departed from. The author instanced by him as (T. Krishnasvamy Iyer) then appeared as Krishnasvamy Iyer (T.), the name designated by the initial being regarded as in some sort, an epithet... It had reduced the cataloging of Indic names to a principle at once more simple and, "as I venture to think, more scientific than that of taking them 'as they stand', viz that all Indians should be catalogued under the personal names".

In the Catalogue of Hindustani Books, published in 1889, the method of rendering the Muslim names was disclosed, which is described as under (Blumhardt, 1889) :

(a) All Muslim names were entered under the personal names.

(b) The patronymic and Nisbah were added only when they were considered necessary.

(c) Takhallus or the pen-names were invariably retained but in subordination to the given names.

(d) Prefix titles were preserved only when considered necessary, for purposes of differentiation, or when an author was usually known by such title.

The above described details, bring out one fundamental point that the nineteenth century foreign cataloguers were ignorant of the prevailing structures of Indic names-of-persons. That was the period when the British rule in the country was in the formative stages. The pattern of naming was also gradually getting influenced by the British culture, and the structures of the Indic names were in the process of getting stabilized. The views of the British cataloguers and the specific practices being followed by them in handling Indic names-of-persons, reveal their non-familiarity in the subject.

It may be added here that during the nineteenth century, and a few decades thereafter, several cataloguing codes were designed by eminent cataloguers. However, they had either remained silent on the issue, or at the most, few codes had prescribed the rules for handling Indic names-of-persons, rather vaguely. Yet, some cataloguing codes had gone even to the extent of clubbing them with the Oriental names. Therefore, to a library cataloguer, the subject of Indic names had remained undefined. The net result of this confusion had brought out chaos in almost all the catalogues. Instead of being a serving tool, a catalogue of that time, had thus become inadvertently, an instrument of misguiding the users, in many instances. In other words, searching a publication by the name of its contributor had become almost impossible.

2.3 RANGANATHAN'S EARLIER CONTRIBUTION

With the emergence of Ranganathan on the horizons of the library science in India, the subject caught his attention. This had occurred while designing the Classified Catalogue Code. In its first edition in 1934, Ranganathan had enumerated the features of the Indic names-of-persons creating problems in cataloguing. They are listed as given below (Ranganathan, 1964):

1. The number of words in it;
2. Their grammatical nature;
3. Their functions;
4. Their sequence;
5. Their relative potency in alphabetisation; and
6. The complexities in their structure.

In the light of the above mentioned problem areas, names from different linguistic regions of the country were analysed and based on the same, Ranganathan was able to prescribe rules governing Hindu and Muslim names from the stand point of their structure, more elaborately than any other catalogue code did earlier. After the publication of the Classified Catalogue Code in 1934, he carried out further research in the subject. His contribution however, was the result of the work carried out for almost two decades, practically single handed. Thereafter, several other cataloguers had emerged on to the scene, and their findings in different facets of the subject brought more clarity. Ranganathan (1938) had also brought out the "Theory of Library Catalogue" which included a chapter on Hindu homonyms and Muslim names. Another book of Ranganathan (1950) discussed Hindu names of the authors.

Though Ranganathan was a naturalised citizen of the country, but considering the vast magnitude of the work involved in handling names-of-persons, from all parts of the country, and covering all religions he was fully aware of his own limitations. Hence, in 1934, he made an appeal to the library professionals in the country, to compile directories of the names consisting of personal names, caste names, house or other kinds of patronymic ones in different parts of the country (Saxena, 1952). This appeal however, has had only a limited response.

Sivaraman (1940) gave his views on the subject. A joint contribution by Ranganathan and Sivaraman (1940), analysed the faults committed by the British cataloguers in entering the Hindu names- of-persons. The authors pleaded to take the Classified Catalogue Code as a standard guide for entering a Hindu name.

2.4 UNESCO PROJECT ON ASIAN NAMES

A parallel endeavour of Ranganathan had been to take up the issue of cataloguing of the Indic names-of-persons at the international level. He was successful in obtaining a "Project on Asian Names" sanctioned by the United Nations Educational, Scientific and Cultural Organization (Unesco), in 1951. Dr. S.R.Ranganathan was named as the Rapporteur-General of the Project. Bhattacharyya (1969) described the series of events concerning the Project, in the following words :

"On 25 March 1951, a meeting of the Second Conference of the Indian National Commission for Unesco held in Delhi under the Chairmanship of Torres-Bodet, the Director General of Unesco, approved the following resolution of Ranganathan:

'That an Asian Committee be set up [by the Conference of Unesco National Commissions to be held at Bangkok in 1951] to produce an authoritative set of rules for the rendering of Asian Names in bibliographical entries.'

The same resolution was also approved by the First Conference of [the] Asian Librarians and the Ninth All India Library Conference held at Indore on 14 May 1951.

The document, Unesco/Reg Conf 11/16 dated 14 September 1951 stated that the proposed Project would be in keeping with the Unesco's programme. A meeting of Mr. Carter, the Head of the Libraries Division of Unesco, with a group of Indian Librarians in Delhi on 25 November 1951 formulated the contents and the stages of the Project. The Regional Conference in Bangkok held from 26 November to 10 December 1951 resolved as follows:

(4) That consideration should be given to the proposals from the Indian Library Association to undertake the tasks outlined in document, Unesco/Reg Conf/11/16 as follows:

(a) Establishment of a committee for framing standard rules for the rendering of Asian names in bibliographical and catalogue entries.'

On 6 January 1952, Ranganathan (1952) prepared a draft Working Paper on the project and circulated it to all the probable participating countries, soliciting opinions. In May 1952, several countries sent their general approval of the draft Working Paper. At its meeting held from 21 to 25 April 1952, Unesco's Provisional International Committee on Bibliography and Documentation held in Paris approved the Project and assignment of it to India.

On 12 May 1952, the Indian Library Association assigned the Project to the care of Ranganathan. From May 1952 to January 1953, Ranganathan did field work and held group meetings in different states in India and in Ceylon. He also had discussion on the subject with the Muslims in Delhi and by correspondence with the librarians in Indonesia, Malaya, and Siam, about the structure etc. of the names in the respective linguistic groups.

In May 1953, a pamphlet embodying the findings arrived at by this investigation was circulated to the participating countries (Ranganathan, 1953a). Replies were received on the contents of the pamphlet from Ceylon, Indo-China, Indonesia, Pakistan, Siam, Vietnam, and the Indian Standards Institution. The final report was dispatched to Unesco on 31 October 1953. An important principle formulated in the report on the basis of the Canon of Prepotence was as follows:

The entry word, in a Name-of-Person, should be chosen from among that group of words occurring in a multi-worded term chosen for use as heading, that is more numerous than the groups of the other words occurring in it. For, the probability for the same word, to be used as entry word in several headings, is inversely proportional to the numerousness of the group from which the word is chosen; and the smaller this probability, the greater will be the concentration of Potency in the entry word. This statistical principle is responsible - unconscious though it might have been-for the choice of the family name as the entry word in rendering a Western Name-of-Person in a heading. So also this principle is responsible for the choice of the personal name as the entry word in rendering a South Indian Name-of-Person in a heading. Sec. 72 and 8 of the Annexture to the report contained the following general findings:

'72 It is impossible to make all the cultural groups of the world to conform to a single efficient standard in Name Formation. But it is possible to agree upon a single efficient standard for printing the name on the title-page. This will easily guide readers in changing over from Title-Page-Name to Entry-Name and vice-versa.

'8 Laying down of a standard for Title-Page-Name by all concerned including Unseco, ISO, IFLA, FID, and the corresponding bodies in the several countries (along lines suggested below or in alternative ways)

1. The Entry Word or Entry Word-Group, as the case may be, should be printed in Black Face.

2. The Honorific Words, to be omitted in the Entry Name, should not be printed on the Title Page. If printed, they should be in Roman Cap and lower case, preferably in different lines and in a font of smaller size.

3. Any titular word, which should be included among the Additional Words following the Entry Word (or Entry Word-Group) should be printed in italics.

4. Pseudonym should be separated from real name and printed in a distinctive style in a separate block.

5. Compound Family Names and Compound Individual Names should be hyphenated if the practice of the language does not admit of their being written as one word or if the author habitually separates them.'"

Apart from the broad description of the important facts connected with the Unesco Project on Asian Names reproduced above by Bhattacharyya, it has also been noted that the Bulletin of the Indian

Library Association (Notes and news, 1952), had reported the progress made in the Project including the field work done by Ranganathan. During this period, a periodical article by Ranganathan (1953c) revealed the work done by him by visiting different linguistic areas of the country. After having detailed discussion with the local persons interested in the subject, and from the similarities of the pattern of the names falling within a region, a general pattern emerged. However, the task of drawing up the problematic names needing special treatment was entrusted to the local bodies. Likewise, in another article, Ranganathan (1953b) had hoped that a uniform practice would be adopted by the persons for their names in all the Asian countries. This would enable to frame some workable rules for rendering the names from Asia.

In response to Ranganathan's appeal in 1934, Saxena (1952) came forward on the cataloguing problems of the names-of-persons from Uttar Pradesh. He brought out that the usage of the family names came only after the middle of the nineteenth century as a prominent influence of the Western culture. Sub-caste names in general and alla (= family name) were made to become surnames. Breaking of personal names into two meaningless parts and their absurdity were illustrated. As made out by him, the sequence of the words in a given name, if no surname is used, be not altered. Leading principles involved in identifying substantive words were highlighted.

The final report on Asian Names was submitted to Unesco in October 1953. Though, remained unpublished, it covered Asian names-of- persons more extensively, and therefore, can be regarded as a milestone in the research activities connected with the subject. Indic names forming a sub-set of the Asian names, were covered quite extensively. However, the report lacked in achieving its goals on account of the following reasons :

1. Selecting the heading from a group of words having a more numerous reservoir, than the set of words in the other group, has been recommended. This has been called by Dr. Ranganathan as the 'Statistical principle'. The counter arguments against the above prescription, are as given under:

(a) The sociology of naming system in any linguistic region of the country, does not follow a rigorous mathematical path. Otherwise, the potency of words in Indic names-of-persons could not have been changed with the period of time, and with the shifting of the geographic regions of the country.

(b) Variation in the structure of the Indic names-of-persons could not have come about merely by attaining a higher educational level.

(c) It is rather difficult to assess the numerousness of one group of the words used in some parts of the names in comparison with the other, in many linguistic belts.

(d) Merely by having a large number of words in a specified group, does not mean that words are chosen at random. In fact, every linguistic society delimits its universe of names to a few popular words (Abdul Huq, 1976a). For instance, in the Hindus, Brahma, Ganesh, Krishna, Ram, Shyam, Kamla, Siva, Sita, Parvati, Shanti, and so on are used in a very large number of names. Similarly, among the Muslims, Mohammad, Ahmed, Abdul, etc. are in extreme popular usage in the names-of- persons.

Hence, if an alphabetical listing of the names-of-persons is brought out, in such a way that the entry word is made always in the personal name, there would be very heavy concentration of the entries under the most popular names.

2. Laying down a standard for the Title-page of a book, at the international level, and getting it implemented, appear utopia. Several national standards like IS : 790 - 1956; IS : 791 -1956; IS : 792 - 1956 (revised in 1964); IS : 793 - 1956; and IS : 794 - 1956 were promulgated in India, and despite earnest and repeated appeals to the publishers and authors by such an eminent personality as Ranganathan, they remained unimplemented even in our own country, by most of the publishers. Further, cataloguing principles are also used in indexing micro-documents. All the complications as are generally observed in the case of books are also encountered by the indexers, and in all kinds of the micro-documents, easy identification as can be achieved from the so called standard author's statement in a monograph, can not be obtained. In this context, it may be clarified that IS : 790 - 1987 is the latest standard on the subject. The other standards namely IS : 791 - 1956, IS: 792 - 1964, and IS : 794 - 1956 have now been superseded by the new revision of IS: 790 - 1987 while IS : 793 - 1956 stands withdrawn.

Another cataloguer of repute of the early fifties was B. Sengupta. His first contribution (Sengupta, 1952) on Asian names examined the provisions of the then existing ALA Code on the rendering the names-of-persons from Asia in the following contexts:

(a) Varying spellings of Indic names-of-persons;

(b) South Indian names;

(c) Muslim names; and

(d) Names-of-persons from the Far East.

Sengupta's findings on the South Indian names were in full conformity with those of Ranganathan. The article was quite timely, in view of the "Project on Asian Names" being in progress then.

After submitting the Report on Asian Names to the Unesco, Ranganathan became convinced that Indic names-of-persons could not be handled exhaustively merely by framing a few cataloguing rules. He suggested the drawing up of a long list of names for each language, which would be helpful in deciding the element(s) in the heading of a catalogue. He felt that the cost of such a work would be prohibitive and therefore suggested the alternative of providing the standard statement on the author's name on the verso of the title page. He pleaded for adoption of such an international standard so that the problem would be solved for all times to come (Ranganathan, 1954c). On similar lines, another paper was contributed (Ranganathan, 1954a). He made use of other forums for projecting his views. He strongly pleaded for adoption of an international standard for the title page at the meeting of ISO/TC 46 on documentation held at Stuttgarh, West Germany from 30 August-1 Sept 1956 (Ranganathan, 1957a). He made out a strong case for such an international standard stating that fruitful cataloguing manpower would be wasted otherwise. Similarly, in yet another paper, surnames and forenames were analysed to conclude that a catalogue code would be too complicated to incorporate all such practices. Also, different parts of a name were examined and a case for an international standard on the title-page was proposed (Ranganathan, 1954b).

The book "Headings and canons" critically examined and compared the provisions in five different catalogue codes on the basis of the canons of cataloguing (Ranganathan, 1955a).

Ranganathan (1955b) also delivered a forceful speech at the "Third International Congress of Libraries and Documentation Centers" held at Brussels in September 1955 where in he demanded that the author himself should indicate the entry element in his name, as he was the most competent person to do so.

2.5 ISI CONVENTION - 1957

One session of the Third Annual Convention of the then Indian Standards Institution (Presently, the Bureau of Indian Standards) held in Madras (Chennai) in 1957 was devoted to the problems of the Indic names in cataloguing. Three of the technical papers presented at the meet, are cited below :

A joint paper (Puranik and Phadnis, 1957) mentioned some of the existing peculiarities of Indic names belonging to diverse cultural groups in the country, citing examples from the Telephone Directory of Delhi and the Who's Who and pointing to the lack of uniformity in rendering the names-of-persons. It Suggested standardization as a remedy and also, carried a brief review of the published literature. Specific areas needing further investigation were identified. This paper was published afterwards with a different title (Puranik and Phadnis, 1958-59).

The second paper dealing with the structure of the Indic names stressed the need for uniformity in the usage of surnames, for documentation work and library purposes (Mukerjee, 1957). Other related problems such as the use of several double worded family names, and titles used as surnames, were also discussed in this paper.

Ranganathan (1957b) shared his own experience with the Documentation Committee (EC 2) in arriving at a series of standards for the preliminary pages of a book. He also discussed their implications, and made a strong plea for implementing these standards, for the supplementary author's statement.

Sengupta (1958) made an elaborate survey of the Hindu names from Uttar Pradesh, Punjab, West Bengal, Andhra Pradesh, Karnataka, Tamilnadu, Kerala and the western parts of the country. Evolution of Bengali family names was carried out in detail. Sikh clan names and tribal names often employed as surnames, were appended.

During the later half of the nineteenth century, while the British rule was getting stabilized, Indian writers fashioned their names according to rhetorical fancies and had modified or transformed their names in accordance with the rules of foreign language and Western pronunciation. During this period individual authors adopted a system of their own, very often incorrect. However, the frequency of adopting anglicised given names had diminished or virtually vanished in recent times, the Western modifications of the surnames had continued in some parts of the country. In addition, variant or diversified spellings of the names as used by many authors had compounded the problems. It was therefore, suggested that the spellings of the surnames be smoothened down to a standardized form. The other parts of the name need not be changed (Sengupta, 1959b). On similar lines, another publication also emerged (Sengupta, 1959a)

Another contribution of Sengupta (1959d) proposed a case for retention of the anglicised as well as the vernacular form of a name, with the system of cross-references. The smoothening of the spellings of the entry words would solve almost one half of the problems. Comparison of the rules of rendering the Muslim names, in different cataloguing codes was also made. In another paper, the scope was restricted to the books in which the names of the authors were printed in the Roman alphabets. Smoothening the spellings of the surnames was suggested. Inter-alia, it was stressed that the names of some well known persons known under some specific part of their names, need not be changed despite the fact that some of the authors might have adopted grammatical wrong approach (Sengupta, 1959c).

In another contribution, Ranganathan (1959a) elaborated nine levels of standardization efforts, to be agreed upon for the formulation of an international catalogue code, and pleaded for the adoption of the standard for printing the name of the author on the verso of the title page.

Yet in another paper, Ranganathan (1959b) discussed the features of the names-of-persons such as the number of words, their grammatical nature, their functions, their sequence, their relative potency, the complexities in their structure, etc. He observed that the West had brought the usage of family names in certain class of the names-of-persons. Some persons were dropping their surnames, in recent times. It was therefore, very difficult for a cataloguer not brought up in the culture of the author, to render the names correctly. He advocated the printing of the name of the writer on the verso of the title page conforming to IS 793- 1956, so that the wastage of time involved in searching the entry elements of the personal authors could be avoided.

A review paper on the contribution of Sharify in the area of cataloguing Persian works was presented (Parthasarathy, 1959). Different elements of Persian names-of-persons were listed with their probable place of occurrence. This article, though not directly related to the present research, is useful in analysing the Muslim names of the country.

Another paper of Sharify (1960) drawn from his book was also published.

Emergence of Bengali family names was the theme of one of the papers (Mookerjee, 1959). It listed quite a large number of different Bengali family names, along with their meanings derived from the official positions occupied by the persons, during the Muslim period in Bengal. Also, a fairly comprehensive listing of the surnames used in the Bengali names-of-persons was included.

2.6 EFFORTS BY THE IFLA

In 1957, the Council of the International Federation of Library Associations (IFLA), decided to hold a world conference to seek agreement on certain basic cataloguing principles. A Preliminary Meeting took place in London from 19 to 25th July, 1959, to work out details of the proposed conference. India was represented by Sengupta who had contributed a working paper, for discussion in the Meeting. A unanimous decision to convene the International Conference at an early date was taken, and the subject matter was divided into specific problem areas to be dealt with by the specialists. Indian representative was allotted 'Problems of the Indic Names in relation to an Integrated Alphabetical Library Catalogue in Roman Script' with a request to submit a revised working paper for discussion. It was also suggested that Indian librarians and other specialists from as wide an area as possible, be consulted before hand.

Indian Association of Special Libraries and Information Centres (IASLIC) took up the job of eliciting opinions of the Indian library professionals and other experts with a view to assisting the Indian delegate in drafting the working paper for the proposed International Conference. The first Symposium (IASLIC, 1960) on 'Cataloguing Problems and Principles with regard to Indic Names' was held at Calcutta in January, 1960. The working paper of Sengupta was circulated, well in advance, and comments were solicited (IASLIC, 1959). The progress made in the Symposium was followed up by inviting opinions of different state library associations in the country. In consideration of the importance of the subject at the national and international levels, IASLIC had decided, after considerable preparation and publicity, to convene another Seminar on Indic Names at Calcutta from Dec. 30, 1960 to Jan. 1, 1961. The scope and outline of the working papers for the Seminar, were laid down (Sengupta, 1960a). Similarly, in another article, Sengupta (1960b) made some passing observations on Indic names. He briefly enumerated some of the problems encountered by the cataloguers while dealing with Indic names-of-persons.

Ranganathan (1960) felt that no catalogue code could prescribe a set of rules adequate to handle Indic names, since the practices were so much varied that all categories of the names could not be covered by the same. He prescribed a statistical formula under which it was to be determined whether the reservoir of providing surnames in a cultural group is larger than the same of the given names. Based on the test, it could be determined whether the entry be made under a surname or in a given name. However, he had apprehensions about this formula yielding correct results for all linguistic groups. Therefore, he advocated that the author must mention on the verso of the title-page, as to how his name be treated in a cataloguing system. This would solve all the problems in rendering Indic names-of-persons at one stroke.

Double-worded Marathi surnames and their origin, were discussed (Belsare, 1960). Analysis revealed that some double worded family names contained such removable words as buva, ji, etc. Except the surnames having one of these words, all other two worded family names were recommended to be rendered as such. Specific cataloguing rules for treatment of the Marathi names were proposed.

A comparison of the methods of Ranganathan and Sengupta, in relation to the Indic names-of-persons was made (Subba Rao, 1961b). Different practices adopted by the Indian National Bibliography, in the context of the directives of the IASLIC Seminar were reviewed. In order to evolve a national code, the standard statement of the author, on the back of the title-page was strongly advocated as a feasible solution.

Transliteration of Arabic, Persian and Urdu words into Roman script was discussed and a method of standardizing the same was suggested (Moquitul Hasan, 1961). This would be helpful in rendering the Muslim names, in an integrated catalogue.

On the eve of the International Conference on Cataloguing Principles held at Paris, Ranganathan (1961) pointed out the impracticability of rendering all the Indic names-of-persons with the help of a few cataloguing rules, mainly because of the non- conformity of family names to a uniform pattern. Some surnames were double-worded. Even in a given linguistic area the practices of naming had undergone transformation over a period of time. Hence, to solve the problems, he proposed that the authors should disclose the full form of their names on the verso of the title-page.

Sengupta (1961) proposed the Working Paper for the IASLIC Seminar. It was widely circulated among the experts, state level library associations, and other professional bodies, several months before the Seminar. Later on, the IASLIC (1961a) brought out the proceedings of the Seminar together with the technical papers and the important speeches by some of the prominent people who attended the same. Gist of the deliberations is incorporated here:

Sen (1961) while inaugurating the Seminar, lauded the holding of the Seminar on such an important issue as that of the Indic names in the following words :

"The very fact that, an attempt is being made to standardize 'Indic Names' makes the subject very intriguing even to a layman. India has so many different languages, so many scripts and so many diverse ways of expressing personal names that not only the librarians, but the readers also very often get lost in the maze of such diversities. It is perhaps in this field where man gets utmost freedom - the world of names is not a world of order - it is more or less anarchy. If you can bring order in this area of chaos, even though limited to authorship only - yours will be an achievement of great importance."

Mitra (1961) the then Vice-Chancellor of the University of Calcutta, being the Chief Guest welcomed all and wished a success in resolving the problems of the Indic names-of-persons in cataloguing.

In his address, the President of the Seminar (Kesavan, 1961) referred to the paper of Ranganathan, where in the very propriety of holding the proposed international conference, at Paris to consider the Indic names-of-persons in cataloguing had been questioned. Hence, Kesavan directed the Seminar to look in the face fully. Also, the formula of statistics proposed by Ranganathan for entering an Indic name, be examined.

Shukla (1961b), the Director of the Seminar introduced the theme by highlighting the importance of the catalogue of a library, particularly in view of the expansion of the academic and public library services, and added that"any mistake made at this stage [in cataloguing] would be reflected not only in the service but would be very difficult to correct at a later stage'.

Important technical papers contributed to a widening of the understanding of the subject are summarised below :

1. The paper of Sengupta (1961) was the key paper, covering names in different phases of history and included almost all the linguistic groups of the country. Religious minorities were also discussed. Quite a comprehensive study of the existing cataloguing codes in relation to the Indic names, was made, and rules for their entering were suggested. This paper with modifications became the working paper for the IFLA's Conference.

2. Hingwe (1961) proposed certain guidelines for smoothening the spellings of Marathi surnames having a common word. This would improve and bring better accessibility in a catalogue.

3. Balasubramanyan (1961) dealt with the names-of-persons from South India, particularly from the structure point of view. The entry of a name having the normal structure, was recommended under the personal name. However, 'the problem arises when an author adopts unconventional sequence. As all such possibilities can not be accommodated in any cataloguing code, author's practice has to be strictly followed'. Feminine names need to be entered under their given names. Among the names of the Christians, he could see no uniformity in the structure. The author supported standardizing of the variant spellings of both personal and family names.

4. Rao (1961) proposed legislation for standardizing Indic names and pleaded that popularization of the surnames even in such areas where it is customary to call by personal names, may be encouraged.

5. Subba Rao (1961a) observed that the transliteration table for all the Indian languages was inhospitable. Hence, another transliteration method was proposed from Telugu to English. Analysis of Telugu names-of-persons was done in detail. Three specific parts of a South Indian name were identified. They are listed as under :

i. Pre substantive part including (a) Place, Job, Ancestor, Attribute etc., (b) God, Father; (c) Auxiliary; (d) Descriptive; (ii) Substantive (iii) Post substantive, with varying sequence where all the parts need not be present. Telugu names were covered quite extensively.

6. Jamil Ahmed and Sengupta (1961) analysed Indic Muslim names in the context of the existing catalogue codes. They arrived at some pragmatic ways of handling them in a cataloguing system.

In addition, a comprehensive annotated bibliography on Indic names was compiled by Saha et. al. (1961) which formed a part of the Proceedings. It also served as a useful tool in the survey of the relevant literature.

In the five plenary sessions of the Seminar, different facets of the problem were thoroughly discussed. Also, working groups on different linguistic areas were formed, to discuss the matter jointly, and to suggest specific solutions. The outcome of the deliberations as summarised were (IASLIC, 1961a):

Group I - East India

The representatives of the panel on Bengali names preferred the forename or the personal name, for the main entry word in an alphabetical catalogue.

Representatives from the Oriya language, however, decided in favour of the surnames.

Group II - South India

A name-of-person from Kannada, Malayalam, Tamil and Telugu speaking regions, is to be entered normally under the given name. The personal name is either the penultimate or the ultimate word in a name. Specific exceptions should however, be made in cases where the author has provided clear indication of his desire to be known otherwise.

Group III - West India

The group decided in favour of family name for the leading section of the main entry in a catalogue.

Group IV & V - North India (Hindi, Punjabi, and Urdu)

The usage of family names being not common in this region, personal name was preferred for the main entry. Exceptions be made in case of authors intending to be known otherwise.

The findings of the Seminar were incorporated in the form of resolutions passed unanimously, which were explained in detail by Dr. Shukla (1961a), the Director of the Seminar with suitable examples by way of illustration. The resolutions are given as below (IASLIC, 1961c):

1. In an integrated alphabetical catalogue in Roman alphabets entries for different works by one and the same author should be brought together under only one specific Author Heading, regardless of the forms of name he has adopted.

2. Considering the diverse nature of different cultural and linguistic groups in India it has been expressed unanimously that no practical

purpose could be served by having one uniform rule for Author Headings; hence it is decided that different cultural and linguistic groups should have freedom to determine the most potent part or parts of the names (either the personal name or surname) for the purpose of Author Heading.

3. Distinct variant linguistic forms of names of persons having one common etymological origin should be treated as separate names for the purpose of the Alphabetical Catalogue.

4. Different spellings used for basically same entry word for an author's name when rendered in Roman alphabets should be standardized and used as such in an Alphabetical Catalogue.

5. After having decided that standardization of spellings of authors' names should be made in all appropriate cases this Seminar requests the IASLIC immediately to form a Committee comprising representatives of the National Library, Indian National Bibliography and experienced librarians and persons specially interested in the subject for finding out ways and means to standardize spellings of authors' names and report within six months to IASLIC.

After the Seminar was over a special committee consisting of several experts was constituted by the IASLIC, to standardize the variant forms of the surnames. The Committee adopted a standardized list of surnames in its meeting held on 16th April, 1961 (IASLIC, 1961d). Similarly, a schedule of the anglicized Marathi surnames was also adopted (IASLIC, 1961b).

The IASLIC Seminar on Indic Names can be described as a successful event in firmly laying down the broad principles and guidelines governing the rendering of the Indic names-of-persons in an integrated alphabetical catalogue. However, it failed in its mission, on account of the following reasons :

a) It dealt with Indic names-of-persons in a superfluous manner without going deep into the sociological aspects of naming.

b) Its coverage was confined mainly to a few prominent linguistic regions. Specific problems relating to smaller units of different cultural regions were not taken into account.

c) By and large, Indian feminine names were neglected. In some papers, only vague and casual reference was made.

d) Several findings and subsequent recommendations on the treatment of names-of-persons from different linguistic belts of the country, were not in conformity with the usage.

e) Religious minorities such as Muslims and Christians, were not investigated in the broader context of different linguistic groups. They were covered rather in a general way, as one group in the entire country.

f) Persons belonging to the Buddhism from Ladakh and Sikkim were not studied.

g) Sindhi names-of-persons did not figure at all in any of the presentations.

h) Konkani names from Goa and nearby areas were not covered. by any one present in the Seminar.

i) Foreign influences other than the British ones, were not taken into account.

Based on the discussions in the IASLIC Seminar, and after inclusion of the comments from several learned societies in the country, such as the Sahitya Akademi, Asiatic Society, National Library, Delhi Public Library, etc., the key paper of Sengupta, was once again revised (Sengupta, 1963) and thereafter, it was presented at the "International Conference on Cataloguing Principles' in October, 1961 at Paris. The Conference accepted all the recommendations of the IASLIC Seminar on Indic Names in their totality (IFLA, 1963).

In making the International Conference on Cataloguing, at Paris a success, specific efforts were made to post the delegates with the regular developments taking place. An English translated publication (Poindron, 1961) covered the subject matter quite comprehensively. It was written originally in French.

Another relevant and useful paper presented in the above International Conference was a joint contribution of Fazal Elahi et. al. (1961) from Pakistan. It was a fairly a detailed analysis of the Muslim names from India and Pakistan. Each component part of the name structure, was discussed, and specific suggestions were made. It was recommended that the order of preference in the choice of the entry, be (1) takhallus; (2) surname if used at the rear; (3) original order of the name elements to be retained where it denotes personal name alone; and (4) laqab if suffixed to given name. Inversion of the word "Mohammad" in some specific cases, was recommended, provided the name consisted of at least three component parts. Similarly, "Khan" was treated as a family name in a three worded name. Otherwise, it could be safely taken as a part of the personal name. Muslim feminine names were also covered. List of words generally used as surnames, was drawn up.

Based on the contributions of Sengupta and Fazal Elahi, priniples governing the rendering of Indic names-of-persons in a catalogue were laid down. They are enumerated as given below (IFLA, 1963)

For Muslim names-of-persons

1. The authors practice is to be followed if it is systematically and consistently used, even if he violates the strict grammatical structure.

2. Where an author uses consistently some part of his name in the manner in which the surnames are used in the West, that part should be the entry word.

3. In cases where the entry word, particularly the part of the name used as surname, appears in various Romanised spellings, reference should be made from a standardized spellings to the spellings actually used by the author. The authors' spellings should be the entry word.

4. When an author uses a pen name or a poetic name and is identified by it, this name should be the entry word, immediately followed by other parts relating to NISBA with other names or parts of name inverted. Reference is to be made from other parts whenever necessary.

5. Compound names should be entered under the first part of the name, with reference from the second part.

6. A woman author should be entered under the personal name, with reference from the name not chosen as main entry. If she is married, the entry should be under the personal name followed by the maiden name (in brackets). Reference is to be made from the name not chosen as the main entry.

7. When the name consists of two elements each of which is a proper name, the entire name will be written as such without inversion.

8. A Westernized form of a name consistently and regularly used by a Muslim author in his publications in European languages (and in the Roman alphabets) should be used as such in catalogues listing publications in European languages (and in Roman script) only. But if the author has also written in Urdu, Arabic or Persian under a vernacular

form of name, a reference is to be given from this to the Westernized form.

For non-Muslims

1. When an Indic personal name includes a surname, last name or the part of the name used in the manner in which surnames are used in the West, the entry word should be such surnames, last name or the part used as surname, provided that it is consistently used by the author in his original writings either in vernacular or in Roman script, provided further that it is not subordinated to or compounded with the personal name as the names of authors from certain parts of south and in the Punjabi names generally. In arriving at this principle, the practice of authors only (who are proportionately less in number than non-authors of the population) has been taken into consideration.

2. The varying orthographic forms of different surnames due to transliteration or assimilation of the names of the character of a foreign language should be standardized as far as practicable for ease in consultation.

The principles accepted by the "International Conference on Cataloguing Principles" organised by International Federation of the Library Associations (IFLA), in October 1961 are pragmatic and helpful. However, the problems were tackled from a theoretical frame-of-reference and in-depth study of the problems did not take place. Hence, all the drawbacks associated with the IASLIC Seminar findings on Indic Names, also found a place in the out come of the International Conference.

Kaula (1962) had lamented on the black-out of the Indian School of Thought on Cataloguing at the Paris Conference. It was regretted that the Conference did not even hear the view-point of printing the name of the author on the back of the title page of each book. Similarly, Ranganathan (1962a) examined in detail, the preliminary official report of the Paris Conference, clause by clause recommendations. Alternative suggestions were provided, wherever needed. He felt that the Conference was biased and paid little attention on the books of the future. It was therefore, recommended for adoption of the standard practices adopted by the then Indian Standards Institution as a step in facilitating cataloguing of future publications.

Ranganathan (1962b) called for adopting a new approach in respect of the books of the future. He recommended to the International

Conference on Cataloguing the wisdom, in order to avoid wastage of the cataloguing energy, of promoting the international adoption on the Indian standard on 'Supplement to Author Statement' to be printed on the back of the title page.

In a review paper, the Indian Library Association (1963) requested the regional library associations and institutions in the country, to translate the principle of 'rendering the names as per the usage in the country of which the author is a citizen' by disclosing their naming practices, and advised them to publicise them.

Sarkar (1963) observed that Indic names, though linear in appearance, were in fact radial in their character. They were a complicated apparatus for identification of a person by means of (1) personal name; (2) father's name; (3) domicile; (4) surname via clan/caste/profession; (5) honorific, feudal or academic attachments. The basic problem was that neither forename nor surname was universally acceptable as the primary key for the identification of persons in the country. Thus, the major cataloguing vacuum remained and encouraged a by-passing by multiple means in catalogues.

Viswanathan (1965) emphasised the need for entering an Indic name under his personal name in all parts of the country. If however, an Indian author disclosed only the last part of his name in full form, and had converted the other parts in initials, the entry word could be chosen as per his usage, i.e. the last part of his name.

Mittal and Gupta (1966) covered the subject in their book meant for the students, but the treatment is scanty and wanting in many respects. Similarly, some passing remarks were made by Pearson (1966).

The analysis of Mangla (1966) on Punjabi names was quite comprehensive in scope. Sikh and Hindu names were both covered adequately. Three lists dealing with the auxiliaries; surnames; and the prefix-titles were appended.

A statistical study on the fields of information used in the catalogue cards of the Library of Congress, for the books, revealed that 74.7 % main entries were made under the personal names (Avram, et. al., 1967)). However, the study encompasses publications from all the countries, and hence can not be decisive as far as Indic names are concerned. It was undertaken as a part of the home-work for the automation project at the Library of Congress.

A review of the provisions of AACR 1967 established that they were at variance with the findings of the Paris Conference on Cataloguing Principles (Sengupta, 1968).

Hindu names-of-persons from Bengal were discussed (Khan, 1969). However, apart from acknowledging the views of Sengupta, the article adds very little to what is known on the subject.

Lambert (1969) found that over 30 library authorities in England, were having some provision for the books in different vernacular languages of India and Pakistan, and others were planning to do so. Some of them were taking the help of their users in cataloguing the material.

On the issue of the entry word, the opinion of the experts in several linguistic regions of the country was sharply divided (Ranganathan, 1969a). For instance, some strongly felt that the personal name be the entry word, where as some others believed that the family name be given the status of the entry element in a catalogue. The practice of naming was found changing with time. Double worded surnames complicated the matter further. All these problems had resulted in wastage of time and resources of the cataloguer. The call therefore, to adopt the Indian Standard, for the title-page was to be assessed in the context. A similar standard at the international level was also proposed. If adopted cataloguing codes got reduced to a simple directive to adhere to the choice of the author.

The Causal factors in the wrong choice of entry-words for Indic names-of-persons in catalogue, were analysed (Goil, 1969). Non- familiarity with the structures of the names from different regions of the country, was identified as the root cause. Three different ways of writing the names were found and Real surnames and Pseudo surnames were defined, and listed for the Aggarwal Vaishya community.

A comparative study of the treatment of Hindi names in different catalogue codes was made (Jain, 1969). It was found that none of the 19 codes existing then could provide specific rules for the cataloguing of the author's names. Even Ranganathan touched the problems only peripherally. Other Indian cataloguers also did not provide adequately for handling the names-of-persons from the Hindi region. Sengupta covered only the names from Uttar Pradesh, which is only a part of the Hindi heartland. The author appealed to the professionals in resolving the problems.

The concept of Recall value was advocated, for entering the names of the authors (Ranganathan, 1969b). In name-of-person heading for South Indian writers, Recall value was concentrated in the given names. On the other hand, in a Western name, it was found concentrated in the surname. However, it could not be known whether the concentration of the Recall value led to the cataloguing rules on the choice of the entry word, in a Western name-of-person, or the cataloguing convention had caused the concentration of the Recall value. Yet, till 1595, personal names were preferred in the catalogue heading for the Western names.

A review by Bhattacharyya (1969), covered almost the entire literature on cataloguing research in India. Starting with the contribution of Ranganathan from 1934 to 1950, all the major contributions to areas of cataloguing by different persons, were studied. Indic names-of-persons too were discussed.

Different categories of Kashmiri surnames, their origin, structure, and derivation were analysed in a study (Kaul, 1970). Double-worded family names, takhallus and changing of surnames among the Kashmiris were described. Also, a list of commonly used surnames in the Valley along with their variants, was appended. In each case, a standard form of family name was suggested.

Problems due to divergent structures in the Indic names,particularly belonging to the Muslims of India and Pakistan were addressed in a Master's degree dissertation submitted to Dhaka University in 1963. The summary of this work was published (Badiur Rahman, 1970). Other issues such as variation in spellings employed in for one and the same name; cataloguing in the local languages vs English, etc. were examined in the summary with an earnest appeal to the then Pakistan Library Association to convene a national conference to study the problems and solve the same.

Ranganathan (1971) appreciated the difficulties of the International Conference on Cataloguing Principles held at Paris in 1961, in arriving at a single simplified practice. Therefore, alternative practices were to be conceived. There were two steps involved in the new method. The removable attachment to a name would be omitted. Then, it would be assessed whether the entry word in the name-of-person was drawn from the most numerous word-groups. This would satisfy the Canon of Prepotence. However, he contradicted himself in observing that in Bengali cultural group, the method might not be appropriate. So also was the case with North Mysore. The strange ways in which people permuted different words in their names, were endless. Some of them even dissected the prepotent word into two parts and reduced all the words and the first word of the dissected word into initial, and mentioned in full only the second part of that name.

Chand (1971) described the variety of forms in the occurrence of the Indic Muslim names-of-persons. Structures of the names along with usual attachment parts were analysed. Critical examination of the provisions of the existing catalogue codes was also made. Helpful suggestions were given.

Elaborate clarification on the usage of family names in the names-of-persons belonging to the Hindi heartland, in a study is both informative and useful (Jain, 1972). Other aspects of naming practices in the zone, were also discussed. Structural differences between North Indian and South Indian names-of-persons were brought out (Sharma, 1973). Many North Indians did not have surname in their names, and in line with their practice, foreign cataloguers tend to commit mistakes in rendering such names when they took the second word of the forename as the family name. In addition, no consensus opinion was available on the larger question of establishment of the norms for the main entries for modern Indic names. Neither forename nor surname was found to be a consistently potent one in a modern Indic name.

A critical examination of the provisions of the AACR 1967 was attempted (Bhattacharyya, 1973). However, it did not add much to the knowledge of the subject beyond reiterating Ranganathan's suggesting to make changes in the ALA Code of 1949, for the Indic names.

Dogra (1973) dealt Indic Muslim names quite extensively. His analysis of the parts of the names-of-persons was scientific and relevant.

A comprehensive work by Sengupta (1974a) revised thrice has a chapter on Indic names that is quite sketchy. The book also carried a separate article as an Appendix (Sengupta, 1974b).

Muslim names from Bengal, differ from those in other regions of the sub-continent, as Bengali is a non-Arabic language (Abdul Huq, 1974). Though, most of the words used in the Bengali Muslim names had originated from the Arabic culture, their form was very much influenced by the Bengali culture. Hence, they could not be tackled adequately with the prescriptions meant for the Muslim names, in general. Some useful guidelines were provided to overcome the problem. On similar lines, another article appeared in which Hindu names-of-persons were also covered (Abdul Huq, 1979). Similarly, Saif-ul-Islam (1980) gave an analysis of the Bengali Muslim names and recommended specific measures for their handling.

Prevalent structures of the Hindu names-of-persons from different parts of the country, were illustrated in a paper (Uppal, 1975). The tendency to abbreviate certain parts of names by some authors was critically examined with the help of the Canon of Ascertainability.

Problems associated with very long Indic names-of-persons were studied in depth by Gupta, et. al. (1975). Implications of such lengthy names for the computerisation of a library catalogue were examined and it was concluded that if the picture value of surname data field was kept at 12, nearly 6 % of the names were worst affected in such a case, and 1 % if the same was increased to 16. South Indian names appeared longer when the personal name and caste name were taken together. Similarly, double or more worded surnames were the source of lengthy Bengali names.

In a generic contribution, Abdul Huq (1976a) dealt with the names-of-persons from several countries in cataloguing. Indic names too were covered. An important unpublished study of the author on the quantification of the name entries carried out at the St. John's University was reported (Abdul Huq, 1976b?).

Nanda and Datta (1975-79) observed that the part 'Singh' in a Sikh name should not be chosen as the entry word. Place name too did not deserve the status of the entry word in a Muslim name. However, in case of Bengali names, both the vernacular and anglicised forms might be used as entry word.

Indic names-of-persons were studied in relation to the time period of their bearers (Dogra, 1976). Classical names in the Vedic time period, were discussed. Caste system among the Hindus in the Hindi speaking belt and its influence on the names-of- persons, were examined. Structure of the names with emphasis on prefix title, personal name, family name, and pen-name were included. A list of commonly used prefixes was drawn up. The style of writing a given name in the split form, was illustrated. Three appendices covering surnames, names of the Hindi writers, and family names with variant form, were provided. In his rejoinder, Jain (1982) criticised Dogra, and came forward with his view points to the contrary.

Two different methods of cataloguing Urdu books were described (Kaula, 1977). The former method covered cataloguing in Urdu language. The other method was to catalogue them through the Urdu system, in the English language. The paper focused on the former method. The problems arose out of the script and romanization, appeared to be confusing. The process of correct choice of the main heading was prescribed. The author pleaded for the incorporation of the standard information on the name of the author, in the supplementary page of the book.

Musicians adopted peculiar structures of their names, and this could be a source of confusion (Rangra, 1977). Analysis of the name structures of several Musicians, was presented.

Dave (1977) carried out investigation, as a part of his Master's degree dissertation. He tried to cover quite a number of communities. However, his analysis was limited to the published literature.

Pearson (1978) attempted to bring out a few important features in the structure of the East Indian names-of-persons. Muslim names-of-persons and Bengali names were analysed in the Indian context. The matter was complicated, as each language had its own naming system. In addition to the usual categories of the names, there were caste names which were further complicating the matter. Word division was never a strong point amongst the Hindus and when adopting a Westernized form of names, words were divided in ways which would never exist in the original.

In his monograph, Kaul (1980) attempted to discuss Indic names. The attempt was superfluous with the recommendations made there in lacking specificity. It contained an excellent annotated bibliography on Indic names.

Serwar Hossain (1980 - 81) examined the factors which dampened the cataloguing efforts in Bangladesh. He attributed the poor progress by the cataloguers in their country, to absence of proper catalogue code. The paper also contained a reasonably good analysis of the Bengali Muslim names.

Rait (1981; 1983a; and 1983b) contributed to the knowledge in the subject by identifying different elements of the Indic names-of- persons suitable for the choice of the entry. She also identified the words which were unfit for the entry and evolved broad principles to be followed in the transliteration of the names. She emphasised the importance of ism (given name) and drew attention to the existence of other words such as laqabs, khitabs, kunyah and takhallus in the names in the analysis of the parts of the Muslim names. She also held the view that the existing catalogue codes were not of much help especially to the foreigners in spotting the entry word.

In yet another paper, Rait (1984) made a survey on the provision for the Indic languages in the catalogues of several British public libraries. She found that several libraries were depending on the help of their readers, in cataloguing the books in the native languages.

Mohammed Haroon (1984) came forward to provide detailed prescriptions for the indexing and cataloguing of Indic Muslim names-of-persons. He covered almost all the possible structures of the Muslim names. However, it failed in dealing with the subject, on account of the following reasons :

1. It linked Indic Muslim names, with the Arabic names-of-persons;

2. Religious linguistic areas were not covered;

3. Prescriptions recommended were highly influenced by the approach of Ranganathan;

4. Unnecessarily, the subject was over-complicated.

On the investigation of the potent word in the names of the Indian Muslims, an interesting experiment was conducted, by inquiring from the users as to which part of the names was most potent for their purposes (Gupta and Mohammed Haroon, 1986). Based on the analysis, cataloguing rules were proposed. The response of the users was viewed in the light of the Canons of Cataloguing.

Kaushik (1986) carried out a detailed investigation into the treatment of Indic names in AACR II as a part of his Master's degree programme in Library Science, at the Florida State University, Tallahassee (U.S.A.). However, he confined his work to the masculine names. His work was quite sketchy.

An unpublished paper was widely circulated to the delegates attending the National Seminar of the IASLIC (Pal and Das, 1988). Existing problems of the Indic names were highlighted in the paper. They suggested that the next conference of the IASLIC might be devoted exclusively in resolving the major problems of the transliteration of Indic names.

Sociological account of naming practices, prevailing in several linguistic communities of the country was attempted. The significance of surname or family name in denoting religion, linguistic area, sub-caste, clan, and even lineage affiliations was described. The varna model of the Hindus, provided a useful framework of the system. The process of Sanskritization, under which lower caste persons adopted the family names of the higher castes, in the process of social mobility, was described. The names-of-persons of the Sikhs and other cultural groups were discussed in detail. Anglicised or other formats of the names adopted by overseas Indians were also analysed (Jayaraman, 1989).

Because of the varying practices in the naming structure, no fixed rules could be laid down for the Asian names-of-persons (Nasreen Akhtar, 1989). The names from different Asian cultures were discussed and general guidelines provided.

Another dimension of the subject, in the context of developing an algorithm for identifying elements/parts of Indic names was discussed (Srivastava and Rajaraman, 1991). Based on their study, an expert system was designed. It recognised the phonetic information contained in an Indic name which in turn, depended on the language. In this case, Sanskrit was chosen as the basic language. It however, failed in dealing with different varieties of the names-of-persons.

Some paragraphs were devoted to the Oriental names with a sketchy treatment of the Indic names (Piggott, 1990). Likewise, Girja Kumar and Krishan Kumar (1982) analysed Indic names from different linguistic parts of the country. A fairly comprehensive list of words used as auxiliaries, employed in North India, was provided. Names-of-persons from West Bengal, Tamilnadu, Kerala, Karnataka, Andhra Pradesh, Gujarat and Maharashtra, were covered. Minority groups such as Sikhs, Muslims, and Christians, were also included and based on these, recommendations in conformity to the AACR, were made. On similar lines, another analysis was presented (Krishan Kumar, 1993). However, the treatment in both the books, is superfluous and recommendations are vague.

On Muslim names-of-persons, Ali Houissa (1993) presented his analysis. Though, this article was meant for Arabic names, it covered some of the features of names from Indian origin also.

Madhuri Devi (1993) submitted her Ph. D. thesis in the Manipur University, on the problems of the names-of-persons from the North-East states in cataloguing.

Principles governing the treatment of Indic names arrived at the International Conference on Cataloguing Principles held in Paris in 1961, were thoroughly examined, in the context of the three successive editions of the AACR (Mookerjee and Neogi, 1994). They found that the proposed entry of the name of an author, was in accordance with the usage of the country of which the author was a citizen, or this being impossible, by agreed usage, in the language in which most of his works were published, was an irrelevant and undiscover criterion.

Part II Literature on Socio-cultural aspects

There have been several useful publications dealing with the sociological aspects of the naming processes in the country. The relevant among them have been described as under :

Kalb (1962) reported that in South India, little babies were often weighed down with their father's name, clan name, village name and own name.

A comprehensive description of the Marathi family names, was provided (Ketkar, 1924). The origin of the Marathi surnames is very old, and is dated back to 12th century or even earlier.

The main reasons for changing the names-of-persons, belonging to the Hindi linguistic area were enumerated. Socio-cultural aspects were considered (Mehrotra, 1979). In another paper, Mehrotra (1982) described the naming practices prevailing in the Hindi heartland, and felt that the names-of-persons were more than mere labeling devices.

Coverage of the Indic names-of-persons and analysis of the variables controlling the naming practices in the country were included (Karnow, 1966). Family names such as 'Doctor' in the Parsee community, were reported rather in an amusing style. If a person bearing such a surname is also a medical practioner, he would thus be referred to as Dr. Doctor. Similarly, the family name of late Prime Minister of India was merely the designation of a degree "Bachelor of Arts".

As a part of the prevailing social practices of the Muslims in South India, some aspects of the names-of-persons were studied (Hussain Khan, 1994). Specific family names among the members of a specified community, were explained. In the forward to the above book, Prof. Gopala Sarana (1994) recorded a very important observation about the Muslims of Gulwar in Gulbarga, which is reproduced as under :

"It is in this context of coexistence that Muslims have imbibed more of the Hindu sentiments, norms and values rather than vice-versa. As such, they reveal a number of similarities with Hindus in the social practices and traditions, especially pertaining to their marriage, kinship and family life. This in no way means the marriage and kinship of Muslims of Guliwar is identical to that of Hindus in all respects... The way in which prescribed body of rules and religious norms governing their family life and interpersonal kin network are interpreted and translated into practice, hinge on the local socio - cultural conditions in which they live."

Srinivas (1966) described the caste patterned society of the Hindus. Its changing facets in the modern times, were presented. In particular, two contrary distinct social phenomena namely 'Sanskritization' and 'Westernization' were found to have profoundly influenced the mutilation of original names. Both of these had however, emerged only after the independence. In another contribution (Basham, 1967), caste pattern prevailing in the Hindus, Muslims, and other minorities were discussed. Likewise, among the Brahmins of North India, peculiar family names denoting the status of the fore-fathers, were used (Mishra, 1949). Their origin was explained in a lucid manner.

Commenting upon why some Indians change their names in their mid- life, which was akin to changing horses in mid stream, Raghunath (1996) stated that one compelling reason could be the ceaseless rubbing they obtained from their peers over their unfortunate names. Few examples of some names were provided.

A detailed analysis of the Telugu names-of-persons, was provided (Gupta, 1993). Though, this article was written for a common man, it is found quite useful. On Tamil names, Subhadra Krishnamurthy (1983) made an interesting analysis. Similarly, a popular write- up connecting the nickname with the identification of a person, appeared (Parthasarathy, 1997).

Marathi surnames were analysed quite elaborately by Soni (1992). His observation to treat pen-names as family names is quite relevant.

The Illustrated Weekly of India had brought out a series of articles on different communities. Each write-up contained a note on the names-of-persons of the community discussed. The following segments of the Indic names-of-persons were covered :

1. Khatris (Chopra, 1971a) from Punjab; and on their caste names (Chopra, 1971b);

2. Sikhs (Randhawa, 1969) from Punjab, and their names (Gill, 1969);

3. Kashmiri Pandits (Rifaquat Ali, 1970a) from the Kashmir Valley; and their surnames (Rifaquat Ali, 1970b));

4. Kayasthas (Dayal, 1971) from the Hindi speaking belt; and on their family names (Saxena, 1971);

5. Sindhis (Gauba, 1969a); and their names (Gauba, 1969b);

6. Parsees (Bulsara, 1969); and on their surnames (Kanga, 1969);

7. Saraswat names (Patil, 1970b); and on their surnames (Patil, 1970a);

8. Iyers (Trivadi, 1970a) and Iyengars (Srinivasachar, 1970a); and on the pattern of their family names (Trivadi, 1970b) and (Srinivasachar, 1970b)

Anthropological Survey of India had undertaken a massive project on the cultural and sociological aspects of different linguistic states in the country. Naming practices prevailing in different parts, also formed a small but important part of the project. Several volumes of the project work, have so far been published. Their details are given as below :

1. Andaman and Nicobar (Singh, 1994a). It contained useful articles by Justin (1994); Subbakrishna (1994); and Sarkar (1994).

2. Dadara and Nagar Haveli (Singh, 1994b). A chapter by Sinha (1994c) was interesting.

3. Daman and Diu (Singh, 1994c). Several chapters were found helpful. They were written by Sinha (1994a, 1994b, and 1994d).

4. Delhi (Singh, 1996b). It covered an article by Lakshmi (1996) and another by Pachouri (1996). Both of these are educational in several aspects of naming process.

5. Goa (Singh, 1993a). It included several chapters. One was by Biswas (1993), three were by Rao (1993a, 1993b and 1993c) and another two by Supner (1993a, and 1993b) were useful. In addition, its introduction by Shirodkar et al. (1993) and a translated paper by Periera (1940) were found beneficial.

6. Himachal Pradesh (Singh, 1996c). Its introduction by Sankhyan (1996) contained new information on the influence of the Tibetan culture.

7. Lakshwadeep (Singh, 1993b). Several chapters by Tandan (1993a, 1993b, 1994c, 1994d) were helpful.

8. Pondicherry (Singh, 1994d). A chapter by Naidu (1994) was quite useful.

9. Sikkim (Singh, 1993c). Three chapters by Ghatak (1993a, 1993b, 1993c) and two chapters by Ghosal (1993a, 1993b) contained a lot of relevant information.

In addition, the under - mentioned reference works have also been consulted, which are covering the entire country:

1. Communities, segments, synonyms, surnames and titles (Singh, 1996a).

2. Scheduled castes (Singh, 1994e).

3. Scheduled tribes (Singh, 1994f).

Published gazetteers from different parts of the country are easily available. They are helpful in throwing some light on the subject of the names-of-persons. Similarly, there have been some other publications relevant to the subject. The following publications are useful in the present work:

Himalayan gazetteer (Atkinson, 1882);

Tribes and castes of Cochin (Anantha Krishna Iyer, 1912);

Panjab castes; races, castes and tribes of Panjab (Ibbetson, 1916);

Orissa gazetteer (Senapati and Sahu, 1968);

Tribes of Andhra Pradesh (Shashi, 1995);

Social and cultural history of Kerala (Sreedhara Menon 1979);

Social life in Himachal Pradesh (Shashi, 1971);

The Census of India 1991 (1995) has been quite helpful in describing the population of each linguistic area. It also lists different minorities. However, due to disturbed conditions, census could not be held in Jammu and Kashmir. The figures for the 1981 Census are available. Sindhi population data could not be obtained as the pertinent volume has not yet been published. The NIC terminal at Hyderabad could answer the query (Census of India 1981).

Mehrotra (1994) edited a very useful book on Indic names. It contained chapters on Kashmiri names (Khan, 1994) and (Koul, 1994); Gujarati names (Mistry, 1994); Marathi names (Dhongde, 1994); Bengali names (Sircar, 1994); Oriya names (Patnaik, 1994); Telugu names (Sjoberg, 1994); Kannada names (Mrigeppa, 1994) and Malayalam names (Rajasekharan Nair, 1994). Similarly, on Sindhi culture, Thakur (1959) produced a useful book. It also discussed family names of Sindhis.

Koul (1924) presented the evolution of Kashmiri surnames, from several nick-names, in an amusing way. Some information on female names of Andamani tribals, was provided (Ranjit Daniels, 1996). Likewise, a scanty discussion on Indic names was made (Smith, 1950).

Part III - Provisions in AACR 2

Anglo-American Cataloguing Rule 2 provides specific rules for handling Indic names in cataloguing, under 22.25. There are two broad categorisation of the Indic names included in it. They are listed as under:

1. Rule No. 22.25A	Early names pertaining to those persons who had flourished before the middle of the nineteenth century.
2. Rule No. 22.25B	Modern Indic names borne by the persons flourishing after the middle of the nineteenth century.

For the purpose of the present research work, only the later category is relevant. Further, it is observed that the middle of the nineteenth century (1850) selected as the cut - off year between the ancient and the modern period, is not very appropriate. Hence, in the present work, the turn of the century (1900) is specifically taken as the cut-off year, which is more logical, on account of the under mentioned reasons

1. British rule in the country had spread in almost all the parts of the country. Even in the areas or regions, being governed directly by the native rulers, British supremacy was fully recognised. On the other hand, in 1850, there had been confusion regarding the status of the British, in a major part of the country.

2. The English educational system had become in 1900, fully operational. The first few universities in the country were established by the British only in 1857. Hence, no university was existing in the country in 1850.

3. The transformation in the new structure of the Indic names-of-persons, and the usage of the anglicised names, due to Western influence, had started getting stabilized around 1900. On the other hand, there was hardly any discernible change in the names in 1850.

4. There had been hardly any publication, contributed by the Indians, particularly in English language, around 1850. On the other hand, quite a few Indian publications had emerged after 1900.

Having decided on the demarcation year as 1900, a perusal of the AACR reveals that there are 4 specific rules for handling the modern Indic names. These are :

Rule No. 22.25B1 Modern Indic names - General

Rule No. 22.25B2 South Indian names

Rule No. 22.25B3 Sikh names

Rule No. 22.25B4 Religious names

Analysis of Modern Indic names under the rule no.22.25B1, has revealed the following problems:

1. The rule 22.25B1 directs entering an Indic name from all parts of the country, except from South India and barring Sikhs, under the surname, or under a name that the person is known to have used as a surname. If, however there is no surname, enter under the last name. In order to implement the specific rule, 5 illustrative examples have been provided. The rule suffers from the following errors and inadequacies:

(i) Surname has not been defined. In other words, nothing has been stated or clarified as to what constitutes a surname in an over all Indian scenario.

(ii) V.K. Krishna Menon is a South Indian name. It has been erroneously included in the example, which is wrong. It would have been appropriate to discuss it under South Indian names. In this name, two surnames are present. The first one is the initial of his vernacular surname (Vengalil) and the other is his caste denoting surname coming from the mother's side, If the prescription is implemented, either the entry be prepared under Menon or under the full expansion of the initial V. Yet, the example strangely suggests to prepare the entry under Krishna Menon, which is correct, without explanation.

(iii) Indrajit Singh has been rendered under Singh. This is a non-Sikh name. Perhaps, it has been taken for granted that Singh is the surname.

As the entire name is the personal name and in the absence of the known preference of the author, the entry has to be prepared under Indrajit Singh.

(iv) The entry of Lal Bahadur Shastri has been correctly prescribed under Shastri. However, the reasoning is wrong. Shastri here is neither a family name, nor a religious title, nor a reinforcement to another surname, as explained in the AACR. It is just the designation of a vernacular degree, meaning "Bachelor of Arts" used as the prominent part of his name. It can be considered as an appendage to the name. It assumed the place of his surname as of now, all his family members make use of Shastri as their surname. This has been despite none possessing the degree.

(v) No mention of the prefix titles has been made, though the practice is wide-spread particularly in North India.

(vi) If no surname is used in a name, the last part generally is an impotent but essential word. Hence, the prescription to render such a name under the last word may produce queer results and obscure the identity of the person.

(vii) Religious minorities from different linguistic regions, have not been given consideration.

(Viii) No sub-rule has been presented for Buddhist names from Sikkim and Ladakh, even though their names-of-persons are different.

(ix) Indian Muslim names have not been included. Treating them at par with Arabic names may lead to incoherent cataloguing.

(x) It does not talk of the British Indian titles conferred on a few distinguished Indians, and used as prefixes to some of the names.

(xi) Names-of-persons from the Western and Eastern parts of the country, have not been covered.

(xii) The prescription does not provide for resolving the problems of the vernacular and anglicised surnames.

(xiii) Multi-worded surnames are not included.

(xiv) Specific suffix attachments such as the pen - name, etc. are not prescribed.

In dealing with the South Indian names, the prescription under 22.25B2 is more or less similar to the earlier rule. It directs to enter a

South Indian name under the personal name provided no surname is used in the name. However, if a surname is present, it does not tell as to how the same is to be treated? Probably, the prescription is to render a South Indian name under the surname, if employed. The under mentioned problems vitiate the total validity of the rule:

(i) It does not indicate where the surname occurs in a South Indian name-of-person. Besides, it does not define the surname in the context of the southern parts of the country.

(ii) The prescription together with the illustrative examples, is silent on multi-worded given names.

(iii) The name of Sir Chettur Sankaran Nair (given as a modal entry), rendered correctly is not in conformity with the rule. Here, the entry ought to have been made under Chettur which as per AACR 2 is the house name or the vernacular family name of the bearer or under Nair which is a caste denoting surname. However, it may be clarified here that Chettur is a place name and not the house name.

(iv) In the particular example of O.P. Josaph, O. has been explained as the initial of Oorakath which is the house name. A house name in Kerala is the vernacular surname. Hence, the illustration of rendering his name under the given name is a contradiction of the prescription, though the end result is correct.

(v) In Sarvepalli Radhkrishnan, Sarvepalli has been taken as a village name, and hence, the entry has been prescribed under the given name. Here, the end result is correct, but the logic is wrong. The word Sarvepalli is also a place name. However, it can't be ascertained whether the same Sarvepalli is appearing in Dr. Radhakrishnan's name or there might have been another village under the same name. In any case, the family of Radhkrishnan has nothing to do with the place bearing the name Sarvepalli. It is his intiperu or house name also known as surname and as such should have been the entry word according to the rule.

In respect of Sikh names-of-persons, the prescription is rather amusing. It directs to enter a Sikh name who does not use Singh or Kaur as a surname, under the first of his or her name (the given name). The following observations negate the validity of the rule :

(i) Singh or Kaur is never used as a surname. In fact both of these words are forming part of most of the masculine and feminine given names respectively. They are generic names devoid of any individualising capacity.

(ii) If a Sikh name is ending with a family name, no specific guidance or rule has been prescribed.

(iii) Usage of takhallus (pen-name) which is also prevailing among the Punjabi names, has not been discussed.

(iv) No mention of the prefixes, has been made, though they are used in several names.

Religious names under 22.25B4 have been correctly prescribed under the given names. The religious titles prefixed to the names, have been inverted.

A very relevant publication in which the decisions and the interpretation of the rules of the AACR 2 were consolidated together, which the Library of Congress, the National Library of Canada, the British Library and the National Library of Australia have made to govern their use of AACR 2nd revision (AACR 2R), and including the amendments 1993 (Howarth, 1994). However, the treatment is vague, scanty and insufficient to deal the vast subject of Indic names-of-persons.

From the analysis of the relevant published literature, it can be concluded that sufficient investigation has not been made in determining the various dimensions of the problems of the Indic names. This has resulted in vague, incorrect and inadequate prescriptions in the AACR. Even other cataloguing codes do not provide adequate solutions. Hence, in the present research work, sociological investigation on the existing naming practices, in various linguistic regions, has been specifically carried out so that a comprehensive picture emerges and guides the cataloguers and indexers, in making the right choice. Based on such an in-depth study of naming practices, cataloguing rules have been framed which are aimed at resolving the aberrations in AACR 2.

Chapter III

INDIC NAMES - CHARACTERISTICS

3.1 IMPORTANCE OF NAMES-OF-PERSONS

In a library catalogue, the name-of-person (author's name) is an important ingredient as it constitutes one of the largest categories of headings. As per one study conducted at the Library of Congress (Avram et. al., 1967), 74.7% of the main entries were of personal name entries. In another study (Abdul Huq, 1976b?), in a medium size university library, 38 % of all the entries including added and subject entries were found to pertain to personal names. Further, the catalogue of a library being the basic tool of accessing the collection, author's name constitutes an important approach to individual volumes in the collection. In fact, it is only next in importance to the subject approach. Hence, extensive study of the names-of-persons becomes very important in framing the rules for their proper handling in cataloguing.

In European and North American names-of-persons, there is usually a fixed place for forename, second name and the surname. Therefore, the rules of cataloguing prescribed for their treatment are capable of dealing with them satisfactorily. In Indic names-of- persons, on the other hand, any conceivable sequence could be there (Ranganathan, 1959b) and word division has never been uniform (Pearson, 1978). For instance, one word may appear as given name in some cases, where as the same may be used as surname in yet others, and even it may denote a courtesy term used as a prefix title, in some specific names. Similarly, a word may be written as a unit-word in some area, while the same might be written split, in some other area.

Thus, the puzzling diversity displayed immensely by a variety of Indic names, pose serious problems in cataloguing. The cataloguer can overcome these difficulties only by having an in-depth understanding of the complexities associated with the Indic names particularly the taxonomy of their component parts. An Indic name-of-person, in general denotes among other things, the following attributes (Karnow, 1966):

(a) Regional origin;

(b) Religious following;

(c) Caste affiliation;

(d) Profession, past or present; and

(e) Educational level.

In addition, the degree of stabilization in the words used in the Indic names-of-persons, is less developed (Pearson, 1978). In contrast to these, European and North American names are generally independent of the above listed attributes, and the stability factor is very high.

3.2 FAMILY NAMES

It may be noted that the usage of the family names in the Indic names-of-persons is not an Indian practice. In fact, it has emerged and adopted by many Indians only after the advent of the British rule. Its flourishing after the independence of the country, is linked with the enlargement of the educational facilities. Yet, it has not become universal in all the linguistic parts of the country, and there is evidence that several persons have abandoned the usage of surnames.

As the tradition of employing the surnames in Indic names has come from an alien culture, and a variety of practices in this regard are in vogue in different parts of the country, it is observed that the potency of surname is not uniformly distributed in all the linguistic regions. There are regions where two types of surnames are used. Similarly, there are areas where no family names are existing. All these add to the confusion. In other words, it is not very clear as to what constitutes a family name in the over all Indian context.

Ranganathan (1964) defined a family name " as a word or word group normally inherited by a person as denoting the name of his family, and it consists of proper noun(s)". It is also denoted by the terms 'Surname' and 'Last Name'. However, this definition may be valid for a European or North American name, but does not hold good in the Indian context. For instance, prefix titles are also inherited by the persons particularly in North India which generally denote the caste, or other status of the person. In addition, in some linguistic regions, such as the Telugu and Malayalam speaking areas, vernacular surnames are inherited and employed as essential elements in the names. However, they are not equivalent to the surnames as used in the Western world.

Another factor for non-acceptance of the above definition is that if every person in India is inheriting some surname, then how is it that many persons do not use surname at all. And if a surname were to be inherited, why do some persons change the same to some other form or to drop it altogether, in their names ? At times, surnames used even by two brothers may differ in form.

Hence, a family name is a word or word-group consisting of proper noun(s) or sometimes by common noun, reflecting the caste status or some other background of the bearer, used as the end part of the name. In some cases, surnames are devised by the persons by themselves. In some linguistic regions such as Telugu and Malayalam speaking states, house name (the equivalent of the surname) occurs in the beginning of the name. But, it does not fall into the definition of a family name, as understood in the Western sense. A house name in such a name-of-person is the least important element.

Regarding the principle of kinship under which the family name is passed on to the next lower generation, Jayaraman (1989) has described the process in the following words :

"Traditionally, most Hindus, Sikhs, Jains and Buddhists subscribe to the patrilineal principle of kinship, which means that property, office and family name were all transmitted in the male line, from father to son. Under this system, a girl retained her father's family name until she is married when she took her husband's [family] name. A major exception to the patrilineal rule was the Nayars, a few other castes in Kerala, and a few tribal groups such as Khasi and Garo in Assam, who followed the matrilineal principle. In this latter system, a person (male or female) inherits the family name, office, and property of the mother and mother's brother and not of the father."

Thus, under the matrilineal system, there is generally no change in a feminine name-of-person, after the marriage. To put it in other words, a woman continues to be known by her maiden name, even after her marriage. In addition, if the father and son are both employing caste attachments along with their personal names, both of them may be present in the full form of the name. Thus, two caste appellations can be discernible in a few names-of- persons from Kerala.

However, during the recent times the system of matriliny has weakened. The reasons for such a change are many. As per Singh (1993b) the growing emphasis on pre-marital virginity of women, sexual consistency in marriage and patrilineal authority over children, are all concerned with the patrilineal ideology. Similarly, among the Muslims of Kerala, the matrilineal system is declining as a result of the ideology and practice of Islam, which as a religion born in semitic ambience, upheld patrilineal norms and paternal authority (Singh, 1993b). This is reflected in changing of a few female names even under the matrilineal system, after marriage.

Relative importance of surnames, as used in the Indic names varies from one linguistic area to another. In the entire South Indian states for instance, family name is not as important an element as given name is, for addressing the person. It is simply used as a qualifying epithet. Hence, a family name in the southern belt is an essential but impotent attachment to the names, for cataloguing purposes. In other zones, a family name if employed by an author, assumes a very important role. Similarly, if no family name occurs in a name, the personal name becomes important.

3.3 PERSONAL NAME

Another important component of a name-of-person is the personal name. It is a word or a set of words used to denote a person. In contrast to a family name, which is common to all the members of a family, personal names of all individuals are different. It is also known as given name, and is equivalent of the Christian name in the Western world. It is different from a nick name, in the sense that a nick name is employed to refer to an individual within a close and intimate circle and is generally not in usage in the wider public forums. For the present purpose, only personal names are relevant.

Apart from the personal names, there is another category of names in which a person assumes some name generally a false one, intended to conceal his identity. It is known as pseudonym. In the present work, however, pseudonyms have not been included, as they form a separate subject of study.

In the northern and eastern portions of the country, generally personal names are single worded, though a tendency to break them into two parts, is prevailing. This practice of splitting the given names misleads a cataloguer not familiar with the system, to believe that the personal name is consisting of two independent words. In reality, the second word is merely a complementary component, supporting the first word. Jain (1972) has called it an added name. Thus, if no surname is suffixed to a personal name, the catalogue entry is to be prepared in its natural sequence.

In the western parts of the country, personal names are generally single worded. Even if a given name is complex, having more than one word, the practice of rendering it in a unit worded form, is prevailing. This is helpful in the identification of the given name.

In the southern parts of the country, quite a large number of given names are single worded and only a few ones are complex or multi-worded. If a personal name has more than one word, the general practice is to render the same as separate words. Here also, some persons are dissecting their personal names, in rare instances.

3.4 STARTER WORD : SURNAME OR FORENAME

As an Indic name-of-person generally consists of more than one element, the foremost problem confronting the cataloguers and indexers, is to decide whether the entry be prepared under the surname or in the forename. In this regard, Ranganathan (1954b) prescribed a mathematical formula under which the numerousness of personal names is to be judged from the number of words in the reservoir of the family names. As per this formula, the entry has to be prepared under the words falling into the larger group. If this formulation is to be applied, perhaps all categories of the Indic names would qualify to be rendered under the given names. This has been so as the number of the family names in each linguistic region is fewer than the words contributing to the formation of the personal names. In other words, all the main entries have to be prepared under the given names.

Sengupta (1959c) rejected the above proposition, and felt that though forenames were far more 'numerous and heterogeneous' in comparison to the words used as surnames which were 'amenable to categorization and standardization', it was no argument to enter authors under their forenames. He felt that the decision should be taken as per the usage of different components of the names in each linguistic belt.

IASLIC Seminar on Indic Names, held in Calcutta, had formed separate linguistic groups, and after deliberations, each group indicated its preference either in favour of forename or surname. The end results which had come out in several linguistic groups, are surprisingly contrary to the findings of this research. Group leaders representing different linguistic areas, after consulting their members felt that Bengali names be entered under forenames, whereas Oriya speaking authors were preferred in their family names. Similarly, Hindi and Punjabi names were recommended to be rendered under the forenames (IASLIC, 1961a). Probably, many cataloguers present in the Seminar, were carried away by the logic of the towering personality of Ranganathan.

After a careful study of the problems of the Indic names in cataloguing, it is suggested that in those areas where some system of employing words or word groups at the end part of the names is prevailing, and when such words or word groups in public usage are recognised as the family names, entry is to be prepared under the surname. In terms of linguistic belts, except in the southern states (Andhra Pradesh, Tamilnadu, Kerala and Karnataka), it is the family name under which an entry is to be preferred. However, there are several exceptions. For instance, an author may not use any family name, the choice then is limited to the given name. If a pen-name has been used as an additional suffix, and it becomes more popular, preference has to be given to it, even if the surname is also present in the name. Further, in the state of Karnataka, there is a particular area possessing strong Maratha influence. In this part, surname is employed in the same manner as used in a Marathi name-of-person, the entry is to be prepared under the surname. In the remaining geographic area of the South India, it is generally the personal name under which a catalogue entry is to be prepared.

Again, there is a further exception in dealing with the Indic name-of-person particularly from South India. Several authors represent all the parts of their names by initials except the last word, which sometimes, is only a small part of the given name, and is generally incapable of standing alone, in many instances. The only option then left before a cataloguer is to elevate such an impotent attachment word to the level of the main entry element. An impotent word, as per Ranganathan (1953a), underlines absence of any capacity to individualise a person, all by itself. Its capacity is as poor as that of a common noun. Yet, the preference of the author for his name, has always to be respected. However, if the preference can not be ascertained, prevailing social norms on the structural pattern of the names have to be followed.

Similarly, an author may use anglicised form of his family name for instance, in his publications in the English language. He may however, stick to the vernacular version of his surname in the books contributed in the vernacular language. As a further extension of it, if a translation of such a book is published, and if the translator is not aware about the existence of the two different forms of the same family name, it might be quite possible that the name-of-person, including the surname, is literally transcribed into the foreign language. Therefore, the prescription to the problem can be enumerated as given below :

(a) The form of the family name is chosen as per the usage of the author in that language of the work. This would be irrespective of the form appearing in the work. The form of the family name not chosen as the entry, has to be provided for by the cross-references. Yet, in respect of those authors employing only one form of their surnames, only the form used, is to be retained.

(b) In an integrated form of a catalogue, the form would be the one in which the author has been widely known among the users.

The European culture had during the pre-independence period, immensely contributed to the inventing of the usage of some irremovable attachments to the Indic names-of-persons as the most important part of the names. A word or word-group attached to an Indic name may indicate ancestry, caste, class, occupation, official rank, title, academic distinction, place of residence or some such attributes of the fore-fathers, during the far-off days (Sengupta, 1958).

Subba Rao (1961b) also held a similar view-point, and has specifically connected the matter with the migration of some educated Indians, to England, for obtaining higher education, and in taking the Indian Civil Services examination held in England, during the British period, in the following words :

"It so happened when a few Indians went to the West for higher studies or [for appearing in the] civil service, the society there shortened their longish names to Reddy, Rao, Mukherji, Mulay, and so on. These endings are so distinct in the Western society that the peculiar minority could be easily identified. Forename was never called to function. On return, in the civil service and in high society which did not include the majority of the people, the supposed surnames had currency. For an educated citizen of the forename group when service took into surname areas, a suitable contraction of the personal name was turned into surname. Instead of longer forename, a shortened title, caste name, or word of patronymic significance (surname !) was enough for identification."

The above observation of Subba Rao was meant primarily for the persons falling in the elite groups. But, now a common man is also indulging in such shortenings of his name. Some have gone beyond it, and are using some part of their personal names as if it were a family name. The reasons for such transformation can be enumerated as given below :

(a) Availability of higher education facility to any level in the country;

(b) Increasing mobility of the common man to other linguistic regions;

(c) Enlarging the visual media; and

(d) Imitating some of the unusual practices of the important persons falling in the elite groups such as the top bureaucrats, educationists, pleaders, politicians, and so on.

The above mentioned factors in one way or the other, have resulted in over simplifying and rationalising the pattern of the names-of-persons in almost all the linguistic regions of the country. In other words, usage of such attachments (the last part) having practically no significance in the names, is continuously showing an upward trend. This has been contrary to the predictions made by Ranganathan (1954b), who had forecasted in the particular context of the southern Indian names, that 'the very impotency associated with such attachment words would soon kill them'.

Another peculiar situation is discernible in which an author may write his name in vernacular form, in his publications in the local language. Generally, full form of the name-of-person is employed in any of the vernacular languages. However, he may use anglicised format of his name in his publications in the English language (Sengupta, 1961). There are several variations. The most commonly used one is to reduce several parts of the name into initials. If the library possesses publications in English as well as in the local language, it can create problems to the cataloguer in relating the two forms of his name, in the catalogue.

During the IASLIC Seminar on rendering of the Indic names, the opinion of the cataloguers was highly divided over the entry element. Some participants favoured personal name as the main entry element. Others were keen that surname be made the entry word. Therefore, the Seminar had resolved (IASLIC, 1961c) that 'considering the diverse nature of different cultural and linguistic groups in India, it has been expressed unanimously that no practical purpose could be served by having one uniform rule for Author headings'. 'Hence' the resolution continued, 'it is decided that different cultural and linguistic groups should have freedom to determine the most potent parts of the names (either the personal name or surname) for the purpose of Author heading'.

Shukla (1961a), the Director of the IASLIC Seminar on Indic Names however, had come forward with some pragmatic and useful alternatives. They would certainly be of immense help to a cataloguer not familiar with the culture of the author. They are described as under:

1. Various linguistic and cultural groups to compile comprehensive bibliographical works for literature past and present, with appropriate author headings, which will also help the cataloguers of other areas;

2. To rely on authoritative work done in this direction by the Indian National Bibliography and various state central libraries; and

3. To work for the standard author statement on the back of the title page of a book.

In this context, it is observed that success in the above suggestions has been very limited, and consistency could not be maintained in all the cases. The third and the last one however, could not be accepted by most of the publishers and authors.

Ranganathan having devoted considerable time and energy in pursuit of resolving the problems of the Indic name-of-persons in cataloguing, ultimately became frustrated. He has observed the impracticability of any one cultural group deciding the mode of rendering the names-of-persons of all the cultural groups in the country. He strongly felt that the author alone knows about the structure of his name. He writes (Ranganathan, 1964), 'the one person who knows the Entry Element and the Secondary Element in a Name-of-person is the person himself. International economy and efficiency in cataloguing require that the author should indicate in his documents the Entry Element and the Secondary Element in his name, along with the lines laid down in the Indian Standard IS 792 - 1962 specification for title page and back of title page of a book. This is to be printed at the back of the title page of a book, or in a suitable place in any other kind of document'. This, according to him, appears to be the only right solution to secure accuracy and consistency in rendering a name-of-person.

However, in spite of the observation made as above, together with the adoption of several Indian Standards in the country, and an earnest appeal to all the authors and publishers, by such an eminent personality as Dr. S.R. Ranganathan, nothing substantially could be achieved, and the problems associated with the Indic names in cataloguing have continued unabated.

3.5 FEATURES OF INDIC NAMES

The Indic name-of-person is linked to the caste based Hindu society. It generally reflects the identity, status, and levels of aspirations (Singh, 1996a) of the bearer. In studying Indic names-of-persons, one has to understand the true nature of the prevailing social-infrastructure in the country, which has been knit into a firm fabric of an age old system of a variety of castes based on specific professions or occupations. These caste groups are more or less standardized throughout the country, though they are known in different parts by varying names. Their number in any region is large and a family generally earns its livelihood through the age old specific occupation of the particular caste with which it is associated. Thus, changing the mode of occupation outside the permissible range for a caste, may not widely take place. These castes are further fragmented into sub-castes. Events of intimate social intercourse such as matrimonial alliances, etc. may not occur in a big way, away from the sub-castes and the local area. In other words, Indian society is quite immobile in its behaviour. It has brought inertia to the cultural change. Another factor worth reporting here, is that to a large extent, society is male dominated. Female names are often changed, partly or in toto, after marriage as per the local customs prevailing. This reflects the dependent status of a woman (Singh, 1996a).

In order to have further grasp on the understanding of the existing caste pattern system, it is a prerequisite to define the varna model of the Hindus. Under this model, the entire society is fragmented into four distinct varnas based on specific occupations. The most highly placed varna is of Brahmins (i.e. learned people involved in learning, teaching , and or performing other religious rituals); followed by the Kshatriyas (or the warriors). Vaisyas come third in the hierarchy and are involved in trade and business. The last one pertains to Sudras, responsible for performing all the menial jobs. In the present caste system which evolved over a long period of time among a number of communities, it is rather difficult to identify the broad varna to which a particular caste belongs. This is true of almost all the castes except the Brahmins and a few low ranking castes of the Sudra (Srinivas, 1966).

However, the great diversity existing in the Indian culture, as displayed in different parts of the country, has a cementing bond in the form of a common religion, viz. Hinduism, which is practised by the vast majority of its inhabitants. The religious foundations are so much deep that a number of other religions which had come later and flourished in the country, have failed to shatter this bond and became Indianised to a large extent. For instance, Islam preaches a casteless social order, and does not permit discrimination on the basis of caste or perpetuation of the same at the social and religious levels among its followers. Yet, in India, Muslim society has also developed some what a similar system based on castes derived from specific professions, and these castes are placed in a fixed hierarchy (Basham, 1967). Similar is the case with other religious groups such as Sikhs, Buddhists, Christians, and so on. In the matter of names, linguistic group, along with specific religion, is the prime determinant of the broad structure of the pattern of the same. Deep understanding of the different castes prevailing in a region resolve many complexities associated with the names-of-persons. The other factors could be the educational level of the person and whether the family has moved out to another linguistic belt, permanently.

In placing the caste system into the varna model of the Hindus, Srinivas (1966) has described two contrary phenomena taking place simultaneously in the Indian society. One of them is 'Sanskritization' under which, a lower caste tends to acquire a higher status in the hierarchy over a period of two to three generations, with persons belonging to the middle level backward castes observing the life cycle rituals including food habits, ideas and culture of the higher castes. The converse of this phenomena is 'Westernization', under which higher caste people move into the lower hierarchy by abandoning their rituals, and by bringing in drastic changes in their food habits, etc. In this respect, it can be stated that Westernization is the net result of increasing English education, fast urbanisation and rapid industrialization. Similarly, 'Sanskritization' has emerged because of the concept of equality of all the persons at the social plane, in a democratic set-up.

In the context of Indic names-of-persons, it is observed that the process of 'Sanskritization' has provided an opportunity to adopt surnames denoting higher caste status, by the people of the lower castes (Jayaraman, 1989). This reflects both the process of upward mobility and of sharing among communities of the regional heritage in the cultural-linguistic context (Singh, 1996a). Likewise, in the other process of Westernization, many of the higher caste Hindus have abandoned the usage of their caste denoting features in their names. Yet, during the recent years, the Dalits have resisted the trend of adopting the family names of the higher caste Hindus, and a few persons belonging to the higher castes, have started employing surnames of the lower caste groups, so as to obtain different concessions and facilities available to the persons of the lower castes (Singh, 1996a).

The above processes of Sanskritization and Westernization have not only affected the Hindu society alone, they are found in other religious groups as well. For instance, Ibbetson (1916) has recorded a popular Persian proverb prevailing in Panjab which states 'The first year I was a weaver (Julaha); the next year a Shekh. This year, if prices rise I shall be a Saiyad'. On the other hand, quite a few Muslims have also abandoned the caste appellations in their names.

3.5.1 Names from different parts

After a perusal of a large number of the names-of-persons from different linguistic parts of the country, specific generic observations can be made. That names-of-persons of North are shorter in length, simpler in structure and straight forward as compared to the names of the South which generally carry other features such as the name of the father, village, house etc. Another important characteristic is that surnames derived from the caste structure, find widespread usage in the North, they are employed very occasionally in the South, and that too restricted to a few leading high castes. In terms of potency, end part of a North Indian name-of-person carries more strength if it happens to be the family name, than the same in South India. In South India, personal names are generally derived from the names of the Hindu Gods or their innumeral manifestations, where as in the northern parts, there are additional sources of obtaining the given names.

The names-of-persons from West India, generally include several similarities of the same found in the northern parts. For example, personal name in both the regions, is generally placed in the beginning. Also, some commonalities are discernible with the South Indian names. Names in both the regions, do generally include the name of the father or husband, as the case may be. Hence, by knowing the name-of-person, the name of the father is also known. This makes it easy to trace the line upwards or downwards, through the names (Mukerjee; 1957). East India, from the names point of view, is very much similar to the northern parts, since the basic structure of the names in both the parts, is the same. However, usage of some of the anglicised words as the surnames is quite common in the eastern parts of the country, particularly in West Bengal and Orrisa. In addition, multi-worded surnames are often employed in the eastern states.

Another generic observation in the practice of rendering the personal names, is that in the northern and eastern parts of the country, they are generally broken in two parts, and both the parts are rendered as if each one is an independent word. Yet, they have to be read together. In the Western India, breaking of the personal names is not generally resorted to. In general, personal names are written in a unified basis, as one word. In the southern parts, both the practices are in vogue. That some names are split as an exception, and some others are not.

In the southern states of Tamilnadu, and Kerala, quite a number of masculine personal names are ending with 'an'. However, if caste names are also suffixed, it is observed that 'an' is generally dropped out in the given names, as per the rules of the local grammar. Likewise, in Andhra Pradesh, 'iya' or 'lu' if used in a personal name, may be abandoned if the caste feature is also suffixed. Thus, to a cataloguer not familiar with the process, a new name may apparently be created, if caste name is attached, afterwards.

3.5.2 Problems of Migration

In personal names, varying styles as per diversified usages have emerged in different linguistic parts of the country. Thus, Ramachandran of Kerala or Tamilnadu may become Ramachandra in Karnataka; Ramchandraiah or Ramachandrayya in Andhra Pradesh. In North India, his name may become Ram Chander or Ram Chand. As a rule of the thumb, any name ending with 'an' as Gopalakrishnan, 'am' such as Santhanam or nath as Viswanath is generally from Kerala or Tamilnadu (Jayaraman, 1989). Similarly, 'iah', 'iya', yya or 'lu' could be the endings of some of the personal names from Andhra Pradesh.

In addition to a slight phonetic change in the personal name, immigration to another linguistic belt can sometimes, also bring transformation in the structure of the name-of-person. For instance, a female from North India named as Anuradha Pandey had become Pandey Anuradha (or simply P. Anuradha) in Andhra Pradesh. She was afterwards known in Tamilnadu as Damodar Anuradha or D. Anuradha. Damodar is the first part of the name of her father. In Karnataka, migration from the Marathi area to another also brings change in structure, in a few names. The situation is so much baffling that it becomes a serious problem in analysing the parts of some names of Karnataka.

Similarly, Gatta Raghunath of Andhra Pradesh has become Raghu Nath Gatta or R.N. Gatta in Uttar Pradesh. Yet, he was known officially as Raghunath Seshagirirao Gatta in Maharashtra. Sheshagirirao is the name of his father, and Gatta is his house name.

In the eastern parts of the country, the letter 'v' is pronounced as 'b', resulting in a slight phonetic variation in a few names. The personal name of the author of this work Devendra Kumar, was written as Debendra Kumar, in West Bengal, which was quite baffling even to him.

On immigration to foreign countries, some Indians have deformed their names, in an attempt to make them look native. For instance, in Australia a person having his personal name as Gopalaraman, initially became Gopala Raman. On shortening his name became G. Raman and finally got transformed as Garry Raman. Another person, Janakiraman has become Jon Raman or John Raman. Similarly, Joginder Singh and Baskar Rao have also anglicised their names as Joe Singh and Bill Rao respectively. The anglicisation of the Indian names-of-persons has become quite common in foreign countries like Australia and the United States (Jayaraman, 1989).

3.5.3 Religious Minorities

The above described generalisations in a broad sense, are applicable primarily to the Hindu society. The other religious groups may generally adopt the prevailing structure of the names-of- persons. In some other cases, influence may be seen marginally and yet in some societies, its impact is not felt. In general, in the matter of following a particular structure of the names, religious minorities form a sub-set of the regional demography. Buddhists, Christians and Jains, though are separate religious groups, are generally following the Hindu pattern of names. Even words employed in the names are commonly used. Yet, the names-of- persons of Buddhists of Ladakh and Sikkim are different as their naming pattern is after the Tibetans.

Sometimes, an educated individual may adopt anglicised model to shorten his name. It is observed that this practice, in recent decades, has been increasing. In this respect, it can be further added that if any author expresses his explicit desire to treat any part of his or her name in a preferred way, which may be based on logical approach or otherwise, the work of the cataloguer becomes easy. But, it has been observed that a large number of the Indic authors don't do so, thereby complicating the process of deciding the entry element.

3.5.4 Tribal Communities

There are several tribal communities inhabiting almost in all the parts of the country. They are different from a caste group. The members of a tribe claim their descent from the aborigines. Educationally, they are generally backward, and are employed in primitive trades. Each tribe is residing in a small geographic track, and is consisting mostly of a small group. Some tribes are so small that they number only a few hundreds. Each tribe is having its own religion, traditions and history. Based on these, it has been stratified into several divisions. These divisions are now used as family names.

In respect of the tribal names-of-persons, Singh (1996a) has recorded his observation in the following words :

"The tribes of middle India and elsewhere in the north-east name their children after the day on which they are born. Some of them even repeat the name of the grandfather for male grand children.... A section of tribes who became Sanskritized adopted Brahmanical gotras. Those who became Christians added clan names and emphasized clans, or the native category of exogamous divisions, as part of the name to avoid incest, a practice which is widespread all over tribal middle India and the north-east.

It is possible to measure the extent of acculturation of tribes by personal names. There are prototypes of tribal names all over tribal middle India, which male and female members adopt, after days, weeks and months, as mentioned above, and after festivals, qualities, drought and famine, plants, flowers, birds and animals, colour, etc. With Sanskritization, tribals have borrowed the names of gods and goddesses, and of epic and Puranic heroes and heroines. When members of tribal communities converted to Christianity, they particularly - the Catholics - assumed the names of Christian saints. The Protestants adopted the names of Christian gods and goddesses or plain secular names. In recent years, with the indigenization, even the Indianization of Christianity, the adoption of Indian names is encouraged, apart from continuing the old practice of lending Hindi and Tamil equivalents of Christian saints' names."

3.5.5 Other Foreign Influences

Apart from the prominent impact of the British culture, which is still continuing in either distorting a few surnames or in contracting the major component parts of the names-of-persons, there have also been other influences of some other foreign cultures. These have come into play due to the fact that some specific parts of the country, had remained under their rule. In general, the structure of the names has remained unaffected. Yet, some words used in the names have been transformed so as to suit the tongue of the foreign rulers. Their description is given as below :

(a) French influence;

(b) Portuguese domination.

In the present work, both the features have been covered, in relation to the changes in the names-of-persons. Similarly, some persons claiming their descent from the Arab world are continuing with the Arabic pattern. This has also been discussed.

3.6 PREFIXES AND SUFFIXES

In North India, there is a tendency to use some honorific titles as prefixes to the names-of-persons. They generally denote the caste status, profession (past or present), etc. Sometimes, conferred titles are also prefixed to the names. The conferred titles were bestowed by the local rulers as well as as by the British rulers. The British Indian titles were:

Among Hindus:	Diwan Bahadur,	Rai Bahadur,	Rao Bahadur
		Rai Sahib,	Rao Sahib
Among Muslims:	Khan Bahadur,	Khan Sahib	
In Sikhs:	Sardar Bahadur		

Most of the prefixes are single worded, though as an exception, they can also be double-worded. All of them are needed to be dropped at the time of cataloguing as they generally denote specific features of caste affiliations to which people belong. In some other names profession denoting or the local self assumed titles could also be employed. Yet, some specific titles have to be preserved in exceptional instances, described as under :

(a) Indian titles conferred, by the former British rulers. Similarly all the Royal British titles awarded by the British Government in England.

(b) A prefix title by usage has become part of the name. In the Muslim names, specific titles have been recommended for retention. Similarly, prefixes used in the names of the erstwhile rulers of the princely states and titles prefixed to the names of saints etc. have been proposed for preservation. Among the Hindus, such titles occur rarely. Yet, it is for the discretion of the cataloguer to decide the matter.

(c) Prefix title employed in the name of father or husband, as the case may be, in those areas where the same is also forming an integral part of the name.

Some prefix titles could be of permanent nature, denoting specific features such as caste or social status. They can also be used by all the members of a family. Another category includes those titles which have been earned by the persons. They are conveying specific profession, educational attainment, religious order, etc. of the individuals. Such titles are not in usage by the persons not possessing the same accomplishment. Beside these categories, there exists yet another class in which specific distinguished persons have monopolised specific titles. However, in all the cases, the prefix titles have to be omitted. Yet, a confusion can be created when one observes that some personal names are formed by the words usually employed as prefix titles. In such situations, they form integral portion of the names, and hence, they can not be abandoned.

Apart from the prefix titles, a variety of suffixes are also employed in some of the Indic names-of-persons. However, they are used while addressing others and hence they are seldom in usage in the names. If any suffix word is present in a name, it is generally ignored. Yet, if a suffix attachment has been used as if it were a family name, the entry in a catalogue has to be prepared under it, provided of course, it is not subordinate to the given name.

During the freedom struggle, in order to accommodate a large number of Indian students who had abandoned their studies, several educational institutions of national importance, as called by Mahatma Gandhi, had started functioning in various parts of the country. As they were not having the requisite legal sanction from the government to award degrees, during the British rule, Indian vernacular equivalents for the educational accomplishments in the form of various degree titles were chosen. However, there has been no uniformity in the nomenclature and each educational institution had selected its own degree titles. Some of the titles are still continuing. In this respect, it is observed that certain persons in possession of the degree, are using the degree designations as the end part of their names. Few among them may even employ them as Western types of surnames, where as some may employ them purely as decorative part of their names. If they are intended to be used as surnames, the same must be deployed in all the names-of-persons of the family. In such a situation, the entry is to be prepared under it, otherwise it is to be ignored.

The context of usage of the honorific titles in some of the names is perhaps applicable to all the linguistic regions of the country and covers most of the religions. Yet, the titles are changing from one region to another. It is observed that a particular word may be purely an honourable puff in one area, it may become a permanent feature of names in some other area. Again in one linguistic belt, it may be employed before the names where as in some other area, the same may be used in the end part of the names. In addition, during the pre-independence era, it had been the practice to bestow a variety of distinguished royal titles on the chosen few by the native rulers. These titles once conferred were often employed as prefixes, in the names of the recipients, in a few instances. As these titles were conferred by the authorities other than the British they have to be ignored at the time of cataloguing. Yet, a serious anomaly may arise when one notices that the titles bestowed on individuals many years ago, have been used as family titles, afterwards, in some cases. In this way, some specific titles have gained their status from a superfluous puff to the most important part of the names.

3.6.1 Takhallus

Takhallus is a distinct word or word group generally devised by the writer in order to get popularity in the wider forum, and acquire an identity for his literary contributions. It is also known as literary name, pen-name, or upnam. In rare cases it may be affectionately coined by the public. The inherent potency of a pen-name can be judged by the fact, that the person is generally identified by the takhallus, if used. In general, the common practice is to employ it as the last part of the name. Some important characteristic features of a takhallus, can be enumerated as given below :

1. It is generally a single worded entity, though some poets or writers also add the place name in it. If the name of the place or some other feature is added, the takhallus becomes double - worded. In cataloguing, both the words have to be taken together.

2. It is usually devised by the person himself. In rare instances, it has also been affectionately bestowed by the public. Yet, its acceptability by the person as a part of his name, makes it a literary name.

3. Generally, a takhallus remains fixed for a person. It is consistently employed in his name. In exceptional cases, some persons possess more than one pen-name.

4. It is employed in the names-of-persons, along with other parts such as the personal name, family name, etc. In those cases where specific features as the village name and/or father's name, etc. are forming part of the names, all such component parts are retained as such, together with the pen-name.

5. The usage of the literary - name has been found all over the country and it is used in the names-of-persons of the diverse religious groups. Nevertheless, in the northern parts of the country, its deployment in the names-of- persons particularly belonging to the Muslims, has been found more.

6. Employment of the takhallus is generally confined to the person. It is very rare that it is also used by the wife and the children.

7. If a takhallus is present in an Indic name-of-person, the bearer of the name, is generally identified by the same. This has been despite presence of the family name in the name.

Ranganathan (1964) considered takhallus as a pseudonym, and has prescribed it to be treated as if it were a false name. He has recommended for its removal at the time of its rendering in a cataloguing system. However, the findings of this research are contrary to this view-point. A takhallus is not to conceal the identity of the author. On the other hand, the full form of the name-of-person including the family name, is also disclosed. Hence, to regard it as a pseudonym, is not correct. As a matter of fact, it has been devised to get the author more acceptability in the public. Soni (1992) has considered it as the family name. Hence, our prescription in AACR 2 is as under :

1. Takhallus be treated as an irremovable and essential word in a name-of-person.

2. Main catalogue entry is to be prepared under a takhallus, even if such elements like family name, are also present.

3.7 OTHER PROBLEMS OF THE SURNAMES

As explained above, there are several practices of using family names, in the names-of-persons. However, in the context of cataloguing, we are considering them as surnames only if they are occurring as the last part of the names. The other forms of the family names appearing as the first part of the names, have been found subordinate to the given names. Hence, for the present work, they have been treated as essential but impotent prefix attachments. The following practices are in vogue in different parts of the country :

1. A word or word-group travelling through the male line, in a family. It is generally found to be the case in most of the regions of the country. The major exception to it, is the community of Nairs and a few others in Kerala.

2. Two different words as a combination of the surname of the mother and the family name of the father. There may or may not be any connecting symbol between the two surnames. This has been prevailing in some names among the Christians of Goa.

3. A group of two family names in which the first word is Kaul. The entry is to be prepared under the other word, as Kaul is a word of affection. This practice is found in Kashmir. Yet, if Kaul alone is used as the surname, the entry is to be prepared under it, as it is also a family name in Kashmir.

4. Two family names, written together as a single group. The first one is the maiden family name, and the other is the surname of the husband. This is found in rare instances, in a married female's name.

3.7.1 Multi-worded Family Names

The surnames could be single worded, in some linguistic area, whereas two, three or sometimes even four worded family names are also in vogue in some other region. Again, the practice of their rendering may also vary as sometimes they are written in a unit worded form, some other time, distinctly and yet in some exceptional cases, in both the forms. As surnames are employed in combination to the personal names, which could be single worded or multi-worded, (and in certain areas also included is the name of the father, and/or village/house name, etc.), they may pose tremendous problems to a cataloguer in recognising them easily.

The employment of other features as the village name, grand father's name and father's name in a traditional name may not be exactly same as being adopted by an educated person of a similar background. The phenomenon is found more profound in respect of the names-of-persons whose families had immigrated to some other cultural belt, permanently. It is observed that in a few names, the person himself sets his own preferences to treat his father's name, the village/house name or the auxiliary as the most important component part of his name. The cataloguer in such situations, is bound to abide by the illogical preferences of the person.

3.8 CHANGE OF NAME

In addition to the problems described above, some persons change their names some what at a later stage of their life. The reasons for it can be enumerated as under (Ranganathan, 1954a) :

1. Marriage for a female;

2. Hereditary title;

3. Change in secular or religious status;

4. Urge for false name (pseudonym) born out of shyness, fear or shear willfulness;

5. Law, as it happened in Japan and Siam, by enforcing the adoption of surname;

6. Imitation caused by contact with other cultural groups;

7. Recession from the result of imitation as it is now happening in North India;

8. Any other cause.

3.9. STRUCTURE OF THE NAMES

From the stand point of the structure of different elements in the names-of-persons, the country can be divided into four parts, described as under:

(a) North India

The given name is generally followed by the family name. However, the usage of surname in the names has not yet become universal. In addition, some persons may also bear some prefix title denoting their caste status, or the profession (present or past), and so on. Further, it is observed that the personal name is usually broken in two parts, and both the parts are made to stand as if they are separate words, which they are not.

(b) East India

The structure of the names is the same as used in North India. Surname comes after the given name. Again, as prevailing in North India, personal names are broken into two parts, and both are rendered as separate words though they convey meaning only when read together in the context. The usage of family names in the names, is fairly high to such an extent that almost all the names possess the same in the end. Two types of family names namely the vernacular and the anglicised forms are in employment in a few instances. In addition, some family names are multi-worded. Yet, the usage of prefix titles is almost negligible. In Sikkimi and Andaman and Nicobari names, both the practices are in vogue. That some names may include family names, some others may not.

(c) West India

In the Western parts of the country, the name of the father or husband, as the case may be is suffixed to the personal name. The surname comes in the rear end, and is usually the third component of a name-of-person. In addition the personal name is generally rendered in a unit worded form, and the usage of prefix titles is not prevailing.

(d) South India

The structure of the names, pose a varied picture. In Tamilnadu, father's or husband's name is generally prefixed. In addition, village name is also used as a further prefix. Some names may also bear the caste name as a suffix. The personal name is the most important part of a Tamil name. It either comes in the rear end or one word before the last word. In Andhra Pradesh and Kerala, house name is the first component followed by the other parts. In Karnataka, several structures of the names are existing.

It has been observed that within a single cultural region generally a standardized pattern of names is used. Any deviation from the pattern on account of a variety of factors, could be nearly uniformly distributed in the entire linguistic area. Yet, in a certain specific belt, more than one pattern may be followed. This study identifies the problem and provides a logical solution.

3.9.1 Conclusion

The present composition of the states in the country, formed on the linguistic considerations, is very much helpful in unifying all the diversified cultural regions. This aspect is quite effective in resolving the problem of identifying names. Conversely, from a specific pattern of a name-of-person, one can know the cultural background of the bearer. In other words, if the cultural background of an author can be ascertained, pattern of his name can be easily understood and specific entry element can be identified. The present study has been designed to study the names-of-persons, from different cultural regions as represented by the variety of states. Hindi heartland is however, composed of a number of states, and a union territory, as an exception. Similarly, Jammu and Kashmir consists of Kashmiri, Ladakhi and Dogri languages and Sikkim possesses Lepcha, Bhutia and Nepali languages.

The above discussion can be summarised by stating that the Indic names-of-persons, though linear in appearance, are radial in their character (Sarkar, 1963). There is no uniformity or consistency in the usage of the parts in the names belonging to all the linguistic regions of the country, and the potency of the words goes on changing with the shifting of the geographic belt. In other words, it is generally not possible to describe the exact position of any particular part of the names. These have resulted in creating confusion. In addition, employment of the honorific, feudal, academic or esteemed terms in Indic names, is compounding the problems. The present research work has been undertaken to provide more clarity on the prevailing structures in the Indic names-of-persons from all the linguistic regions of the country and covering the major religious minorities. This would help a cataloguer to deal with Indic names in logic and correct manner.

Chapter IV

North Indian Names

4.1 NORTH INDIA

4.1.1 General

The vast geographic zone covering the states of Bihar, Haryana, Himachal Pradesh, Jammu and Kashmir, Madhya Pradesh, Punjab, Rajasthan, Uttar Pradesh together with Chandigarh (at present, a union territory) and Delhi (the National Capital Territory) constitutes North India. In terms of different zones of the country, the other four zones being (1) East India; (2) North-East India; (3) South India; and (4) the West India.

Several languages are spoken in North India. They include Hindi or Urdu, Punjabi, Kashmiri, Dogri, and Ladakhi. Each language has several dialects, which are generally used at the spoken level only. At the written level, all the dialects of a language are generally combined together. Based on the languages used in each region, the zone can be divided into the following linguistic belts, each covering the specified religious groups.

1. Hindi and Urdu: Hindus, Muslims, Sikhs, Jains and Buddhists have been included. Sikhs are discussed under Punjabi names. The names-of-persons have been discussed under the following two heads:

   (a) Hindi Names; and

   (b) Muslims Names

2. Punjabi Hindu and Sikh religious groups are studied.

3. Jammu and Kashmiri — It consists of three linguistic regions, viz : Kashmiri : Hindus and Muslims are covered;

Ladakhi: Buddhists are included;

Dogri: Hindus are included. However, their names-of-persons are similar to those of Punjabis. Hence, they are not dealt with extensively.

The demographic composition of North India, is such that Hindus are in vast majority in all the states, barring Jammu and Kashmir and Punjab. Muslims rank second population wise. Jains and Buddhists inhabiting in this zone have naming pattern similar to the Hindus. Yet, the Buddhists of Ladakh are quite different and hence, their naming practices have been separately dealt with under Jammu and Kashmiri names.

Investigation on the social practices of the naming has been described in the following pages

4.2 HINDI NAMES

4.2.1 General

Hindi heartland as it is generally known, is located in the northern part of the country, and is the largest single linguistic region of our country, in terms of area and population. This Hindi speaking area occupies 1, 355, 455 sq. km. (roughly 41% of the country's land) with about 367 million people (about 45% of the national population) inhabit in this region (Census of India 1991, 1995). In demographic composition, Hindus constitute the vast majority, followed by Muslims, Sikhs and Jains in that order.

To the north of the Hindi speaking region, lie Jammu and Kashmir, Tibet (i.e. China) and Nepal and to the north-east and south-east are West Bengal and Orissa. It borders Andhra Pradesh and Maharashtra in the south, and is contiguous with Gujarat and Punjab in the south-west and north-west. Pakistan's frontier is in the north-west of the Hindi heartland.

Several dialects of Hindi are spoken in different regions of the Hindi speaking belt. Important dialects are (Dogra, 1976): Awadhi, Brijbhasha, Bundelkhandi, Chhattisgarhi, Hariyanavi, Hindustani, Khari Boli, Maithli, Maghadhi, Western Boli, etc. Muslims living in this area speak Urdu.

4.2.2 General Features

Names-of-persons from the Hindi speaking area generally have two distinct components. The first component is the personal name and is generally followed in the end by his family name or surname. The given name identifies the person whereas the surname signifies the family of his descent. Both put together form the full name. The given name of an individual normally consists of a single word, which may be simple or compound. In case the given name is a compound one, which it very often is (Sengupta, 1961), it is generally broken down into two or more parts, and rendered as if they were separate words. This style of splitting the personal names into parts is mainly due to some imitative urge to have two forenames, and subsequently two initials when abbreviated (Ranganathan, 1954c). However, the second part is invariably read in conjunction with the first part. The second part of this resultant split is now known as auxiliary, which is irremovable. Few personal names may have more than two words, and thus possess more than one auxiliary. On the other hand, there are individuals who do not employ any surname and hence, their names are confined to their personal names.

Examples:	**Masculine Names**	**Feminine Names**
	Ajit Prasad Jain	Kamla Sanghi
	Babu Jagjivan Ram	Kusum Lata Sharma
	Kewal Krishna Srivastava	Lovely Singh
	Ram Manohar Lohia	Narayani Devi
	Rajindra Prasad	Ram Dulari Sinha
	Shri Ram Sharma	Tarkeshwari Sinha
	Vedehi Charan Parashar	Usha Singh

4.2.3 Past Trend

On carefully observing the past trend, one finds that a vast majority of Hindi speaking person's names did not carry family names even at the beginning of the twentieth century. In times prior to that, surnames were practically non-existent (Saxena, 1952). The so called surname, where it was used, was either a common epithet in the personal names in a family or a name customarily employed as such or merely a supplementary name (Sengupta, 1958). This was found to have no potency. Therefore, names-of- persons had carried a remarkable uniformity as most of them were single worded. In other words, in the far-off days names of Hindi speaking people were simple, straight and easy to handle.

If one examines how different names are rendered in Hindi language, it transpires that abbreviations in names do not make sense. In academic certificates like degrees and diplomas, they are always written in full form. In the vernacular, a personal name is generally rendered as a single worded entity (Goil, 1969). However, when the same is written in the Roman script, the general trend is to break it into two parts. In some instances, because of the influence of the modern education, a new trend has emerged in which splitting of the given names has been resorted to in the vernacular language too. Yet, in the English language, invariably the practice of breaking the given name into two parts is followed. Specific examples given here with the vernacular and their English versions illustrate the point beyond any ambiguity.

Masculine Names	**Feminine names**
Bholanath = Bhola Nath	Amaikaur = Amai Kaur
Krishnachandra = Krishna Chandra	Kusumlata=KusumLata
Ramlal = Ram Lal	Latakumari = Lata Kumari
Ramprakash = Ram Prakash	Narayanidevi= Narayani Devi
Shivshankar = Shiv Shankar	Sitabai = Sita Bai

During the British rule, the practice of using the family names was confined to a small section of the educated. But with the advent of independence and with more and more people receiving the education, usage of surnames/family names in the names-of- persons showed an upward trend, thus confirming the observation that the Western education prompted Indians to use the surnames.

4.2.4 Surnames

As per R.S. Saxena (1952), 'a U.P. [or for that specific purpose, the entire Hindi speaking belt] sub - caste name differs from an English surname. The latter is confined only to one patriarchal family, that is borne only down the male line. But, a sub - caste name of U.P. embraces diverse families and is borne along every male and every female line [in several instances]. Marriage is restricted to sub-castes'.

In respect of surnames, it is found that an overwhelming majority of them are representative, in one way or the other, of the caste or vocation with which one is associated. They can be grouped in two broad categories, mentioned below (Goil, 1969):

(a) Real family names (b) Pseudo family names

Real family names are generally based on the "Gotra" system of the Hindus, prevalent among all the castes. The other sources of family names are vocation, mode of worship, residency, and learnedness, particularly in relation to the Vedas, of the ancestors (Goil, 1969). In some specific instances, designations of the Indian academic degrees have become surnames. For example, the under mentioned are the Real family names employed among the Vaishya (Aggarwal) community, based on their 16 or 17 gotras (Goil, 1969):

1. Goil	7. Mangal	13. Dahran
2. Garga	8. Singhal	14. Tungal
3. Bansal	9. Jindal	15. Kuchhal
4. Kansal	10. Tayal	16. Varsheney
5. Mittal	11. Mudgal	17. Khandelwal
6. Rastogi	12. Ahran	

In addition to the group of surnames described above, some families were identified, hundreds of years ago, with some specific features or accomplishments, which have been indicated by the surnames adopted. To denote such accomplishments with respect to Vedas for instance, the following family names are used in some Brahmin families (Mishra, 1949):

Surname	**Other/short form**	**Meaning**
Chaturvedi	Choubey	Having mastery over all the four Vedas.

Trivedi	Tripathy, Tyari (Atkinson, 1882) Tiwari	Possessing full knowledge of at least three Vedas. Another version is that they were performing puja three times a day.
Dwivedi	Dubey	Having command over at least in two Vedas.

Similarly, some important vocations practised by the Brahmins during the good olden days, have been employed as family names. A sample of such surnames is given below (Mishra, 1949):

Surname	**Other form**	**Meaning**
Agnihotri	Agyari	Profession of performing 'Agnihotri' or yagna.
Awasthi		Profession of performing 'Awasth' yagna.
Dikshit		Whose fore-fathers were donors of higher education ("Diksha"). Another view is that those who had received the diksha.
Joshi	Jyotishi or Jusi (Atkinson, 1882)	Descendants of palmists.
Mishra		Whose ancestors were performing "Misra" yagna. An other view is that Misra means an all round expert in several professions.
Upadhyaya	Ojha, or Jha	Descendants of teachers imparting religious education.
Pandey		Descendants of teachers.
Pathak		Their fore-fathers were in the profession of teaching. Yet, the popular belief is that their ancestors were performing puja once in a day. Another view is that they were expert in at least one of the Vedas.

Vajpeyi	Whose ancestors were per forming 'Vajpeyi' yagna.

It has been observed that the above described surnames have been made to descend from one generation to another, through the male line, over a long period of time and in the present context, their usage has nothing to do with their true meaning.

Educationally, the Kayastha community is one of the most advanced segments of the Hindi heartland. They claim their descent from Maharaja Chitragupta. During the Muslim era, their ancestors were in the fore-front among the Hindus, to learn Persian, and thus were identified with the educated elite groups. Similarly, with the advent of the British rule, they were amongst the first to learn English and became lawyers, civil servants, and judges (Dayal, 1971). Their sub-caste names are often used as surnames, described as under (Saxena, 1971):

Surname	**Meaning**
Asthana	Their ancestor was given astha or eight kinds of pearls by the Maharaja of Banaras.
Ambasth	Their fore-fathers were worshiping Goddess Amba.
Nigam	Their ancestor learned all the major Sanskrit texts of Hindu religion such as Vedas and Shashtras.
Kulsreshta	Their fore-father "Atindruja" is said to be the most amenable son of Maharaja Chitragupta.
Bhatnagar	Originating from the fortress town of Bhatner.
Saxena	Descendants of the friends of army (= Saka + Sena).

The other sub-castes of Kayasthas, which figure as family names are Gaur, Karan, Khare, Mathur, and Srivastava. In addition, alla (denoting some specific features like occupation, residency, etc.) is also employed as surname in many Kayastha families. A sample of such family names is given below :

Bisaria, Johri, Rupenwal, Sabbarwal

Surnames were also derived from the names of the places or the regions where the families had lived (Jain, 1972). People who came from some parts of the country, and settled permanently in another part, could not do away with the roots to their original places which gradually took the place of their surnames. A sample of such family names derived from the regions, is given as under:

Bagri, Bengali, Marwari, Punjabi, Sindhi

Apart from the names of the regions, there are families using the place names as their family names. In the hilly districts of Uttar Pradesh, in the Garwal region, most of the family names are derived from their village of origin. In some cases, the names of the present villages are used as surnames. Sometimes, names are suitably modified. An illustration of such family names is given as under (Atkinson, 1882):

Family Name	**Village Name**
Anethwal	Aneth
Bhartula	Bhartuli
Chapaliya	Chapal
Dhaundyal	Dhaund
Dimri	Dimar
Kotyal	Koti
Lakhera	Lakhera
Mamagai	Mama
Nainwal	Nail
Pokhryal	Pokhri
Raturi	Ratura
Salani	Salana

In Rajasthan, a few family names derived from the place names with or without modifications, are used in the names-of-persons. On enquiry, it was revealed that it is generally after a family moves out permanently to a new place, does the name of the original native place get quite often used as a surname.

Examples:	**Surnames**	**Meaning**
	Ajmeria	Resident of Ajmer
	Ameria	Belonging to Amer
	Jhunjhunwala	Coming from Jhunjhunu
	Ramdev	A name of a village

In Haryana, some names-of-persons may include the name of the village in the end part, employed as the surname. Om Prakaŝh Chotala, the present Chief Minister of the state carries the name of his village "Chotala" on the pattern of the surname, though, his father Devi Lal does not have it in his name. This practice it appears, has percolated from the neighbouring Punjab where prominent politicians quite often, use village names as surnames.

Likewise, in the Chattisgarh region of Madhya Pradesh, Patel is employed as a family name which was an official title of position, many years ago. Similarly, Risaldar was another title of position, has also been employed as a surname.

Again, in the hilly districts of U.P. Negi, Bisht and Rawat are employed as surnames among the Rajputs. Negi means perquisite or due and was a title given to any one holding military or civil employment under the former Rajas. Bisht, or more correctly, visisht, means good, respectable and was a title, more than a real caste name, though in the present context it has acquired a permanent caste denotation. Similarly, Rawat, means a senior or officer such as pradhan, and has now grown also into a caste appellation (Atkinson, 1882).

In the Hindi heartland, it is observed that certain persons use the designations of the Indian vernacular degrees, as their surnames. In this respect, it is found that some persons may use them merely as academic epithets, whereas some other individuals use them on the pattern of the Western surnames. The under- mentioned degree titles are mostly used:

Degree Title	**Meaning**
Acharya	Master of Arts
Prabhakar	Bachelor of Arts in Hindi
Sastri	Bachelor of Arts
Siddhantalankar	Bachelor of Arts
Vachaspati	Master of Arts
Vedalankar	Bachelor of Arts, specilised in Vedas.
Vidyalankar	Bachelor of Arts
Vidya-vachaspati	Doctor of Philosophy

Lal Bahadur Shastri, the late Prime Minister of India, was awarded the Shastri degree, and used the same as the end part of his name. His caste denoting family name was Srivastava which he never used. Strangely his wife and all his sons also use Shastri, in the end part of their names though they don't possess the degree. It appears that the degree title has now become their family name. In such a specific situation, if a personality is identified through his academic qualification, the same should be used as the entry element (Uppal, 1975). However, Ranganathan (1957b) did not agree with this prescription. He believed that the degree designation was to be dropped, and the entry be made under Lal Bahadur.

On the other hand, Bhola Paswan Shastri, a former Chief Minister of Bihar suffixed his name with the degree title (Shastri) merely as a qualifying word. His caste representing surname "Paswan" was also used in his name. Therefore, in such a situation, both the words would be used in rendering his name. In other words, Paswan Shastri would be used as the entry element.

The illustration of the family names described above, is applicable in all the castes of Hindus in North India. Among the dalit community of Chamars, family names are generally based on gotras derived from the names of their ancestors, or after totem. Some of them used by the Jatav sub-caste, are enumerated as under (Singh, 1994e):

Bargoti	Neem	Sagar
Dabar	Pipal	Soor

4.2.5 Takhallus or Upnam

Some individuals, particularly poets and writers, often employ pen-names under which they generally write. This pen-name, known as Takhallus in Urdu, and Upnam in Hindi, is used by them in their names, at the end. Jain (1972) feels that it is 'nom de plume' of poets and writers, and is equivalent to some extent to what in English is called a pseudonym. In this regard, it is observed that in a few exceptional cases, it remains superfluous, and is therefore, disregarded in rendering. But, in most cases, the individuals are known only by the same, and their identity is totally lost if the same is not reckoned with their names.

Examples:	**Masculine Names**	**Feminine Names**
	Chandra Dhar Sharma Guleri	Indira [Sharma] Indu

Ram Dhari Singh Dinkar — Sarojini Pritam

Shyam Singh Shashi

Surya Kant Tripathi Nirala

Upendra Nath Ashka

In certain cases, it has been noted that the poetic name of an individual (i.e. Takhallus) has been employed by all the members of the family, afterwards, as if it were a family name, though they are neither poets nor writers. An illustration of such pen- names, is given as under:

Name of the Husband	Wife's name	Child's name
Ghanshyam Pankaj	Vinita Pankaj	
Haribansa Rai Bachchan	Teji Bachchan	Amitabh Bachchan
Robin Shaw Pushpa	Gita Pushpa Shaw	
Upendra Nath Ashka	Kaushalya Ashka	Nilabh Ashka

An analogy of the takhallus has been used by several persons particularly a few prominent politicians. They make use of some catchy word, and suffix the same in the end part of their names.

Examples : Bhagwat Jha Azad

Bhola Ram Toofani

Brij Mohan Toofan

Deep Chand Bandhu

Dharam Pal Atal

Jogendra Singh Dharti-pakad

There are generally three different sources of obtaining the takhallus. They are described as under (Jain, 1972):

(a) Some part of the given name of the person such as Bhakta for Guru Bhakta Simha Bhakta, or Rasik in Rasik Lal Tandon have been used.

(b) Place names such as Banarasi, Moradabadi, and so on. In some specific pen-names, place name is further added, so as to make the pen-name, double worded.

(c) Any other word or word-group, as per the desire of the person. For example Navin is the pen-name of Bal Krishna Sharma Navin. Similarly, Neeraj is the pen-name for Gopal Prasad Saxena Neeraj.

A literary name is generally assumed by the person, though in rare instances, it can be affectionately bestowed on by the public. Yet, its acceptance by the individual makes it a part of his name. In cataloguing, the entry is to be prepared under the pen-name if used by an author. However, there is an exception to it. If an obvious place name is used as the takhallus, entry is to be avoided under it. Such a literary name is to be retained in sub-ordination to other parts.

4.2.6 Other sources of Surname

Another class of the family names comprises auxiliary words. In Bihar and eastern U.P. such surnames are widely used among Kayasthas and Rajputs. It appears that these words were a part of the given names of their fore-fathers, a few generations ago. However, now they acquired the status of family names, and are being used as such.

Examples:		
	Anand	Prakash
	Datta	Prasad
	Dayal	Rai or its anglicised form Ray.
	Kumar	Ram
	Lal	Sahai
	Nath	Singh (In Bihar, its anglicised form Sinha is also used).

If a name ends with an auxiliary, it could either be a part of the personal name without the surname, or a name in which the auxiliary word has been used as a family name. This can be a source of confusion. However, by carefully examining the name, one can reach a conclusion whether the last part of the name is the surname or not. To resolve the conflict and to know its correct status, the following clues are suggested.

(a) If the last part is the family name, there would usually be at least another auxiliary word present in the name. In this context, it may be added that this clue is quite vague. Thus, if the person has not been identified by the last word, the entry is to be avoided in the end part.

Examples: Bipin Bihari Lal

Jaya Prakash Singh

Murli Manohar Prasad Singh

Ram Narayan Prasad

(b) If a masculine auxiliary is employed in a feminine name, it can be safely taken as the case of a family name. In this respect, it is observed that auxiliaries employed in masculine names alone are used as surnames.

Examples: Naintara Kumar

Ritu Singh

Usha Prakash

(c) The practice of contracting the name by an author can lead to a correct assessment of the status of the auxiliary. If all the component parts of the name are shortened into initials except the last part, the auxiliary word can be safely taken as the surname.

Full Name-of-person	**Shortened form**	**Entry Element**
Anugrah Narayan Singh	A.N. Singh	Singh
Devendra Pal Singh	D.P. Singh	Singh
Har Nandan Lal	H.N. Lal	Lal
Rajendra Prasad Kumar	R.P. Kumar	Kumar
Satyendra Narayan Singh	S.N. Singh	Singh

During the recent times, some individuals are employing their present or immediate past vocations as their surnames. Even though the vocation has been changed in a few instances, the surname is continued. As the vocation or occupation, had been in vogue at the most a few generations ago, family members are fully aware of the specific ancestor carrying the same.

Examples:	**Surname**	**Meaning**
	Lohia	Iron merchant
	Banker	Money lender
	Batashewale	A particular sweet maker

Chandiwale	Silver ornaments dealer
Johri	Gold and precious gems dealer
Pilot	Aeroplane crew driver
Rangwale	Colour industry owner or seller of its products
Saraf	Precious metal dealer
Shawlwale	Merchant dealing in shawls

Thus, it can be concluded that whatever may have been the form, derivation, meaning or association of a family name, in the present context, it is just a surname used as the most important part of the names-of-persons.

4.2.7 Pseudo Surnames

Pseudo surnames are very generic descriptors used to denote caste or sub-caste of the bearer. They are used by a wide cross-section of the community. Among the Aggarwal Vaishya, the words given below are used as pseudo family names (Goil, 1969):

Aggarwal, Gupta, [Jain], Vaishya

4.2.8 Two worded surnames

In the Hindi speaking area, specific individuals make use of two-worded surname in their names. One of them denotes the caste background, and the other represents some other feature such as academic accomplishment, place name, profession, auxiliary, etc. In such cases, both the words are retained in the same sequence, as appearing in the name.

Examples:

Names-of-persons	Entry words
Mohan Lal Jain Saraf	Jain Saraf
Bhola Paswan Shastri	Paswan Shastri
Kripa Nand Tripathy Ujela	Tripathy Ujela
Raj Nath Sonkar Shastri	Sonkar Shastri

In rare instances, specific females have retained their maiden surname as such, and in addition have added their married family name also. Such a compound surname possesses two surnames. In cataloguing both the surnames have to be taken together.

Example : Indira Bahuguna Joshi,

4.2.9.1 Tribal surnames

Tribals and aborigines in general, have the same pattern of names as found in the Hindu society. Each tribal group has its own social divisions and further sub-divisions among them. For instance, the Thotia community of the Gonds in Madhya Pradesh, is divided into phratries. Each phratry is a cluster of clans and has a definite number of deities. These clan names are employed as family names. Some of them are listed as under (Singh; 1994f):

Akhe	Kurma	Tumrisar
Dhurva	Sairam	Yuna

Similarly, in the mid - Himalayan or Pangi range in Himachal Pradesh, which remained inaccessible till recently, the inhabitants mainly Buddhists maintained close cultural affinity with Tibet. Their priest the Lama gives a Tibetan name to the newly born baby. Their names are (Shashi, 1971):

Masculine Name	**Feminine Names**
Arigyal	Devanpati
Darje	Dumuku
Gyachhe	Paljam
Medang	Tashi
Rigjih	Yagshim
Shaltu	

The names-of-persons of this region are generally double worded. Usage of family name is not prevalent. Hence, they are rendered in the natural sequence in a cataloguing entry. Yet, among the educated class three worded names along with their family names are not uncommon. They need to be handled in the same manner as those of the Hindi speaking region. Some of their family names derived from their clans, are listed as under :

Gyazhingpa, Henir, Khyungpo, Lonchhenpa, Nandu, Nyekpa

4.2.9.2 Problems in Surnames

It is evident from the above discussion that two or more forms of a surname exist which represent the same person. One form presents the surname in full, whereas the other one could be the shorter form. In a few exceptional cases, both or all the forms are in usage by a single author. Thus, Choubey and Chaturvedi; Trivedi, Tripathy and Tiwari; Dubey and Dwivedy could be employed in an interchangeable manner. This aspect must be taken into consideration while dealing with such surnames.

Another complex situation may be created by those names where caste features are employed as surnames. Every person has the option to choose among a variety of specific features for his surname, which denote his caste status with which he is associated. Therefore, it looks really strange particularly to a foreigner to know that sometimes even husband and wife or for that matter, two members of the same family may employ different sets of the family names. In this respect, Hindi family names are different as compared to the same in other linguistic regions.

4.2.9.3 Dropping, Attaching or altering surnames

In some situations, a few persons decided to drop their family names which hitherto had been a part of their names. Distinguished persons in the country resorted to this practice after independence as part of their drive to promote a casteless society.

Examples: Rajendra Prasad (Surname Srivastava was abandoned)

Sriman Narayana (Family name Agarwal was dropped)

Several scholars including Ranganathan (1961) had viewed the phenomenon of dropping the family name as a new trend setter. It has now been established that the above two examples are more an exception rather than the order, and in reality, the usage of surnames has increased, many folds afterwards.

After the family name is dropped, or in the event of no such appellation being in usage, the personal name alone remains. As the given name is generally rendered in a two worded manner, a false impression is created that the second part is the family name, which it is not. Hence, the cataloguer needs to guard against erring in making the correct entry.

There have been instances where the surname or some other part of the name, has either been added, dropped or altered, at some later stage. In this exploratory survey, only 6 such names could be identified. If an author has written under two different family names or names, it is essential to bring all his published works together. Cross-references are effective in such instances. A sample of such names-of-persons in which changes have occurred is given as under :

Original Name	Present Name	Shortened name
Atal Behari Lal Vajpeyi	Atal Behari Vajpeyi	A.B. Vajpeyi
Ghanshyam Das Sharma Pankaj	Ghanshyam Pankaj	
Kamleshwar Nath	Kamleshwar Nath Gupta	K.N. Gupta
Mahendra Kumar Jain Raja	Mahendra Raja Jain	M.R. Jain
Nityanand	Nitya Anand	N. Anand
Virendra Swarup Sinha	Virendra Swarup Saxena	V.S. Saxena

4.2.9.4 Impotent suffixes

There are some individuals, suffixing specific word in their names, indicating their status. The word is simply a qualifying epithet and hence, it can not be granted the status of the entry element. Such suffixes have to be taken along with the given names which are to be rendered in full. An illustration of such names-of-persons is given as below :

Prabhu Dutt Brahmchari, Vijendra Snatak

4.2.9.5 Auxiliaries

As explained earlier, almost all personal names are broken into two parts, with both the words made to stand independently. However, in reality though written as separate words, the second word in isolation conveys no sense and therefore, must invariably be read in conjunction with the first part. The second part is known as auxiliary. There is however, another view point which considers it an added name (Jain, 1972).

The absurdity of breaking the personal names can be understood from the fact that several masculine names may start with a feminine word, and if one looks this part alone, he is bound to be misguided to assume that it is a feminine name. In fact, it is only the auxiliary part which qualifies the first part and makes it a masculine name. An illustration of such names, is given as under :

Personal Name	**Meaning**
Kamla Pati	Refers to the husband of goddess Kamla
Lakshmi Narayan	Denotes Narayan the husband of goddess Lakshmi
Radha Krishna	Signifies Krishna who was emotionally attached to Radha
Sita Ram	That Ram who was the husband of goddess Sita
Uma Maheshwar	Maheshwar is another name for god Shiva. The name refers to Lord Shiva the husband of the goddess Uma.
Vedehi Charan	Vedehi is another name for goddess Sita. The name means that the child is born at the feet of the goddess Sita.

The converse of this in which the first part of a feminine given name may in isolation, conveys a masculine name, is also true. The second part however, when read in conjunction yields a feminine name. A sample of such names is given as under:

Name	**Meaning**
Ram Dulari	A female receiving affection from Lord Rama.
Ram Piyari	Refers to the one who is beloved to Lord Ram.
Ram Vati	A female devoted to Lord Rama.
Siva Piyari	A feminine person who is beloved to Lord Siva.

Another peculiar situation is also noticed in which some given names start with "Shri" or "Sri". The word following it determines whether it is superfluous puff (like Mr. in English), or an integral part of the name. Normally the names of Hindu gods may contain Shri/Sri as an integral part, and hence it can not be ignored. This logic may be true for almost all such names. An illustration of such names is given as under:

Shri Bhagwan	Shri Kant	Shri Ram
Shri Chand	Shri Krishna	Sri Ranjan
Shri Gopal	Shri Lal	Sri Narayana

Likewise, in some specific feminine personal names 'sri' can be the ending part, which is irremovable. A sample of such names is given as under:

Jayasri or Jaya Shri, Padamasri or Padama Shri, Rajasri

As explained above, the given names are split and the second part of it is used as auxiliary. There is an endless list of such words emerged and employed as auxiliaries. However, from among the names examined in this survey, the under mentioned words are often used as auxiliaries in the Hindu masculine names:

Anand	Dhan	Mal or Mull	Roop
Bahadur	Dhar	Mohan	Sahai
Baksh	Dutta or Datta	Narain	Saran
Ballabh	Gopal	Nath	Sarup
Bihari	Kanwar	Pal	Shankar
Chand or Chandra	Karen	Prakash	Singh
Charan	Kishore	Prasad	Swamy
Deo	Kumar	Peatap	
Das	Lal	Ram	
Dayal	Lubhaya	Rattan	

In the feminine personal names, the under-mentioned words are quite widely used as auxiliaries:

Bai	Devi	Lata	Rani
Bala	Kaur		Vanti
Dei	Kumari	Piyari	Vati

The position of the auxiliary should not be altered as it is always fixed and invariably follows the first part of a given name. If a name does not terminate in a family name/surname, the entry has to be made in the straight order in which the words occur.

It is however, to be noted that several personal names are formed mainly with the words often used as auxiliaries. This may cause confusion. The following examples are of such names :

Anand Prakash	Dayal Singh	Lata Kumari	Roop Chand
Bahadur Singh	Devi Dayal	Narayan Singh	Sarup Singh
Bala Kumari	Dhan Singh	Pal Singh	Shankar Kishore
Bihari Lal	Kishore Lal	Prakash Chand	Singh Pal
Chand Ram	Kumar Pal	Pratap Chand	Swamy Dayal
Chandra Prakash	Kunwar Sain	Ram Prakash	
Charan Singh	Om Prakash	Rani Devi	
Dev Anand	Lal Singh	Rattan Lal	

The employment of a particular set of auxiliaries, it has been observed, can be more or less standardized as per the caste status, in a given geographical belt. Yet, it may not be possible to do so in some other region. For instance, while Rajputs of Uttar Pradesh and Bihar use Singh as the auxiliary in their masculine names, Rajputs of Himachal Pradesh do not do so. Among the Harijans, Ram appears to be a favourite auxiliary in Bihar and eastern Uttar Pradesh. Similarly, in Rajasthan, given names of the Jat community may not generally carry the auxiliary Singh, where as in the western Uttar Pradesh, Singh is very often used in the names of the same community.

4.2.9.6 Change of female name after marriage

In Rajasthan and Bihar, it is observed that many girls at the unmarried stage, use Kumari as the auxiliary. However, in the married status, it is replaced by Devi.

Example : A female having her maiden name Nirmala Kumari mar ries to Prakash Chandra Verma, her name becomes after marriage Nirmala Devi Verma.

In most other parts of the Hindi speaking area, the surname only undergoes change. After marriage a woman adopts the family name of her husband and abandons her maiden surname.

Example: If a girl Sushila Kumari Goel marries to Ravi Kumar Gupta, her married name would become Sushila Kumari Gupta.

4.2.9.7 Prefixes in names

Many names-of-persons carry a variety of prefixes. These prefix titles denote specific features like caste, profession, religious or honourary status, etc. and do not normally form a part of the names. Sometimes, they convey affection while addressing. In this survey, it is found that prefixes are used in less than 1% names. They are therefore, edited at the time of cataloguing. Important prefixes employed in names are given as under:

Prefix	Meaning
Acharya	Teacher
Babu	Clerk
Choudhury	Title for martial races
Diwan	Minister
Lala	Petty shopkeeper
Kunwar	Son of a land lord
Mahatma	Pious soul, a saint
Master	School teacher
Munshi	Clerk
Pandey	From a Brahmin caste
Pandit	Belonging to a Brahmin family
Seth	Big business man
Swamy	A saint
Thakur	Warrior
Vaidya	Ayurvedic doctor

However, if there is a British Indian title prefixed to a name, the same has to be retained in an inverted order.

Yet, in some specific names-of-persons, prefix titles have become part of the names to such an extent that the identity of the person is jeopardized by its dropping. In particular, the prefixes employed in the names-of-persons of the erstwhile royal families, and the same used in the names of some well-known saints have been found fit for retention, though in inverted order. A sample of such names is given as below :

Name-of-person	**Catalogue entry**
Swamy Agnivesh	Agnivesh, Swamy
Rajmata Gayatri Devi	Gayatri Devi, Rajmata
Maharaja Karni Singh	Karni Singh, Maharaja
Rao Birendra Singh	Birendra Singh, Rao

Though prefixes are used in the names in the beginning, and are either ignored, or retained in an inverted order as has been recommended above there can be a confusion when one observes that certain names are containing any of these words often used as prefixes. The following examples pertain to such given names :

Babu Ram	Lala Ram	Thakur Das
Diwan Chand	Munshi Ram	Vaidya Nath
Kunwar Sain	Swamy Dayal	

Further, some of the words generally used as prefixes are ambivalent and are also employed as surnames, by the persons of some families. In such names, they acquire a very important position, and the catalogue entry is to be prepared under them. An illustration of such names is given as below :

Hari Kishan Chaudhuri	Tilak Raj Thakur
Narayan Pandit	Man Singh Diwan
Govind Ram Seth	Radhe Mohan Acharya

4.2.9.8 Styles of writing names

There are a variety of ways in which names-of-persons are rendered in the Hindi speaking area. The foremost category pertains to those names in which all the three parts are written in full measures. In such names, the last part is the surname and is the most important part of the name. Therefore, the catalogue entry is to be prepared under it.

<u>Examples</u>:	**Masculine Name**	**Feminine Name**
	Anand Kumar Agarwal	Kanti Bai Vashishtha
	Pratap Singh Kothari	Kusum Lata Sharma
	Ram Niwas Mirdha	Prem Kumari Bhatnagar
	Laloo Prasad Yadav	Shushma Devi Panwar

In the above category, specific persons, because of the influence of the English education, contract both the parts of the personal name or the entire given name if it comprises a single word, and the last part is written in full measures. In this case, the entry has to be prepared under the surname.

<u>Examples</u>:	**Names-of-persons**	**Style of Writing**
	Kamla Gupta	K. Gupta
	Om Prakash Gupta	O.P. Gupta
	Ravindra Kumar Sagar	R.K. Sagar
	Shri Ram Tiwari	S.R. Tiwari

In another category, the middle part is reduced into its initial form. The first part and the last part are written in full form. This practice has emerged because of the influence of the American culture. In this case, the entry is to be made under the last part, that is the surname. An illustration of such names is given as under :

Masculine Names	**Feminine Name**
Jagdish S. Sharma	Girjesh K. Gupta
Khushal S. Panwar	
Lakshman K. Parashar	

In yet another category, no surname is used, and hence, the entire name is the personal name. The main entry is to be in the straight order and no inversion is to be resorted to.

<u>Examples</u>:	**Masculine Name**	**Feminine Name**
	Bal Krishna Das	Shyamala Devi
	Har Nandan Lal	
	Ishwari Prasad	

Rajendra Prasad

Ram Karan Singh

In another peculiar category, no family name is employed but in rare instances the first part(s) of the name is contracted into its initial form. In such a name, the author himself wants to use the auxiliary prominently. The cataloguer is helpless in the situation, and is to abide by even the illogical choice of the author.

Examples:

Full Name	Contracted Name	Entry Word
Arvind Bharti	A. Bharti	Bharti
Bal Krishan Das	B.K. Das	Das
Jaya Prakash Singh	J.P. Singh	Singh
Narender Datta	N. Datta	Datta

4.2.9.9 Father's name as a suffix

Of late, a new trend has emerged in which the full or the part of the father or husband's name is suffixed, and no surname is used. In such a name-of-person, the choice for entry should be the given name of the bearer. An illustration of some such names-of-persons is given as under:

Full Name	Remarks
Ashok Vikram Singh	Vikram Singh is the father's name
Vinay Bharat Ram	He is son of Lala Bharat Ram
Sushma Swaraj	Swaraj is the given name of her husband
Vaishali Abhay Singh	Abhay Singh is the given name of her husband

4.3 PUNJABI NAMES

4.3.1 General

In the year 1966, the composite Punjab state of North-West India got divided on linguistic basis into two separate states. The Punjabi speaking area formed the present Punjab state while the Hindi speaking region became Haryana. Chandigarh, the joint capital for the both was taken over by the Centre, as a union territory on account of a dispute between the two states. Spread over 50, 363 sq. km., Punjab has a population of around 20 million of which 62.95 % are Sikhs and 34.46 % are Hindus (Census of India 1991, 1995).

It may be recalled here that a major portion of the erstwhile province of Punjab has gone to Pakistan when the country was partitioned in 1947, on the basis of religion. The hill districts of whatever remained of Punjab were given to Himachal Pradesh.

4.3.2 Names-of-persons

Punjabi names are similar in the structure to the same from the Hindi speaking area. The first part of a Punjabi name is the given name which, as its like in the Hindi speaking belt, is broken into two parts, with both the words rendered separately (Ranganathan, 1969a). The second word of the personal name is regarded generally as an essential part and may be called the complementary or auxiliary word to the given name. As the usage of family names has not yet become universal, both forms of Punjabi names with and without surnames are in vogue. However, the family name where it occurs, is generally denoted by the last word (Mangla; 1966). Usage of prefix titles in some names also prevail.

Examples:	**Masculine Names**	**Feminine Names**
	Gopi Chand Bhargava	Indira Devi Dhawan
	Giani Zail Singh	Lata Khanna
	Pt. Ram Rattan Sharama	Kaushalya Devi
	Prakash Singh Badal	Kulwant Kaur
	Pratap Singh Kairon	Sudesh Kumari Saluja
	Sardar Swarn Singh	
	Surjit Singh Barnala	

4.3.2.1 Sikh and Non-Sikhs in Punjab

In order to know the features associated with the Punjabi names-of-persons it is desirable to understand relationship among the Sikhs and Hindus. For this purpose, a note has been prepared, which is reproduced as under :

"Sikhism has emerged primarily from Hinduism, and till a few decades ago, it had functioned and flourished merely as a sect of the Hindu religion. In fact, the bondage between both the communities had been so much deep rooted that in many a Hindu families of the Punjab, as per the prevailing tradition, the first born male child was brought up as a Sikh, immediately after his birth. The other male children could remain as non-Sikhs. In the subsequent generations, the children of the Sikh families were the naturalised born Sikhs. In this way, their population had been increasing. In this context, it can be added that the social inter - course between the Sikhs and Hindus had been so much intimate that inter-marriages, dining together, and participating in each others' functions had been taking place frequently. In fact, there was no difference at the social plane, between the two communities. Of late, this close and intimate relationship between the Sikhs and Hindus is on the decline.

As explained above, the Sikhs having evolved from the Hindus are following the same caste based social infra-structure of the Hindu society despite strong teachings of the Sikh Gurus to the contrary. Even the concept of a common kitchen inside the Gurudwaras, could not eradicate the evils of casteism. Thus, all the major castes based on age old professions still exist among the Sikhs. The persons from the down trodden castes are known as "Mazahabi Sikhs". They are traditionally engaged in a variety of menial jobs. The Jat Sikhs, on the other hand, constitute a very influential segment of the Sikh community, particularly in the rural areas. They are primarily landlords deriving their livelihood from agriculture. Together with Rajputs, Jats are constituting nearly 65% of the Sikh population in the state (Randhawa, 1969). The other caste persons belonging to Khatri and Arora, are customarily engaged in business and service. In terms of population figures, the entire Sikh community is around 15 million. They are however, concentrated in the state of Punjab where they are in majority. Further, Punjabi Sikhs are highly mobile, and are generally found in almost all parts of the country."

Since Sikhs and Hindus possess a common heritage, there is no difference in the names-of-persons in both the communities. The minor variations which are discernible, occur only in the usage of certain words at the auxiliary level but not in the basic pattern of the names.

4.3.3 Surnames in names

It may be added that among the Punjabis, usage of family names in the names-of-persons had emerged due to an overwhelming influence of the British culture (Ranganathan, 1964). Prior to the British rule, family names were almost non-existing. Their usage has not been universal as there are many persons whose names do not bear any such appellation. There are several sources of deriving family names in Punjab. Based on their origin, they can be classified into the following groups:

(a) Village Name as Surname

A typical feature of Sikh and Hindu families has been that the names of villages are suffixed to the personal names. These suffixes have been employed more or less as family names. Among the Jat Sikhs, this practice is quite prominent. According to Mangla (1966), certain family names had signified originally the misls (denoting different Sikh jathas or groups which became powerful in Punjab after the last invasion of Ahmed Shah Abdali in 1769 and which divided the entire territory of Punjab among themselves) during the far-off days. The names of the misls, be translated being mostly geographical are, as given below:

Fateh Singh of Ahluwal

Jassa Singh of Ramgarh

Ranjit Singh of Sukerchak

Perhaps, an analogy of the misls obtained from the place names was used to form other surnames as many of the family names are the place names in Punjab. As per another analysis (Singh, 1996a), "because the Sikh community at the religious level is a casteless and equalitarian social order, a section of the Sikhs add place names instead of the got as a suffix". Denzil Ibbetson (1916) has recorded that Dhaliwal (or its variant Dhariwal) had been derived from the name of a village, "Dharanagar". Conversely, several villages have been named after the sub-castes of the Jats. For the present work however, it is less important to go in for such details beyond giving an illustration of such family names as below :

Badal	Dhillon	Randhawa	Sidhu
Barnala	Gill	Sandhu	Talwandi
Brar	Kairon	Sial	

In some cases, adjectives such as 'ia', 'wal', 'wala', or 'walia' (denoting resident of), are added to the village names forming the surnames. A sample of such family names is given as under :

Attariwala	Faizulpuria	Ramoowalia
Bhinderwala	Kartarpuria	
Dalawalia	Longowal	

b) Sub-caste Names as Surnames

Another important class of Punjabi surnames is the one in which the sub-caste names are used as family names. The usage of this type of surnames is more prevalent among the Khatri caste. The sub-caste names had originated from some important anecdotes associated with their ancestors. These sub-caste names are now employed as family names. The description of some sub-castes and their derivation are given as under (Chopra, 1971b):

Surname	Explanation
Beri	They ascribe their name to the fact that their ancestor was born under a Beri tree.
Bhalla	From bhal, spear. Bhallas were reputed to be experts at wielding the spear.
Bhandari	From Bhandar, store. Their ancestors were in charge of the State's grain stores.
Chopra	They are descendants of the persons who were expert gamblers. They were given the title Chaupar, expert in chaupar gambling game of those days.
Chowdhri	Leader of the community.
Dhawan	Corrupted from dhaavan, messenger in the battle-field.
Kakkar	Descendants of Raja Kuckus.
Khanna	From Khan which means one half.
Kochar	From kavach or Armour.
Mahendru	From Maha-Indra or big donors. Also known as Mahendra/ Mahindra.
Sahi	Bankers who were styled Shahji.
Sahni, Sainani, or Saini	Army general.

Seth	Srestha, great.
Tandan	Derived from Tan meaning ready to fight.
Vohra	Expert in special type of fighting formation.

Ibbetson (1916) described the origin of a few surnames of the Punjabis. Their details are given as under :

Surnames	**Explanation**
Bains	One of their ancestor's name was Bains.
Barar	Descendants of a person whose name was 'Bur'.
Bhatia	Originating from a place called 'Bhatner'.
Bhullar	They are said to have sprung from Jat or "Matted hair"of Mahadev whose title is Bhulla Mahadev.
Chahil	Named after the name of their ancestor.
Gil [Gill]	They claim their descent from a person whose name was Gil.
Kapur	From Kapur Chand, the name of their ancestor.
Man	Originated from the personal name of their fore-father.
Mehra	Mahar Chand had been one of their ancestors.
Randhawa	Named after the personal name of their ancestor.
Sarin	During the period of Alla-ul-din, widow remarriage was made legal. Most of the Khatris had gone against this. Yet, a section among them did not resist the move. They were called Sara Ayin or the Muslim customs - hence, they be came Sarin.
Sidhu	Named after their ancestor's name.
Sohal	It was the name of some ancestor.
Virk	It is a sub-caste of Rajputs.

Apart from the surnames described above, there are other family names used among the Khatri community. Some of them are given as under:

Ahuja	Chawla	Khosla	Narang	Sondhi
Bagga	Chug	Lamba	Narula	Suri

Bahal	Dhingra	Luther	Oberoi	Taneja
Bajaj	Dhir	Luthra	Puri	Tuli
Batra	Gujaral	Maini	Sabbarwal	Tuteja
Bhasin	Gulati	Malhotra	Saluja	Vij
Budhiraja	Khetrapal	Mehra	Sethi	Wahi
Chaddha	Khullar	Nagpal	Setia	Walia
Chandak	Kohli	Nanda	Sikka	

Further, Khatri and Verma are the generic surnames which can be used by any person belonging to Khatri caste. Similarly, Arora is other family name of a generic nature.

(c) A name adopted by some ancestors (Mangla, 1966) such as Gambhir, Komal, etc.

(d) Occupation or position held by some ancestors (Mangla, 1966) such as Diwan, Munshi, Pathak and so on.

(e) Auxiliary as a surname

As explained above, the given name is generally broken into two parts. The second part of this split personal name is the auxiliary. Among the Sikhs, in almost all the masculine names, "Singh" is the natural choice for the auxiliary. This has been irrespective of the caste affiliation of the bearer. Likewise, its counterpart "Kaur" is in usage as the auxiliary in most of the feminine personal names. In this context, it may be pointed out that an auxiliary does not have an independent existence, and hence it has to be avoided as the entry element. Ranganathan (1964), considers it is an essential but impotent word.

Yet, in a number of Sikhs belonging to the educated class, and particularly those who had migrated out of the state, are making obvious use of the auxiliary Singh, prominently. In such situations, they hide the other parts of their names by using initials. This process of converting Singh into a prominent word has acquired such a magnified dimension that even the wife and daughters of such a person are sometimes employing 'Singh' as if it was their surname. In such a name where preference of the person has been expressed, the entry has to be prepared under Singh.

However, identification of such a name-of-person in which the auxiliary word Singh has been employed as if it were a family name, is rather a difficult task for a cataloguer. There are a few clues described as under which can be helpful in ascertaining whether the auxiliary has been used as a family name or not:

(1) If the contracted name of the person can be known though some source including the publication and if it is found that except Singh, all the parts of the name have been converted into initial form, it has to be taken as a case in which Singh has been employed as the surname.

(2) Similarly, if the word "Singh" appears in association to a feminine name, it has to be understood to have been used as the surname.

(f) Anglicised form

During the beginning of the present century, some persons had translated their family names into their English equivalents and these translated words were used as the family names. This practice seems dead by now as no such translated surname could be located. Apart from Lal Chand Verman, the first Director General of the Indian Standards Institution (Now, the Bureau of Indian Standards) who transformed his family name Verma into Verman, no other person has been known to have used Verman. The anglicization of Verma into Verman occurred while he was living in Europe before our independence.

Examples:	**Vernacular form**	**Anglicised form**
	Kapur	Camphor
	Tirkha	Sharp
	Verma	Verman

In addition to the family names described above, there are other family names obtained from the gotras (Mangla, 1966). The other generic family names such as Aggarwal, Gupta, Sharma, Vaish, and so on are also used. Their occurrence is in the same manner as found in the Hindi speaking belt.

4.3.4 Takhallus or Pen-name

Some poets and artists of Punjab suffix a unique word known as literary-name, pen-name or the takhallus, to their names (Gill, 1969). Generally, the takhallus becomes so much prominent that the individual is identified by it. A sample of such names is given as under :

Masculine Names		Feminine Name	
Name-of-person	**Entry word**	**Name-of-person**	**Entry word**
Asa Singh Mastana	Mastana	Amrita Pritam	Pritam
Gopal Singh Dardi	Dardi		
Karam Singh Zakhmi	Zakhmi		

4.3.5 Given Names

Personal names in Punjab are very much similar to the ones used in the Hindi speaking area. However, due to slight phonetic variations, different spellings for one and the same name have emerged. These have not been discussed here as they fall outside the scope of the present investigation.

Further, it has been observed that sources of masculine and feminine personal names are common for many names; they differ only at the level of the auxiliary (Jayaraman, 1989).

<u>Examples</u> :

Masculine Names	Feminine Names
Paramjit Singh	Paramjit Kaur
Partap Singh	Partap Kaur
Rajinder Singh	Rajinder Kaur
Surinder Singh	Surinder Kaur

As explained earlier, given names are dissected into two components, and therefore, a Punjabi personal name may generally be consisting of two words. Also, a further splitting of the first part of the personal name has been observed in a few instances. Among the educated communities, it has been observed that all the parts of the names-of-persons, except the last word (i.e. Singh) are converted into initials. In this way, preference has been expressed in favour of the auxiliary.

<u>Examples</u> :

Usual form	Splitted form	Abbreviated form
Indrapal Singh	Indra Pal Singh	I.P. Singh
Kirpal Singh	Kir Pal Singh	K.P. Singh

Inderjeet Singh	Indra Jeet Singh	I.J. Singh
Kawaljeet Singh	Kawal Jeet Singh	K.J. Singh

However, this unusual process of breaking the given names is not common among the feminine names-of-persons. Their personal names generally consist of two words, the second word being Kaur.

During the earliest phases of the British rule, a person had even transformed the first part of his personal name into its English equivalent. A solitary example found to illustrate that the practice has been given up.

Example :	**Punjabi form**	**English form**	**Remarks**
	Chanan Singh	Bright Singh	Chanan = Bright

4.3.6 Prefixes in the names

Analogous with the Hindi speaking belt, prefix titles are also employed in some Punjabi names-of-persons. However, their usage is diminishing day by day. In Punjabi names, the following titles are widely used. They are in addition to the prefix titles described in the Hindi names.

Prefix Title	**Meaning**
Bibi	Respectable word for a woman.
Bhai	Respectful word for a man.
Giani	A degree at the Bachelor's level. Also denoting a religious holy person.
Jathedar	Leader of a jatha or a group.
Nihang	A religious position of the Sikhs.
Sant	A religious leader of high order.
Sardar	Respectable word for a male Sikh.
Sardarni	Honourable word for a Sikh woman.

As these prefixes do not form a part of the names, they are best dropped in cataloguing. Sometimes, these may be required to be preserved and rendered in an inverted order when the same has become a part of the name, and identification of the person is affected by its dropping in cataloguing. The general guideline could be that when it does not lead to crisis of identification, prefixes are to be dropped in cataloguing.

Example:	Name-of-person	Catalogue entry
	Bhai Mahavir	Mahavir, Bhai

Yet, it may be kept in mind that some specific personal names are also formed with the words often used as prefix titles. The cataloguers are advised to deal such names with caution. No part of such name is to be ignored.

Examples: Sant Singh, Sardar Singh

4.3.7 Western Transformed Names

It is observed that quite a number of educated persons are contracting all the parts of their names barring the ultimate component part, into initial form. The end portion could be the caste names, village name, or in some exceptional instances, an auxiliary. Since this unique practice is adopted exclusively in the educated communities, all the names falling in this category are the Western transformed names.

Examples :	Name-of-person	Shortened name
	Mohinder Singh Dhillon	M.S. Dhillon
	Rajinder Kumar Bagga	R.K. Bagga
	Subhash Chand Narang	S.C. Narang

This unusual practice of contracting the names is limited to the masculine names. Females on the other hand, do not generally resort to this practice. They render their names in full form.

4.3.8 Structure of the Names

Broadly, there are two categories of structures used in the names-of-persons. They are described as under :

a) Names without surname

In this category, the entire name is the personal name. Though the name may generally be of two words, the second word has invariably to be read in conjunction with the first one. Therefore, the words in the name need not be inverted, and their rendering has to be done in the natural sequence.

A cataloguer not born and bred in the North Indian culture, may commit a mistake by treating the second part of such a name as the family name, which it is not. Therefore, such names need careful handling.

Examples:	Masculine Names	Feminine Names
	Bhagat Singh	Amrit Devi
	Ishwar Dayal	Kulwant Kaur
	Ram Narayan	
	Swaran Singh	

In the above category, some specific names may also bear prefix titles. As a general rule, all titles have to be omitted, except the British Indian titles and all such prefixes which have become part of the name. An illustration of such names is given as below :

Masculine Names	Entry Words	Feminine Names	Entry Words
Bhai Mahavir	Mahavir, Bhai	Rajkumari Amrit Kaur	Amrit Kaur, Rajkumari
Lala Hardayal	Hardayal	Sardarni Sada Kaur	Sada Kaur
Pt. Kripa Shankar	Kripa Shankar		
Sant Fateh Singh	Fateh Singh		
Vaidya Kishan Lal	Kishan Lal		

(b) Names having family name

From the public usage and the manner in which Punjabi persons are contracting their names, it has been noticed that the family name, if employed, is the most important component part of a name. Hence, the entry be preferred under the surname. Prefix titles if also used, have to be treated in the same manner as described above.

Masculine Names	Entry Word	Feminine Names	Entry word
Ashok Kumar Kapur	Kapur	Asha Rani Dhawan	Dhawan
Gurdiyal Singh Dhillon	Dhillon	Prema Vati Sikka	Sikka
Indra Kumar Gujaral	Gujaral		
Lala Ram Narayan Khatri	Khatri		
Pratap Singh Kairon	Kairon		

In the above illustration, Lala Ram Narayan Khatri is to be rendered as Khatri, Ram Narayan. The prefix title 'Lala' is to be ignored.

(c) Names possessing Pen-name

Entry in such a name be made under the pen-name. Thus, Sudhir Kumar Sudhir be entered as "Sudhir, Sudhir Kumar".

4.4 JAMMU & KASHMIRI NAMES

4.4.1 General

Jammu and Kashmir is the strategically located northern most state of the country. Spread over an area of 222,236 sq. km. the state had a population of about 60 lakhs in 1981 with a break down of 64 % Muslims, 32 % Hindus and Buddhists, Sikhs and others constituting the remaining 4 % (Census of India 1991, 1995). Geographically and ethnically, the state excluding the area still under Pakistan and China's illegal control, can be recognised into three regions. The predominantly Muslim inhabited Kashmir Valley, the Jammu region with a sizeable Hindu population and the highly Buddhist dominated Ladakh. The Kashmir Valley is politically the most active of the regions with all the Chief Ministers of the state hailing, from this area alone. The Valley also contributes richly to the coffers of the state exchequer by attracting tourists from different parts of the world.

The state lies in the extreme north of the country. It is bounded by China in the north, Tibet in the east, Himachal Pradesh and Punjab in the south, and Pakistan in the west.

4.4.2 Kashmir Valley

In the Kashmir Valley, Muslims are in overwhelming majority. From the view point of names-of-persons, they fall into two broad categories. The first one includes those whose fore-fathers got converted to Islam from Hinduism, a few centuries ago. They constitute bulk of the Muslim population (about 90 %).

In the other category are falling those Muslims who are descendants of migrants from the near by countries. Though, they have become Kashmiris, their names are quite different from the other Muslim names. Their numerical strength is small, say about 5 % of the Muslims.

Numerically, Hindus are in utter minority in the Valley, and are constituting about 5 % of the entire population. They all belong to one caste, Brahmin. They call themselves as "Pandits".Muslim society on the other hand, displays a variety of castes, based on specific professions. In addition, almost all the family names currently in usage by the Hindus, are also employed by the Muslims. Even generic family names of the Brahmins such as Bhatt and Pandit are used by several Muslim families.

Viewing Kashmir in historical perspective, it has been found that it had been ruled in succession by Hindus, Buddhists, Påthans, Mughuls, Sikhs and Dogras, each leaving in one way or the other some impressions on the social and cultural life of the Valley. The institution of christening has also been affected. The imprints of the tides of these hectic periods are easily discernible in the names of Kashmiris (Kaul, 1970).

4.4.2.1 Names-of-persons

The names-of-persons from the Kashmir Valley generally have the sequence "Given Name - Surname", though few names may also include some other attachments, and some names may not employ any family name. In structure, Kashmiri names are similar to Hindi names. Surname wherever used, occurs generally in the end part of a name (Ranganathan, 1964).

Examples :

Muslim Names

Masculine Names	**Feminine Names**
Abdul Aziz	Fatima Begum Qureshi
Abdul Rashid Mattoo	Khalida Shah
Abdul Salam Bhat	Mehmuda Begum Peerzada
Bakshi Gulam Mohammad	Sakina Bano
Dildar Ahmed	Sundari Kadir
Mohammed Rafiq Ahmed	Zarina Bano
Moinuddin Akhtar	
Syed Mir Qasim	
Sheikh Mohammed Abdulla	

Hindu Names

Masculine Names	**Feminine Names**
Durga Parshad Dhar	Arundati Zutshi
Jiyalal Kaul	Khem Lata Wakhlu
Maharaja Karan Singh	Pran Pyari
Maharaj Kishen	Sarga Devi Shakdhar
Prithvi Nath Kaula	Shiela Kaul
Surinder Kumar Razdan	
Triloki Nath Khushoo	

4.4.3 Surname

The usage of surnames in the names-of-persons in Kashmir has been so extensive that hardly a person without a surname can be found in the Valley (Kaul, 1970). There are several sources of family names. They include such surnames indicating ancestral profession. In addition, nick-names are also used as surnames. Koul (1924) has described interesting anecdotes associated with the evolution of family names in the following words:

"Besides gotra, each family has a kram or nick-name added to the original name by reason of the head of the family's or any of his ancestor's special calling or because of such peculiar circumstances which had occurred to him. For instance, a man, named Wasdev had a mulberry tree growing in his courtyard and, therefore, he was called Wasdev Tul (mulberry). He, in order to get rid of this nick-name, cut down the tree. But a mund (trunk) remained and people began to call him Wasdev Mund. He then removed the trunk, but by its removal khud (depression) was caused and henceforth people called him Wasdev Khud. He then filled up the depression, but the ground became teng (a little elevated) and he began to be called Wasdev Teng. Thus, exasperated, he left to do any further attempt to remove the cause of his nick-name and it continued to be Teng which is now attached to the names of his descendants."

Surnames falling in the above class, and used frequently among the Hindus of Kashmir are given below :

Ambardar	Jhala	Manwati	Shivpuri
Bakaya	Kachru	Mattoo	Trakru
Bamzai	Kak	Muthu	Thalsoor
Bhan	Kalpush	Panju	Trisal
Dhar	Kaul	Raina	Tikku
Duloo	Kitchlu	Rawal	Tufchi
Gadu	Khushoo	Razdan	Tutu
Gunju	Kunzru	Rishi	Wali
Gurtu	Madan	Sapru	Wanchoo
Hakhoo	Malla	Shakdhar	Warikoo
Haksar	Manwati	Shanlu	Zutshi

Among the Muslim community, the under-mentioned family names are used quite popularly :

Alaia	Gojri	Magrey	Wani
Dar	Khan	Rather	
Gauaie	Malik	Sheikh	

In addition, some generic family names are also used, in the Valley. They are generally caste denoting attachments indicating Brahmin caste among the Hindus. A sample of such surnames is given below :

Bhat, Pandit

Sometimes, the official positions occupied by some ancestors in the past, are also used to denote the family names, though, at present, it is quite rare that any family member is occupying such a position. In fact, some of such positions have become obsolete. Still, the family names are continued after such positions. A sample of such family names is given as under :

Darbari, Kanoongo, Munshi, Khazanchi, Vakil, Wazir

In some families, territorial distinction is employed to denote surnames. There are two categories of such family names. In one category, the original place name or the name of the region from where the family had immigrated, is used. Sometimes, a word such as Parimoo denoting 'outsider' is also in usage. The under - mentioned are some of the examples of such a family names (Kaul,1970).

Garyali, Misri, Nowshahri, Punjabi, Parimoo

In the other category, the name of the village where the person was born, is used to represent the surname. As the place is generally situated in the Valley, such place names have become prominent as family names, in rare instances.

Examples : Batwari, Hajni, Kishtawadi, Lojora, Sopori

As explained above, most of the Muslims in Kashmir are the descendants of the converted Hindus. Even after conversion and remaining part of the Islamic society for hundreds of years, several of them have strangely preserved their caste denomination with them. In the names-of-persons, family names derived from castes or occupations are used in the end.

Examples:

Caste/occupation	Family Name
Barber	Hajjam
Breadmaker	Sofi
Carpenter	Najar
Cloth merchant	Bazaz
Cobbler /Sweeper	Wattal
Goldsmith	Zargar or Sonur
Mason	Dasil
Milkman	Goor
Petty businessman	Sodagar
Trader	Jinsi
Washerman	Dhobi
Weaver	Lone

Besides the groups of surnames described above, few totemic surnames are also existing (Singh, 1996a). The family members however, are not aware as to how such surnames were adopted by their fore-fathers. They are commonly employed by Hindus and Muslims.

Examples:	Surname	Meaning
	Dabroo	Cat
	Gagroo	Rat
	Hak	Green vegetable
	Hangal	Deer
	Haput	Beer
	Kaw	Crow
	Khar	Donkey
	Panzu	Monkey
	Shal	Jackal
	Wangnoo	Brinjal

Similarly, some specific family names are quite unusual and embarassing such as : (Koul, 1994)

Churu	Thief
Thag	Cheat
Thalachoor	Thief of plates
Thapal	Pick-pocket
Thaplu	Snatcher

Almost all family names of the Hindus of the Valley, are in usage by the Muslims too. On enquiry, it came to light that several Muslim families had retained their earlier surnames, even after getting converted to Islam.

4.4.3.1 Two-worded Surnames

The family names described above are all single worded. In addition, double worded surnames are also in use in the state. A sample of such surnames is given below (Kaul, 1970):

Kaul Adalti	Kaul Dembi	Raina Kandroo
Kaul Bamzai	Kaul Duloo	Zargar Sopori
Kaul Bhan	Kaul Jalali	
Kaul Bharti	Kaul Shastri	

Observing the pattern of the two worded family names, it can be stated that the first word in most of them is Kaul, used often in the Valley to denote affection. As this word is usually present in almost all the two worded family names, it may be deemed as essential but impotent word. A catalogue entry has to be made under the second part of such a surname.

In some double worded family names, Kaul is not present, and in such a two worded surname, two different concepts are brought together. One is generally the place of residency, and the other one is the family name. Hence, both the words have to be used as the entry element, and if needed, a cross reference entry under the second part of the surname can be prepared.

The stability of the surnames, among the Muslims in some cases is quite low. For insatance, in a family of three brothers, Munshi, Bhat and Khan were used as three surnames (Khan, 1994).

4.4.3.2 Change of surnames

Several family names are quite funny and ridiculous. Hence, some families have either reformed or changed them to some other format. An illustration of such surnames is given below (Kaul, 1970):

Old Surname	**New Surname**
Fakh	Faque
Hakchar	Haksar
Noel	Nehru

However, the family name 'Nehru' of India's first Prime Minister, had evolved from a Hindi word Nehar meaning a canal. Their original surname was Kaul. Because their family had been living in proximity to a canal, the surname was modified to Kaul Nehru. It was shortened to 'Nehru' afterwards, by Moti Lal Nehru, the father of Jawahar Lal Nehru.

4.4.4 Takhallus

In some names-of-persons of Kashmir Valley, a prominent influence of the Persian culture, is discernible. For instance, several Kashmiri authors are using pen-name in their names (Kaul, 1970). It generally appears in the end part of a name. In this respect, it has been observed that if a literary name has been employed, it generally acquires prominence to such an extent that if it is ignored in cataloguing, it may result in a total loss of identity of the person. Therefore, if a pen-name is used by an author, the entry has to be prepared under it, even when the family name is also present in the name.

Examples:	Masculine Name	Entry Element
	Abdul Rahman Rahi	Rahi
	Dina Nath Nadim	Nadim
	Ghulam Nabi Khayal	Khayal
	Motilal Razdan Saqi	Saqi

4.4.5 Prefix Titles

Prefixes employed in Kashmir, in Muslim names-of-persons, are similar to the ones used in Hindi names. Most of them are removable in nature.

Among the Hindus, only one prefix title is employed. Its usage however, is diminishing day by day.

Example : Pandit

However, some specific titles among the Muslims by usage have become almost a part of the names, and if removed, it may lead to problems in identifying the persons. In Kashmir, such prefixes are considered as surnames. Hence, they are recommended for retention in subordination to other parts.

Examples:	Prefix	Examples
	Bakshi	Bakshi Gulam Mohammad
	Mir	Syed Mir Qasim
	Syed	Syed Mir Qasim
	Sheikh	Sheikh Mohammad Abdulla

In this context, it may be added here that certain persons, in recent times, have started using Mir as if it were a surname. They employ it in the end part of their names. As the title is used intentionally in the end, the purpose is to use it as a family name, in the Western sense. Hence, the entry would go under it.

Examples: Gulam Mohmmad Mir, Nasrullah Mir

4.4.6 Names of Immigrant Muslims

The Muslim families which immigrated from the neighbouring countries such as Iran, Iraq and Afghanistan, some centuries ago, have a different source of deriving their surnames. The surnames are usually the modified forms of the native place names in the alien land where ancestors of the family lived, before migration (Khan, 1994). A sample of their family names is given below:

Family Name	Derivation
Bukhari	Migrant from Bukhara in Afghanistan
Hamdani	Originating from Hamdan in Iran
Gupkari	Migrating from Gupkar
Jilani	Immigrating from Jilan near Baghdad in Iraq
Kabuli	Hailing from Kabul in Afghanistan
Kashani	Original resident of Kashan in Iran

4.4.7 Change of female name after marriage

It is observed that family names are not generally used in the names of Muslim females. Other attachments such as prefix titles and Takhallus are also absent. In the coining of feminine Muslim names, three practices are prevailing lending them to be classified into the following groups:

1. Simple names are written as such in the natural sequence. A name is generally composed of two words, rendered separately. The second word is the auxiliary. After marriage, there can be either no change in her name or the auxiliary can be replaced by "Begum". In some rare instances, the auxiliary is replaced by the short name of the husband.

<u>Examples</u> : Akbar Jahan Begum

Hajira Begum

Zeenat Bano

2. Father's given name in short, is used in place of the auxiliary. After marriage, husband's name is used instead of the name of the father. This particular structure is gaining more popularity, even among the other group of the Muslims. Some masculine names may also bear the same structure. An illustration of such names is given here :

Name-of-person	Explanation
Imtiyaz Qayoom	Son of Abdul Qayoom
Iqra Manzoor	Son of Manzoor Ahmad
Mahbooba Bashir	Wife of Bashir Ahmed
Parvin Shahid	Daughter of Mohammad Shahid

3. Family names are employed. After the marriage, the family name of the husband replaces the surname of the father. This practice is adopted in rare instances. In this respect, it can be added that the auxiliary may or may not be used in the personal name of the female.

Examples: Khlida Shah
Razia Begum Parimoo
Shameema Bano Bhat

However, among the Hindu community, females generally carry the surnames in their names. Before marriage, it is the father's family name, and after marriage, the husband's in place of father's family name.

Examples: Anupama Kachru
Sarga Devi Sakdhar
Vijay Laxmi Munshi

4.4.8 Jammu Hindu names

Hindus are in majority in Jammu region. In the names-of-persons, the pattern, structure and even wordings are the same as in Punjabi names. There are generally three distinct components of a name. The first one is the given name. The middle part is the auxiliary and the end part is the surname. The naming characteristic is the same as those of the Punjabis, and hence, all the features of the Punjabi names are evident here too.

Examples:	Masculine Names	Feminine Names
	Bhim Singh	
	Girdhari Lal Dogra	Sudesh Kumari Mahajan
	Kishan Prasad Gupta	Sushma Chaudhury

Mangat Ram Sharma

Thakur Baldev Singh

4.4.8.1 Surnames

Apart from the surnames denoting the caste/profession of the family as in Punjab, there exists another class of the family names derived from the place names. Some of them are :

Surnames	Meaning
Bhadwal	Originated from Bhaddu
Billawaria	Original resident of Billawar
Jamwal	Resident of Jammu
Sambial	Migrant from Sambha

4.4.9 Ladakhi Names

In the northern part of the state lies a high altitude plateau, known as Ladakh. Though, it forms a part of Jammu and Kashmir, it is culturally close to Tibet. The religion followed by the people here is Tibetan Buddhism. In addition, a large number of refugees from Tibet have also settled here.

In names-of-persons, there appears to be a similarity with the names of Bhutia and Lepcha races from Sikkim. Perhaps, this is so because the languages (including the script) in Sikkim and Ladakh are derived from the Tibetan language. The names-of- persons are generally two worded, and only a few of them are three worded.

Examples :	**Masculine Names**	**Feminine Names**
	Kushok Bakula	Disket Wangmo
	Norbo Gyaltsan	Kunzes Dolma
	Phuntsog Stobdan	Rigzin Yangdol
	Rigzin Jora	Sonam Dolma
	Rigzin Spalbar	Spalzes Angmoo
	Sonam Dorjey	Yangchan Dolma
	Sonam Wangyal	
	Sonam Wanchuk Norboo	
	Thupstan Tsewang	

4.4.9.1 Surnames

Being situated in an isolated corner, and remaining backward in education, the culture of the West has little influence on the naming pattern in Ladakh. In general, the entire name is the personal name. Yet, in exceptional instances, some names-of-persons may bear the following suffixes indicating specific features :

Gurutsring	-	on the name of famous Lama Tsering.
Jora	-	is a martial title.
Oltang	-	Means green pasture.
Shingkan	-	Carpenter.
Wangso	-	Royal dynasty of Nimoo and near by villages.

The above words are used more or less as family names. In the absence of the surname the entire name is to be treated as the given name with its sequence unchanged.

4.4.9.2 Given Names

As mentioned earlier, given names are mostly two worded, though a few among them are of three words. The following meanings have been assigned to some of the words used in the personal names:-

Sonam	= Person with good karma in the previous life.
Tsering	= Tse means life and Ring means long life.
Wangmo	= Powerful

4.4.9.3 Anglicised format

As explained above, most of the names are denoting personal names. All the component parts are of equal importance. Yet, some educated persons, in order to be known by a shorter form of their names, represent the first part of their names by the initial. The last part is generally written in full. In such a name-of-person, the person himself having expressed his desire to be known by the last part, the catalogue entry has to be prepared under the same. Examples are given as below

Masculine Name	**Short form**	**Entry element**
Phuntsog Namgyal	P. Namgyal	Namgyal
Phuntsog Stobdin	P. Stobdin	Stobdin

Feminine Name	Short form	Entry Element
Sonam Dolma	S. Dolma	Dolma

4.4.9.4 Prefixes in names

Like in any other region of the state, specific names may carry prefix titles. They generally denote the religious position or the profession of the bearer. Sometimes, a particular title expressing affection of the community is used as a prefix. A sample of the prefix titles is given as under :

Prefix Title	Meaning
Chocho	Affectionate title by the people. Also respectable term for small girls.
Chomo	Female Buddhist Monk
Gergan	Teacher
Kushak	Buddhist religious head i.e. Head Lama
Lama	Buddhist Monk
Lobzang	Another name for Lama. It is no longer in currency.
Rinboche	Reincarnated Lama

In this context, it may be added that the title "Chocho" has been employed exclusively for a particular woman, Yangchan, who is one of the leaders of the area. She is ordinarily referred to by the people as Chocho Yangchan.

The titles used as prefixes to names-of-persons are not part of the names-of-persons. Hence, they are dropped for the purposes of cataloguing.

4.5 MUSLIM NAMES

4.5.1 General

Most of the Muslims in India are the descendants of the converted people from Hinduism. This conversion had taken place in a phased manner, over a few hundred years. In this process, a hierarchical social order based on caste type system had emerged, among the Muslims, which is continuing even today (Basham, 1967).

These fragmented social divisions on caste basis, are against the basic tenets of Islam, and are not found in the Arab world. As per one version, the social order among the Muslims had come into vogue from the existing caste system, with which all the converted families had been associated. In other words, previous caste affiliations had become the basis for the new social status in the Islamic society in India. Thus, a Brahmin after conversion for instance, might have become part of the Syed family. In pure Islamic system a Syed is a direct descendant of Prophet Mohammed. A Kshatriya on similar lines, perhaps became a Sheikh. Ibbetson (1916) has recorded that one section of Khoja in Ambala was Kayastha. On the other hand any Hindu trader in Punjab, was known after the conversion, by Khojah. As Aroras and Khatris were largely involved in business in Punjab, most of them in Islamic society became Khojas. In some instances, the Islamic social status of the converts had also developed from the whims and fancies of the converting agencies, and people gained higher social status in terms of their caste affiliations, while getting converted to Islam. Hence, the actual connotations of these social groups are different from the same as existing in the Arab world. Atkinson (1882) has described the process as "pious fraud". He adds, "in the plains [of U.P.] all Hindu converts to Islam became Sheikh and with time and money may become Sayyids with a genealogical table ready prepared by an indigent Moulvi showing their direct descent from the Prophet".

Islam had come in India, a couple of centuries after its emergence in Saudi Arabia. In reaching here, it had travelled a long distance, and passed through several countries, having varied cultures. It influenced the prevailing culture, custom, and civilization of all the countries where ever it had gone or passed through. In return, it also received the impact of the locally existing cultures. In this way, some of the original practices prevailing in the Arab world, got modified and these distorted traditions were transmitted in our country. The tides of this process had been far reaching, deep and wide. They could not spare names-of-persons. Thus, one can see that Muslim names- of-persons in India are different from the same in other Islamic countries. They very much differ in form and style (Jamil Ahmed and Sengupta, 1961). Even, within the country, strong influences exerted by different linguistic regions, are easily discernible particularly in the structure of the parts of the names.

Another major factor which had influenced the Muslim names, is that dynasties of different nationalities had ruled the country. Notable among them, were Afghans, Lodis, Turks, Mughuls, Sayyids, etc. The present day Muslim names-of-persons in India, represent a fusion of the practices followed by different Muslim nationalities, tribes, and sects (Jamil Ahmed and Sengupta, 1961). About 48 % of the Indian Muslim names-of-persons are religious. They are of the Arabic or other Middle-East origin. Some of the names of ordinary Muslims in India are Hindu in form, though not in origin (Jamil Ahmed and Sengupta, 1961).

Several authorities in cataloguing, have studied names of Indian Muslims in the past, and have come forward with their recommendations. However, almost all of them have committed the same error of linking Indian Muslim names with Arabic names-of- persons. Though, it is a basic fact that many words employed in a variety of Indian Muslim names have come from different Holy books of Islam, they differ very much in their pronunciation, form and style from other Muslim names. By picking up a very few complex names, most of the authorities have over complicated the matter. Hence, in the present work, a broad spectrum of the names has been taken into consideration to put the matter in the correct perspectives. The analysis presented here, is valid for most of the present day Muslim names in India. The remaining names, described as classical Muslim names, have not been covered extensively here. They have already been studied, in detail, by many scholars and their handling by cataloguers has been well documented.

Indian Muslim names can be assorted into several classes. In the first one are included names of those Muslims who live in the Hindi and Punjabi speaking regions. Names-of-persons falling in both the northern regions carry the same structure. They are being discussed here. The other linguistic regions like Kashmir, West Bengal, Orissa, and southern states of Andhra Pradesh, Tamilnadu, Kerala, and Karnataka have been included along with the names in their specific linguistic groups. Likewise, Muslim names of Gujarat and Maharashtra, have been covered along with Gujarati and Marathi names respectively. Nevertheless, it is observed that the structure and pattern of Indian Muslim names-of-persons are gradually changing, particularly among the educated and urban elites. This is so irrespective of the linguistic area, to which they belong. The names-of-persons discussed here broadly denote this uniform pattern to which Muslims of India are resorting to.

A number of sects exist in the Indian Muslims. These have been wrongly understood to mean castes. In fact, each sect possesses its own caste structure. A sect is based on a specific school of thought, mode of worship, religious leadership, etc. In India, Shia and Sunni are two dominant sects. However, in the names-of-persons, there is hardly any difference between them. It is usual for Shias of the educated class to suffix the names of Imams such as Ali, Hasan, Hussain, etc. to their ordinary names in order to show their creed. But, the names so compounded are often used by Indian Sunnis also (Jamil Ahmed and Sengupta, 1961).

4.5.2 Use of Surname

As per Mohammed Haroon (1984), the present day trend in the names of the Indian Muslims, tends towards the European pattern. Dogra (1973) too has expressed a similar opinion that Urdu writers after the World War I, owing to the strong influence of the West, have become surname conscious. Fazal Elahi, et. al. (1961) also have observed that there has been a growing tendency among the Muslims of India and Pakistan to adopt family names. The findings of this research are in conformity with those of the above authorities. It is observed that in the structure, a Muslim name-of-person possesses similarities with the Hindi or Punjabi speaking person's name.

4.5.3 Parts of a Muslim Name

An Indic Muslim name-of-person generally consists of several components. However, all names may not possess all the component parts, and in some specific names, more than one word may be denoting one single component. Even, there may not be a strict order of the different elements, though they generally appear in the following order

1. Prefix Title

2. Given name

3. Surname

4. Pen-name

1. Prefix Title

Broadly speaking, two types of prefixes are employed in Muslim names-of-persons. These are :

(a) Khitabs; and

(b) Laqabs

Khitab is a distinguished title of honour, generally bestowed by a ruler on his subjects. During the pre-independence period, it was customary for the Muslim rulers, to award official titles at their pleasure, to some distinguished citizens, on specific important occasions. These Royal titles were used as prefixes in many names-of-persons. This practice of conferring Khitabs vanished with the rulers soon after the country became a democratic republic. A Khitab is never passed on to the next generation, and is exclusively employed in the name of the recipient, though there are rare instances of using it as the family name, by the descendants.

Apart from the Indian Muslim rulers, another source of awarding the Khitab to the distinguished Muslims was the British Government in India. Prominent Khitabs bestowed by the British are given below :

Khan Bahadur, Khan Sahib

Khitabs awarded by the British authorities, are to be preserved in an inverted order. As the British rule vanished in 1947, and the present Government of India does not bestow such titles, the usage of the British titles in the names-of-persons is getting diminished day by day. However, there are specific national awards bestowed regularly on some distinguished persons, by the Government of India. But the recipients are forbidden from using them in their names.

Laqab on the other hand, is a title of social importance. It is either self acquired, earned, inherited, or sometimes given by the people. In exceptional instances, it can also be bestowed posthumously by the descendants or the followers (Mohammed Haroon, 1984). As per Sengupta (1952), a Laqab is an honorific or descriptive epithet, sometimes a nickname, often a title. It may indicate any of the following characteristics :

(a) Profession of the bearer;

(b) Accomplishment of a specific level of proficiency in the religious matters;

(c) Completion of pilgrimage in Saudi Arabia, Haj;

(d) Social importance; and

(e) Esteemed and affectionate terms.

The following words are often employed as Laqab (Mohammed Haroon, 1984) :

Aali	Choudhury	Khwaja	Mufti	Sarkar
Aalijah	Faqir	Kunwar	Mulla	Sayyed
Aagha	Hafiz	Malik	Munshi	Shah
Aaqa	Haji	Malikzada	Nawab	Sheikh
Al-haj	Hakeem	Mian	Nawabzada	Sufi
Allama	Huzoor	Mir	Pir	Sultan
Amir	Imam	Mirza	Qari	Ustad
Baba	Khalifa	Mohtaram	Qazi	
Bakshi	Khan	Moulana	Raja	
Beg	Khanam	Moulvi	Sardar	

Mohammed Haroon (1984) and others in cataloguing have categoried Khitabs and Laqabs as non-essential parts of the names as they are generally terms of courtesy, reverence, academic distinction, office, or any other attribute. They all recommended dropping them from the names at the time of cataloguing. However the findings of this work are slightly different. If a Khitab or Laqab by usage has become part of the name, it is to be preserved as a pre-substantive part of the name. Thus, a prefix title is to be retained if it can be established that the person has acquired public image, and popularity, through the title.

Examples:	**Names-of-persons**	**Catalogue entry**
	Khawajah Mohammad Ali	Mohammamad Ali, Khawajah
	Mir Mustaq Ahmad	Mustaq Ahmad, Mir
	Syed Nurul Hassan	Nurul Hassan, Syed

Some confusion might arise when one observes that some names are formed with the words often used as Laqabs. Since the words form integral part of the names, they have to be retained. A sample of such names is given below :

Ali Sardar Jafri	Mir Alam	Nizam Ali	Sayyida Bano
Amir Ali	Mohammad Mian	Sardar Ali	Sultan Ali
Abdul Hakeem	Nawab Ali	Sayyid Ahmad	Shaikh Ali

Further, it is observed that a Laqab is either prefixed or suffixed to a name-of-person. If it is used before a personal name, it is regarded as an honorific, and therefore, disregarded in cataloguing, or it can assume a secondary element, if the holder has acquired his identity through the same. Yet, its status gets drastically changed and becomes the most important if it occurs after the personal name. Often, the intention to suffix it is to use it as the family name.

Examples:	**Masculine Names**	**Feminine Name**
	Ashraf Jehangir Qazi	Pakeezah Sultan
	Ghulam Rasool Sheikh	
	Masud Husain Khan	
	Mohammad Ali Chaudhury	

2. Given Names

Given name of a Muslim, is known as Ism or Alam in Urdu. Its equivalent in the West is christian name. It is a name given at the time of birth. Important characteristics associated with the given names are enumerated as given below :

1. There is no uniformity in the number of words used in the Muslim personal names.

2. Many modern Muslim names are not syntaxtially correct in their structural sequence as Islamic nomenclature in the countries in the Near East. Like many English names, they may comprise words without any grammatical relationship, sometimes consisting of proper nouns (Fazal Elahi, et. al., 1961).

3. Personal names are drawn from several sources. They include the names of prophets, or Muslim saints in expression of one's devotion to Islam or a compound name to express devotion to God (under one of His 99 names), to the Prophet (any one of his 99 names), or to Ali, Hasan, Husain for Shias (Fazal Elahi, et. al., 1961). In addition, the following attributes are also used to form the given names (Chand, 1971):

(a) Colour names such as Kale Khan (Kala = Black) or Lal Mohammad (Lal = Red).

(b) Names of the Heavenly objects; e.g. Khurshid Ahmad (Khurshid = Sun), Shamasuddin (Sams = Sun), Aftab Ahmad (Aftab = Sun), Mehr

Din (Mehr = Moon); Aktari Bai (Aktari is the name of a planet): Mushtary Bano (Mushtary = Jupiter); Najamuddin Ahmad (Najam = star).

(c) Names of Islamic months and seasons, such as Ramzan Khan, Bahar Ahmad. Ramzan is the holy month, and Bahar is the spring season.

(d) Names of animals : Sher Khan (Sher = Lion), Asadullah Khan (Asad = Lion).

(e) Names of flowers, plants : Gul Mohammad (Gul =Rose), Nihal Ahmed (Nihal = Young plant), Shajar Mohammad (Shajar = Small plant).

4. In addition to the words used to form Muslim given names, as listed above, some names as done among the Hindus, are broken into two parts. If a given name is split, both the parts have to be retained together in the natural sequence. Example Khudabaksh is written as Khuda Baksh.

Types of personal names

By having a perusal of the Muslim personal names, the undermentioned classification can be done (Rait, 1983a):

(1) Simple names consisting of single worded personal names. Examples are : Mumtaz, Nayyar, Yahya, Yakub, etc.

(2) Compound names. Most names fall in this class. There are variations, described as under :

(a) It may consist of two personal names rendered as two separate words, e.g. Afzal Ahmad, Nayyer Iqbal, Jahan Ara, Raza Akhtar, Shaukat Bano, Taiyaba Khatun, and so on.

(b) It may comprise two personal names of which the second name is ending in 'i', such that Ismat Rizvi, Manzur Jafri, Sadiq Hashmi, Sukhlain Naqvi, etc.

(c) It may be of two personal names of which the first name is a compound name, such as Izzat Ara Praveen, Shamasuddin Tabrez, Zahiruddin Khurshid, and so on.

It is also observed that a large number of the names begin with the word 'Mohammad'. In general, there are two possibilities, described as under (Fazal Elahi, et. al., 1961):

(a) It can be a secondary element in the given name, if it has been used as the blessing or the part of the family tradition. In such given names, two worded given name is generally following the word, Mohammad. In other words, if a personal name is consisting of three words, of which the first one is Mohammad, the entry has to be prepared under the other two words, by inverting the name.

(b) It can be the main part of the personal name, if it is consisting of merely two words. In such a name, entry is to be prepared in the natural sequence. Examples are given below:

Personal names	**Catalogue entry**
Mohammad Ali	Mohammad Ali
Mohammad Faruq	Mohammad Faruq
Mohammad Abdul Hai	Abdul Hai, Mohammad
Mohammad Farukh Ahmad	Farukh Ahmad, Mohammad

3. Surnames

Strictly speaking, there has never been a system among the Muslims, of having surname or family name. In the classical Muslim names, there is a component called Nisbat, employed in the names. A Nisbat is a distributive adjective indicating the place of birth, origin or dwelling; sect; tribe or family, occupation, trade or profession of the owner (Fazal Elahi, et. al., 1961). Though, in a classical name, there can be more than one Nisbat, in a modern name of a Muslim, the general trend is to select one word. Further, because of the Western influence, the practice is to employ it as if it were a surname. In addition, some Laqabs are also in usage as family names. An illustration of the words frequently employed as family names is given as under (Mohammed Haroon, 1984).

Abbasi	Bakhshi	Fazli	Kaifi	Niazi	Shadani
Abidi	Bari	Fidai	Kar	Nomani	Shamshi
Afaqi	Batt	Firangi	Kashfi	Noorani	Sherwani
Afindi	Bazmi	Firozi	Kazmi	Pasha	Shirani
Afridi	Beg	Ghazali	Khairi	Qadri	Shirazi
Agwani	Bhatti	Ghori	Khalili	Qadyani	Siddiqi
Ahmadi	Bilgrami	Gilani	Khan	Qasmi	Subhani

Ajmali	Bukhari	Hadi	Khani	Qazi	Sulemani
Ajmeri	Burni	Haideri	Kidwai	Qidwai	Surmadi
Akbari	Changezi	Hamdani	Kirmani	Qazilbash	Tayebji
Alfaruqi	Chisti	Hanifi	Lutfi	Qudsi	Tirmizi
Alvi	Choudhury	Haqqi	Madani	Qureshi	Toosi
Amini	Chugtai	Hashmi	Mahdi	Qutbi	Umeri
Anhonvi	Dar	Hijaji	Makki	Rabbani	Urli
Ansari	Daudi	Hindi	Maududi	Rehmani	Usmani
Arfi	Durrani	Hussaini	Mazhari	Rizvi	Wahabi
Arshi	Fahmi	Islahi	Meenai	Sadi	Warisi
Asfahani	Faizee	Israeli	Mehdi	Sabiri	Yadzani
Ashahari	Farahi	Jafri	Mirasi	Sabuhi	Yezdi
Asri	Faridi	Jaisi	Mujeebi	Safrani	Zai
Askari	Farkhi	Jalali	Mush-hadi	Sahbai	Zaidi
Awesi	Farooqi	Jalavi	Musvi	Saiti	Zuberi
Azhari	Farshori	Jamali	Nadvi	Saiyyadain	
Azmi	Farshori	Jilani	Naqvi	Sarwani	
Badakh Shani	Fatimi	Junaidi	Nasiri	Scharwardi	

In North India, Muslims have adopted particular surnames based on their caste affiliations. In this way, some uniformity has emerged in the names-of-persons belonging to one caste group, and it is possible to know the caste background of the bearer from his surname. A sample of such surnames is given as under :

Family Name	Caste
Ansari	Weaver (Singh, 1996a)
Hakeem	Barber
Qureshi	Butchermen (Singh, 1996a)
Rogankar	Oil expeller
Saifi	Blacksmith

Samshi	General merchant
Shah	Fakir (Singh, 1996a)
Salamani	Barber
Siddiqui	Bangle dealer (Singh, 1996a)

However, there is a section among the Muslims, not agreeing to the above logic of linking the surnames directly with castes. In addition, some particular Hindu caste names such as Chauhan, Rajput, Tyagi, and so on are also used as family names, by the Muslims.

In the above list of the words often used as family names among the Muslims, it has been observed that 'Khan' is one such word which is used in some names as the surname, where as it can also be the part of the personal name, in some other names. To determine its correct status, it has to be found out whether the name is of two component parts or more. If it is consisting of only two parts, Khan is to be taken as a part of the given name. Other wise, it has to be treated as the surname (Fazal Elahi et. al., 1961).

<u>Examples</u> :	**Given names**	**Main entry**
	Gaffur Khan	Gaffur Khan
	Farid Khan	Farid Khan
	Mir Osman Ali Khan	Khan, Mir Osman Ali
	Rahmat Ali Khan	Khan, Rahmat Ali

Some specific names may start with Mohammad and end with Khan. In such names, Mohammad has to be inverted, and the other two words have be treated as the personal name.

<u>Examples</u> :

Names-of-persons	**Catalogue Entry**
Mohammad Yakub Khan	Yakub Khan, Mohammad
Mohammad Zardan Khan	Zardan Khan, Mohammad

4. Pen-name

Among the educated and learned people, it has been quite a common practice of using some distinctive word representing the literary name, under which the person contributes his writings. It is known in Urdu, as Takhallus. Generally, it is self acquired though in rare instances, it can be bestowed by the people. It generally forms the last part of a name-of-person. Ranganathan (1964) has described it as a pseudonym, and therefore, he has prescribed its treatment as if it were a real false name. However, the findings of this work are that it is the prominent part of the name under which a poet or writer as the case may be, contributes, and he is generally recognised by it. As all the elements of his name are also disclosed, the intention is not to conceal the identity of the author. On the contrary, it is used to give a distinct identity to the writings in which it appears, considering the fact that the name-of-person is generally too long, to accommodate in a verse. It may be difficult for a common man to remember the full name of the writer. Hence, to treat it as a pseudonym, is not correct. It is herein recommended that the catalogue entry be prepared under the pen-name, if used by an author with the other component parts have to be inverted.

Name-of-person	**Catalogue entry**
Abdul Hafiz Hafiz Jullundhari	Hafiz Jullundhari, Abdul Hafiz
Khwaja Haider Ali Atish	Atish, Khwaja Haider Ali
Shabbir Hasan Josh Malihabadi	Josh Malihabadi, Shabbir Hasan
Syed Altaf Hussain Hali Panipati	Hali Panipati, Syed Altaf Hussain
Syeda Bano Hejab	Hejab, Syeda Bano

5. Other Components

Apart from the components of the Indian Muslim names-of-persons, described above, there are some additional features associated with a few names. Their occurrence however, in the names is very rare. These features are often used in the Arabic names. Yet, in a few exceptional names-of-persons claiming their origin from an Arabic country, employment of such additional features is prevailing. In the other names, such features may appear rather rarely. Their description is given as under :

(a) **Kunyah** : The Kunyah literally means patronymic and sometimes indicates descent (Rait, 1983a). Ranganathan (1964) has declared it an indirect name. It normally consists of 'Abu' (= father), 'bin' (=son), 'bint' (daughter), 'Ibn' (= son) or 'Umm' (= mother). It is generally the practice to name the eldest son or the daughter, as per the kunyah name. However, by taking note of the fact that names are given to infants having no child bearing age, the Kunyah may be false. Again, some Kunyah may be metaphorical, referring to some desired quality (Jamil Ahmed and Sengupta, 1961). An illustration of the Kunyah is given as under :

Kunyah	**Meaning**
Abu Bakr	Father of Bakr
Abu Musa Ali	Ali, the father of Musa
Ibn Inshah	Son of literature
Umm Bilqis	Mother of Bilqis

In Indian sub-continent, some specific personal names are formed from the combination of words appearing to be Kunyah. Yet, the entire is used as the personal name.

(b) **Nasab** : or pedgree, a list of ancestors, immediately following the given name or ism. Each personal name is denoting the given name of the father, grand father and so on. A connecting word such as ibn, or bin (=son of) or bint (= daughter of) is employed to separate the two personal names. The description of such names has been provided under Telugu names.

(c) **Urf** : is the nickname of the person. Ranganthan (1964) feels that it is an alternate name or a pseudonym. However, it has been observed that in general, it is employed to denote the pen-name (i.e. takhallus) of the person in a few instances, and the author gets recognition through it. Hence, the catalogue entry has to be prepared under it. If it not so, it has to be regarded only an added name.

4.5.4 Structure of the names

Based on the diversified practices, several structures have emerged in the Muslim names-of-persons. They are described as under:

(a) Names having the surname

The sequence of the parts used is 'Given name-Surname'. In some names, prefix title is also present. A sample of such names is given as below :-

Masculine Names	**Feminine Names**
Ali Jawad Zaidi	Fahmida Bano Hashmi

Ishrat Ali Rizvi Sanjida Khanam Ansari

Mohammad Ahmad Farooqi

Sartaj Alam Abidi

Sultan Haider Kazmi

In such a name, the entry has to be prepared under the last part of the name, i.e. in the family name. The prefix title, in general has to be ignored. Yet, it is required to be preserved in an inverted order if it had been a British title, or if it has become the part of the name, and the identification of the person is affected. The prefix titles mentioned below are recommended for retention in a Muslim name:

Khwajah, Mir, Mirza, Sheikh, Syed or Syeda

(b) Names without Family Name

There are two categories of such names, described as under :

(a) Names denoting personal names. They are falling in the following three classes :

(i) Simple names of single words. They do not pose any problem.

(ii) Multi-worded personal names :

- double - worded given names in which the second word is ending in 'i'. The entry has to be made under the second word.

- A two worded name in which the first word is a compound word. The catalogue entry is to be preferred in the natural sequence.

- Multi - worded names have to be rendered in the natural sequence, except the names in which the first word is Mohammad. In such a name, the word Mohammad has to be inverted.

(c) Names having some Prefix Title, and no Family Name

The prefix title has to be dropped, in general, barring the specific situations of being either a British title or on becoming the part of the name. The treatment is the same as given above.

(d) Names-of-persons possessing Takhallus

Main entry is to be preferred under the pen-name or the takhallus. The other parts of the name including the surname, if used have to be inverted. The prefix title has either to be removed, or retained as prescribed above. In this respect, it may be stated that some persons add place name after the word used as their literary name. For our purposes, both the words have to be taken together, as the entry elements.

(e) Names suffixed by the Name of Father/Husband

In this class of the names-of-persons, the given name is followed by the name of the father; Among the married females, instead of the father's name, the personal name of her husband is suffixed. In the recent times, this pattern is gaining popularity in the educated class. An illustration of such names is given as under :

Masculine Names	**Feminine Names**
Ahmed Naseem	Niloufar Fakruddin
Baqir Shameem	Sabila Asaf
Irfan Habib	
Khalid Shafiq	

(f) Name suffixed by the auxiliary of the father's name

In rare instances, specific feminine given names may be suffixed by a masculine auxiliary. This is generally taken from the personal name of the father or husband. However, only a solitary example could be obtained which is given as below :

Rais Hai

Since the suffixed word is not a prominent part of the name, the entry has to be prepared under the natural sequence of the name-of-person.

4.6 NORTH INDIAN NAMES IN AACR- 2

From the view point of the pattern of the names-of-persons, the entire North India can be divided into two groups, described as under:

(a) Ladakh area of Jammu and Kashmir, and a small track of Himachal Pradesh, on the frontier of Tibet. Both of these areas have the domination of the Tibetan culture. Persons in both the areas are followers of Buddhism.

(b) In the remaining area of North India, persons are Hindus, Muslims,

Jains, Sikhs or Buddhists. In the structure of the names-of-persons, there exists a remarkable uniformity, in all the states and the union territory. Even Buddhists and Jains follow the same pattern in their names as used by the Hindus.

Based on the categorization given above, certain discernible features associated with the North Indian names-of-persons are presented here :

1. Usage of prefixes

Prefix titles, generally denote the caste affiliations, social status, educational attainment, profession, or some other feature of the bearer or of his dominant ancestor. The practice of using prefix titles in the names-of-persons is mainly prevailing in North India. Their usage is however, getting diminished day by day. In general, all such titles have to be omitted at the time of cataloguing. However, there are specifically two exceptions described as under:

(a) Titles awarded by the British Government in India. They are often used in the names of the recipients. They are never passed on to the next generation. Hence, they have to be retained but only in subordination to the other component parts. This is in conformity with the AACR 2.

(b) Khitabs and Laqabs used in the Muslim names-of-persons have to be ignored. However, by usage, a few among them have become part of the names. Hence, they have to be retained in an inverted order, being subordinate to the other parts. Similarly, among the Hindus, some prefix titles have to be preserved, in rare instances if the identity of the bearer is affected otherwise. In specific, prefix titles used in the names of saints and former rulers and their immediate kins, have been found for retention.

2. Breaking of the personal names

Normally given names are complex, and they are generally broken into two parts. Though, both the component parts become intelligible only when read together. Yet, they are made to stand as if both of them are independent words. Hence, the entry in the second part of the given name is to be avoided, except in the particular context when the author provides his own preference to treat that word as the most important part of his name.

3. Surnames in Names

The tradition of using surnames in the names-of-persons, has not become universal in the entire North India. In addition, changing, dropping or using it, can be seen, in rare instances in the latter part of the life. In this context, it is observed that the surname wherever employed, comes in the rear end of a name-of-person. In public usage, a person is generally identified by his family name and therefore, the main entry is to be prepared under it. The other parts of the name are to be inverted. Prefix if occurring is to be removed, or preserved as directed earlier.

In such names having no family name, the treatment has to be slightly different. The entire name generally is the personal name. Hence, the entry is to be prepared in the full form of the name, without altering the sequence. Yet, there is an exception to this, described as under :

If the last part of a name-of-person has been converted or used as the surname, the main entry is to be made under this part. A feminine name-of-person ending with the name of her father or husband, her personal name should form the entry. However, if the end part is a masculine auxiliary, it is to be treated as the family name.

4. Takhallus in Names

A literary-name generally known in the vernacular circle as Takhallus, is used in the names of some poets and writers. Some prominent politicians, and others, in rare instances may also employ a similar attachment. Wherever such an appellation is employed, it generally assumes an important role. Hence, the main entry is to be prepared under it.

Ladakhi Names-of-persons

In the Ladakhi names-of-persons, usage of family name is an exception. Thus, a name-of-person generally denotes the given name alone, and therefore, it is to be rendered in its natural sequence. However, there are two exceptions to it, described as under :

(a) If a person is using anglicised format of his name, and is found to have contracted all the component parts into initials except the last part which is appearing in its full form, the main entry is to be made under the last part. In such a name however, if any prefix is also used the same is to be dropped.

(b) In rare instances, if a surname is used, the main entry has to made under it.

The under-mentioned prescriptions in cataloguing, for the names-of-persons from North India, are suggested :

N.1 With the exceptions of N.2 to N.4, enter a name-of-person from North India, into his or her pen-name or takhallus, if employed, otherwise under the family name, if used in the end. In the absence of the surname, the entire name as such be treated as the entry element. However, if any prefix title is employed, it is generally ignored, or preserved in inverted form in the following exceptional rare situations:

(a) if it has been a British title;

(b) if, by usage it has become part of the name.

Examples:

Name-of-person	**Entry in AACR 2**
Choudhary Brahm Prakash	Brahm Prakash
Dina Nath Nadim	Nadim, Dina Nath
Indira Sharma Indu	Indu, Indira Sharma
Khwaja Haider Ali Atish	Atish, Khwaja Haider Ali
Mohammad Ahmed Farooqui	Farooqui, Mohammad Ahmed
Rabri Devi	Rabri Devi
Rajendra Prasad	Rajendra Prasad
Rai Bahadur Seth Gujjar Mal Modi	Modi, Gujjar Mal, Rai Bahadur
Rao Birendra Singh	Birendra Singh, Rao
Surya Kant Tripathi Nirala	Nirala, Surya Kant Tripathi
Syeda Bano Hejab	Hejab, Syeda Bano

N.1.1 Enter a North Indian name-of-person under the combination of a two worded surname, if the same contains the family name of the father and of the husband. Or, one part may denote the name of a place and the other is his surname, academic degree or profession. If the author provides no indication to any other way, both the words have to be taken together.

Examples	Name-of-person	Entry in AACR 2
	Bhola Paswan Shastri	Paswan Sastri, Bhola.
	Usha Anand Kapur	Anand Kapur, Usha

N.1.1.1 If however, one portion of the surname has been a word of affection, enter under the other part of the surname. The affectionate word has to be preserved in sub-ordination to the personal name.

Example:	Name-of-person	Entry in AACR 2
	Amar Nath Kaul Adalti	Adalti, Amar Nath Kaul
	Jiya Lal Kaul Jalali	Jalali, Jiya Lal Kaul

N.2 Enter a name-of-person under the last part of his name, if the person gives prominence to it. This could have been despite being irregular in the linguistic belts of North India. Similarly, among the feminine names terminating with a masculine auxiliary, the auxiliary word should form the entry element.

Examples:

Name-of-person	Shortened form	Entry in AACR 2
Kirpal Singh	K.P. Singh	Singh, Kir Pal
Naintara Kumar		Kumar, Naintara
Narender Datta	N. Datta	Datta, Narender
Sonam Dolma	S. Dolma	Dolma, Sonam
Viswanath Pratap Singh	V.P. Singh	Singh,Viswanath Pratap

N.3 Enter a name-of-person under the given name of the bearer if the given name is succeeded by the personal name of the father or husband, provided no surname is used.

Examples:

Names-of-persons	Entry in AACR 2
Irfan Habib	Irfan Habib
Sushma Swaraj	Sushma Swaraj
Vinay Bharat Ram	Vinay Bharat Ram

N.4 Enter a modern person of religious vocation (whether Hindu, Buddhist, or Jain) under the religious name (given name). The religious title prefixed to the name has to be inverted. The suffix if also used, has to be retained as such.

Names-of-persons	**Catalogue Entry**
Mata Nirmala Devi	Nirmala Devi, Mata
Muni Sushil Kumar	Sushil Kumar, Muni
Swamy Chinmayananda	Chinmayanada, Swamy
Swamy Satpal Maharaj	Satpal Maharaj, Swamy

Chapter V

EAST INDIAN NAMES

5.1 EAST INDIA

5.1.1 General

West Bengal and Orissa are the two prominent states of East India. They have many similarities in their culture. Before Bihar was separated from the erstwhile Bengal Presidency, in the beginning of this century, several districts of Orissa, formed a part of the Presidency of Bengal. In the present chapter, Sikkim a new state has also been included in East India, on account of the following reasons:

1. Geographic proximity to the state of West Bengal;

2. Ethnic similarities with the people of the hilly region of West Bengal.

In addition, Andaman and Nicobar Islands located in the Bay of Bengal, presently a union territory, has also been covered under East India. The reasons for doing so are as under :

1. A large number of Bengali Hindu settlers, uprooted from the Muslim Bengal (Presently, Bangladesh), form one of the largest ethnic groups in the territory.

2. Nearest in the main land, from the territory is West Bengal. Though, Tamilnadu is also equidistant from the Andamans, the number of Tamil speaking persons, is far fewer than Bengalis.

East India based on the languages spoken, can be divided into the following groups :

1. Bengali: Hindus and Muslims of West Bengal have been covered;

2. Oriya: Hindus, Muslims and tribals of Orissa have been studied;

3. Sikkimi: The names-of-persons from Sikkim have been investigated. They consist of the following three ethnic groups:

(a) Lepcha - they are the aborigines of the state. They use Lepcha language. Most of them are Buddhists;

(b) Bhutia - They are descendants of the migrants from Tibet. Their language is Bhutia. They are following Tibet Buddhism; and

(c) Nepali - Originally belonging to Nepal. Most of them are Hindus.

4. Andaman and Nicobari Islands- The names-of-persons include several groups, from different parts of India. Their names have been covered under different linguistic heads of this thesis. Similarly, Locals the descendants of the persons who completed their punishment term of more than 10 years, before 1942, also reside. Their names are simple as they do not include surname component such as the caste suffixes, etc. In addition, there are several tribal groups native to the islands. Though, hostile in nature, a section of them have now be come civilized. Their naming pattern has been investigated in this study.

Some sociological aspects of the naming of persons in East India, to be borne in mind while attempting the rendering of these names are briefly described here, in the following pages:

5.2 BENGALI NAMES

5.2.1 General

The partition of Bengal on the eve of the Indian independence in 1947, led to the formation of the state of West Bengal in the Indian Union and the East Bengal (now Bangladesh) of then Pakistan. West Bengal is 88, 752 sq.km. in area and has a population of around 68 million. Hindus are in vast majority (74.72 %), followed by Muslims (23.61 %) (Census of India 1991, 1995).

Situated in the sub-Himalayan eastern part of the country the state is bounded in the west by Bihar, and Orissa in the south. It has frontier with Nepal, in the north, while the Bay of Bengal forms the backdrop in the south. There are two distinct geographic regions in the state. The hilly region in the north popularly known as Gorkhaland, is a small part of the state. It is culturally quite close to the neighbouring hilly state, Sikkim. The names-of-persons from this area have been adequately covered in the sub-chapter on Sikkim. The remaining area is the mainland, excelling in Bengali culture.

5.2.2 Names-of-persons

Bengali names follow the same structure as those employed in North India. There are generally three component parts of a name-of-person. They occur sequentially as proper or personal name; padanta employed to embellish or complete the proper name; and the family name (Sengupta, 1974b).

Examples:	Masculine Names	Feminine Names
	Makhan Chandra Roy	Bharti Kumari Saha
	Sailendra Kumar Mahata	Indrani Kumari Maiti
	Swapan Kumar Banerjee	Nanita Rani Bhowmik
	Utpal Kumar Das	Rita Renu Chaudhury

However, during the recent times, a trend has emerged in which the middle part of the names, i.e. padanta is not being used. Therefore, names-of-persons have become two worded. A sample of such names has been given as under:

Examples:	Masculine Names	Feminine Names
	Ajit Khan	Rita Mukherjee
	Jana Mitra	Sandhya Mondal
	Subrata Bose	Sikha Sarkar

It may be recalled here that the British had entered in the country from Bengal, and therefore, Bengali culture had been among the first few ones to come under the direct influence of the British. In names-of-persons, its impact was felt quite early. Several family names got transformed into their anglicised form.

5.2.2.1 Surnames

The surnames in the state, had originated from a variety of sources. As per Sengupta (1974b), quite a few Hindu family names had emerged from the padanta or the complementary part (an equivalent of the auxiliary) of the given names. As personal names during the far-off days had been mostly single worded, a part of their names, now known as the complementary part, the padanta, an additional epithet, got metamorphosed into the family name. An illustration of such personal names during the fifth century, is given below. The padanta or the complementary part has been underlined :

Dharampalit, Harishchandra, Vasumitra, Sanghamitra, Jayadrath, Agvaghosa, Gurudatta, Haridasa, Visnusarman

In another century or so, the padanta had acquired so much prominence in the names that almost all the masculine names belonging to one family were possessing the same padanta. There is evidence to believe that these families were known in the wider circles, by their padanta. Examples of given names of four brothers of a family possessing a common padanta (chandra) are given below (Sengupta, 1974b):

Harishchandra, Girishchandra,

Rameshchandra, Ganeshchandra

The system had undergone further transformation, at a latter stage, and the padanta became independent, detached from the name. In this way, each name had became two worded entity. The padanta afterwards had become the family name in several non-Brahmin families. These padantas generally depicted some names of gods or celestial bodies. Some of them are listed here (Sengupta, 1974b):

5.2.2.1.1 Padanta used as surname	**Meaning/origin**
Aditya	Sun
Chandra	Moon
Mitra	Sun

Sometimes, specific words denoting Varman (armour), Yasah (fame), or Balam (power) were also employed as padanta.

There are several classes of the family names derived from the padantas. They have been categorised in the following classes (Sengupta, 1974b):

(a) Names of gods and celestial bodies

Surname	**Other form**	**Meaning/origin**
Aich		Corrupted from Aditya
Indra		Rain god
Chandra	Chanda	Moon

De	Deb	Deva or deity-from Jaydeva
Mitra		Sungod
Ruj		Corrupted form of Rudra
Rudra		Shiv
Soma		Moon god

(b) Padantas denoting fame, power, prosperity, and strength

Surname	Other form	Meaning/origin
Bhadra		auspicious
Pai	Boi or Bai	from pati or lord
Bardan		increase
Kirti		fame

(c) Words implying favour or protection from gods

Surname	Other form	Meaning/origin
Datta		bestowed
Dama	Da	bountiful
Palita		protected
Laha		From Naha
Dhara		holder, protector
Gupta		protected
Guha		another name for Kartikeya
Pala		protector
Kar		made protected
Pan	Pain	for Pani or palm of the hand, implying protection

(d) Names of animals

Several animal names originally forming part of the names of the gods such as Narsimha, Dignaga, Panhasti, etc. were employed, in their Sanskrit form, as family names. Subsequently, in some specific cases, they were also drawn by analogy, and a few animal names not forming part of the names were also used as surnames.

Examples:

Surname	Other form	Meaning
Bag		Leopard
Gondak		Rhinoceros
Guin		One possessing many cows
Kara		Buffalo
Hati	Hait	Elephant
Nag	Naga	Cobra
Sinha		Lion

(e) Vocation as family name

In some non-Brahmin families, designation titles of some well-known and established vocations of the past have been used as surnames. However, they denote the status of the ancestors and may not have any relevance to the present.

Examples:

Surname	Other Form	Meaning
Sapure		Snake charmer
Dhaki		Hand held musical sound producing device operator
Bayen		Drum beater
Dhobi		Washerman
Gayan		Singer
Gharami		House maker
Kumar		Earthen pot maker
Napit	Pramik	Barber

(f) Place name and vocation as family name

The Brahmins of the state claim their origin from the vicinity of Kanpur in Uttar Pradesh. But, their surnames are not derived from some prominent caste denoting terms such as Sharma, Chaturvedi, Mishra, Tripathy, etc. or from some more specific features like sub-caste or gotras, etc. as is the case with most of the Brahmins of North India. On the other hand, Bengali Brahmin surnames are primarily based on the profession of teaching i.e. upadhyaya, in the ancient times, coupled with place names (Sengupta, 1974b). An illustration of such family names is given as under :

Surname	Place name
Mukhopadhya	Mukhoti
Bhattacharya	Bhatpara

Another surname Gangopadhyaya had perhaps emerged from the name of the holy river Ganga. As per a popular belief, their ancestors were engaged in performing the funeral rites. Likewise, there are other prominent family names of the Brahmins, such as Bandhopadhya, Chattopadhyaya, and so on.

In the present context, the surnames may not be conveying the profession as implied by them. Yet, they are employed as the most potent part of the names.

(g) Position titles as Surnames

The Islamic rule in the state brought several vocational titles. The families occupying them were identified with such position descriptors, which are now used as family names. Their origin is given as under (Mookerjee, 1959):

Surname	Origin/meaning
Baksi	Pay-master and land revenue clerk
Bhandar Kayastha	Royal post; employed as decoration by the Hindu rulers
Biswas	Village accountant
Chakladar	Chief of a cluster of a few villages known as Chakla
Chaudhuri	In charge of four different forces in the Army. Sometimes, the headman of a village is also known by it
Dastidar	Keeper of the Royal seal
Deshmukh	Chief revenue or police officer of a district
Haldar	Assistant keeper of accounts for a village
Hazari	General of a thousand Army personnel
Khan	Royal title

Kanungo	Revenue officer
Khasnovis	Private secretary, a clerk or an accounts officer
Krori	A revenue officer collecting more than ten million Dam. One Dam = one rupee
Laskar	Title conferred on fit persons in the Army
Mandal	Head of the village
Mir - vahar	Chief of the Fleet or the Admiral of the Fleet
Mullick	Conferred title on zamindars, and jagirdars
Mazumdar	Audit person for the revenue records for the zamindars
Munshi	Secretary for noting down the disposition in the law-courts, and other writing work
Munsiff	Land inspector appointed by zamindars
Mustafi	In charge of the civil records
Ohdedar	Revenue officer to realise the revenue from the zamindars, when they failed to pay
Patranavis	The person who controlled the State's Correspondence Department.
Poddar or Fotadar	Examiners of coins (money)
Pur Kayastha	Old Hindu title generally awarded to the chief writer of the ruler
Ray, Rajan or Roy	A title signifies the honour of having a thousand soldiers
Ray Bahadur	Having three thousand soldiers under him
Samaddar	Inspectors for the crop cultivation.
Sarkar	the chief person in the village
Serkhel	General of the Army i.e. Senapati
Sikdar	Revenue clerk in a small area
Singh	Decorative title for Army officers
Tarafdar	Owner of a portion or taraf of a paragana.

Upadhyaya	A title signifies a Brahmin
Visayee	Chief of a district in Orissa. Also, revenue collector and administrator.

As the official positions described above had almost been hereditary in nature during the Muslim rule, many of the families occupying them had adopted the position descriptors as part of their surnames. The original transformation which had come about several hundred years ago, was to employ the main caste denoting surname followed by the Muslims position title. In this way, two worded family names had come into regular usage. As Kayasthas were mostly in the employment of the government, the typical change had been witnessed more in their family names. Similarly, Muslim rule in the erstwhile eastern parts of the undivided Bengal had been more influential, many more instances of double worded surnames are found in the families of the migrants. An illustration of such multi-worded family names is given as below:

Basu Mullick	Deb Biswas	Nag Chaudhury
Dutt Mazumdar	Khan Chaudhury	Rai Chaudhury

In addition, some surnames such as Das Gupta, Deb Nath, and Sen Gupta are also double-worded, though they have not been derived from the official positions.

Further, individuals belonging to specific Brahmin families, suffixed a title Chakraborthy denoting a magnificent house, during the distant days. It must however, be kept in mind that it denotes the past status of the fore-fathers and does not imply anything in the present situation. It is now an established surname.

5.2.2.1.2 Anglicised Surnames

The British rule in Bengal had brought distortion and over simplification in some of the surnames. As several family names had been quite typical and it must have been difficult for the British, to pronounce them correctly, they might have been suitably amended to suit the convenience of the Foreign rulers. In this way, a new class of surnames had come into existence. Their usage is still continued. They are the anglicised form.

Examples:

Vernacular Form	Anglicised Form
Bandhopadhyaya	Banerjee
Basu	Bose
Dutt	Dutta
Gangopadhyaya	Ganguly
Mukhopadhyaya	Mukherjee
Rai	Ray
Thakur	Tagore

A similar transformation has occurred in some of the multi-worded surnames. The general tendency has been to change one (or more) of the words into the anglicised format. The other word may remain in its vernacular form.

Examples:

Vernacular surname	Anglicised form
Basu Mullik	Bose Mullik
Basu Rai Chaudhury	Bose Ray Chaudhury
Dutt Mazumdar	Datta Mazumdar
Raichaudhury	Ray-chaudhury

Again, it is observed that sometimes, these surnames are rendered distinctly, some other times in a unified way, and yet in some specific instances, in a hyphenated way.

5.2.2.1.3 Shortening the surnames

Some families in modern times, have abandoned the usage of a double worded surnames, and have dropped either of the two component parts of their family name. For instance, some families have preferred not to employ the first part whereas some others decided to continue with the former portion alone. Still, there are families who have continued to use the full format of the two worded family names.

5.2.2.1.4 Three-worded family name

Some specific families have taken to a strange practice of rendering their surname like Raichaudhury distinctly. If the surname also includes a caste appellation as Basu, for instance, the family name becomes three worded. In such a surname, all the three words are to be taken together.

5.2.2.1.5 Two Forms of Family Names

A number of the Bengali writers adopt the anglicised version of their family name for the works authored by them in English language. The same authors while writing their work in the native language however, revert to employing the vernacular form. Yet, there are existing some persons who consistently use only one form of their surname irrespective of the language of the work. In this context, it is observed that sometimes father and son/ daughter may be using different forms of the surnames.

Rabindra Nath Tagore the Nobel laureate in the Bengali literature, had always used Tagore for his works written in English language. On the other hand, he had invariably preferred Thakur as his surname for his contributions in the Bengali language. Therefore, it may be concluded that both the forms are used in an interchangeable manner. This may lead to certain amount of confusion, as can be seen from the undermentioned illustration:

Assuming a specific situation in which the translation of a Bengali work into the English language or vice- versa, has been under taken by a person who is not aware of the existence of two different forms of the surname. It is quite likely that the name of the author might be reproduced as it is existing in the original work. This could be different from the form employed by the contributor in his works in the English language or other wise. The cataloguing in the library, done afterwards may lead to two different entries for one and the same person.

5.2.2.1.6 Usage of ji in surnames

It can be seen from the above discussion that several surnames in the state include ji or any of its variants, as integral part. This ji can not be removed from the same and has to be retained in all such cases. A sample of such surnames is given as under :

Banerji, Bhattacharji, Mukherji, Chatterji

5.2.2.1.7 Name-of-person with out surname

It is observed that every family is possessing a fixed title, employed as the surname in all the names. Yet, in some feminine names, no surname occurs. In such a name-of-person, the entire is the personal name. An illustration of such names of the females, is given as under:

Dhiren Bala, Mahasweta Debi

5.2.3 Prefixes in names

Bengali names-of-persons are different from those of the neighbouring states in the sense that the prefix titles are not generally used. In this regard, it may be stated that the emphasis on the usage of the usual prefixes has been shifted to the rear portion of the names, and in this way, they have been hardened to denote the family names. Yet, as an exception, some distinguished persons have been identified with specific prefixes which are honorific in nature. A sample of such names is given as under :

Name-of-person with prefix	Explanation
Acharya Prafulla Chandra Ray	Acharya = a teacher
Babu Bankim Chandra Chattopadhyaya	Babu means an educated person
Gurudev Rabindra Nath Tagore	Gurudev = A renowned teacher

In the above specific examples, Babu is a prefix title of a very generic nature. It can be used by any person, though, its usage is diminishing recently. Such prefixes if used, are to be ignored in cataloguing.

5.2.4 Personal names

Masculine and feminine personal names in the Bengali culture are generally two worded. The first name is being followed by another word, known as auxiliary, employed to qualify the first name. Yet, a confusion can arise because some surnames are made up of the auxiliary words. Therefore, in such a name two auxiliary words can be present. Yet, with the emergence of a new trend in which no auxiliary is employed, the full name-of-person is of two parts. The first word is the given name followed by the family name. Similarly, if a feminine name is ending with a masculine auxiliary, this auxiliary word can be safely taken as the family name.

5.2.5 Change of female name after marriage

An unmarried Bengali girl generally uses the surname of her father which is replaced by the family name of her husband, after marriage. Yet a trend is appearing in which the woman is adding the surname of her husband after her maiden surname. In such a situation, two surnames are found to be in use by the same person. As this practice is still in evolution not many instances have been noticed. A solitary example of such a name is given as below :

Ketaki Roy Dutta

5.2.6 Muslim Names

The state of West Bengal is possessing the largest Muslim population in the country. This has been despite the ceding of a major chunk of the Muslim dominated geographic area, which has now become a separate country, Bangladesh. The structure of the Muslim names is the same in West Bengal and Bangladesh. Even the names chosen are common in the both the regions. Therefore, in this study, several publications for the names-of-persons from Bangladesh, have been referred to study these names. There are two classes of the Bengali Muslim names, described as under :

1. Names denoting given names alone. In such a name-of-person, no family name occurs;

2. Names possessing family names too, at this end.

Names falling in either class also bear prefix titles. The title generally represents either the family background of the bearer or his profession. In this regard, it is observed that where a prefix is used in a name, no family name generally occurs at the end. A sample of the Bengali Muslim names-of-persons is given as under :

1. Names having surname

Masculine Names	Feminine Names
Abdul Barkat Ataul Ghanikhan Choudhury	Fouzia Khatun Khan
Ali Akbar Khan	Nargis Begum Sircar
Gulam Nabi Chaudhury	Ummeiyaman Bibi Mandal
Kabir Chowdhury	

2. Names not possessing surname

Masculine Names	Feminine Names
Aminul Haka	Dilroba Begum
Anishul Rehman	Khalida Begum
Mir Hamid Akbar	Nadinnisha Khatun

Nazrul Zamal	Nilufar Akhtar
Sheikh Yaseen Husain	Sheikh Abida Begum
Syed Shahidul Husain	Syeda Munsura Khatun

Bengali Muslim names-of-persons are different from the Muslim names from other linguistic regions. There are several reasons for it, enumerated as under (Abdul Huq, 1979):

1. A large number of Bengali Muslim names appear to be of non-Bengali origin, mostly coming from the Middle East.

2. Bengali Muslims have accepted Bengali script, which is a branch of the Indic family, and not the Arabic script, as has been done else where.

3. Bengali language does not possess sufficient number of the alphabets, to represent all the Arabic or Persian sounds.

4. Grammar of the Bengali language is in essence, Sanskrit grammar, and as such it is not equipped to deal with the syntactic arrangement of Arabic, Persian or Urdu nouns and more particularly, phrasal names originating from these languages.

5. Because of the phonetic transformation, Bengali Muslim names are just the groups of words or labels arbitrarily bestowed on them for the purpose of identification, or for referring to them.

Thus, it can be inferred from the reasons enumerated above that a Bengali Muslim name is a Bengali name first and Islamic afterwards. Yet, there are some discernible differences between the names of Hindus and Muslims. They are described as under :

1. Hindus ordinarily use family names in their names, where as not all Muslims employ their surnames(Abdul Huq, 1974).

2. Prefix titles in the names of the Hindus are rarely used. In Muslim names-of-persons, they are used in liberally.

3. Anglicised family names are used in some of the Hindu names-of-persons. Among the Muslims, this phenomenon is non-existent.

4. Multi - worded surnames are used in many Hindu families. This is not generally found among the Bengali Muslims.

5. The prescription for the non-Bengali Muslim names-of-persons, is not necessarily true for a Bengali Muslim name.

5.2.6.1 Family names

There are several sources of family names of the Bengali Muslims. Important among them are described as under :

(a) Specific Muslim family names denoting Muslim attributes like Kazi, Khan, Sheikh, and so on.

(b) Surname of the family before conversion, in the Hindu society, such as Brahma, Chatterji, Ganguly, Shastri, Sinha, Thakur, etc.

(c) Family names derived from the Muslim positions, as used by the Hindus like Biswas, Haldhar, Majumdar, etc.

5.2.6.2 Structure of the names

Apart from the two structures used in the Muslim names-of-persons, there exists another one generally employed by the females. In this, the given name of a woman is followed by the name or a part of the name of the husband. An illustration of such names is given below:

Fouzia Hossain, Nargis Zafar, Nilufar Akhter, Siddiqua Zaman

In addition, some Muslims as an exception, use their family name in the beginning or in the middle of the name. Such surnames could be single or multi worded. They are found less potent than the other parts of the name. A sample of such names is given as under :

Names-of-persons	**Entry-word**
Abdul Burkat Ataul Ghanikhan Choudhury	Choudhury
Khan Ataur Rahman	Rahmam
Khan Muhammad Saif-ul-Islam	Saif-ul-Islam

Another structure of the names is also used. In such names, no surname is used. The first word is Mohammad which is succeeded by two more words. In such a name, Mohammad is to be treated as the secondary part of the name. This pattern is confined to the masculine names only. In cataloguing, Mohammad is to be inverted. Similarly, Khan is to be treated as the part of the personal name if the entire name is of two words. If the name has three or more words, Khan is to be considered as the family name. A sample of the names falling in the category are:

Names-of-persons	Catalogue entry
Islam Khan	Islam Khan
Mohammad Abdur Rashid	Abdur Rashid, Mohammad
Mohammad Rehman Khan	Rehman Khan, Mohammad
Mohammad Zahirul Islam	Zahirul Islam, Mohammad

5.3 ORIYA NAMES

5.3.1 General

Orissa is a small state on the east coast of the country, that had come into existence on April 1, 1936 out of the Madras Presidency, Bihar and the Central Provinces. 25 Oriya speaking princely states were merged into this state, after the country became independent. Encircled by Bihar in the north, Bengal in the north-east, Andhra Pradesh in the south-east and Madhya Pradesh in the west, the state's long coastal line in the east is washed by the Bay of Bengal, the state has an area of 155, 707 sq. km. and a population of around 32 million with a demographic break-up of 94.67% Hindus, about 2% Christians, and 1.83% Muslims (Census of India - 1991, 1995).

5.3.2 General Features of Names

Culturally, the state has acquired a distinct identity through the border districts of neighbouring states which exert their influence, tending to make it a composite one. The basic pattern of the names-of-persons is similar to the names of North Indians, with the last part of a name generally denoting the family name (Ranganathan, 1964). The first component of a full name, is the given name which may be single or double worded. If the personal name is made up of two words, the second word is always the complementary to the first part and is irremovable.

Examples:	Masculine Names	Feminine Names
	Basant Kumar Das	Adarmani Mohanty
	Kanhu Charan Lenka	Basant Manjari Debi
	Pravat Kumar Samantaray	Kanak Lata Acharya
	Raghunath Behra	Krishnapriya Panda

Ram Charan Bhoi	Mahamaya Dalai
Prafulla Kumar Patnaik	Mamata Rani Patsahani
Pratap Kesri Deo	Nandini Satpathy
Ramesh Chandra Mishra	Sujata Kumari Nayak
Vishnu Charan Pradhan	

In the southern part of the state, name of the native place or the surname is prefixed in some instances, to the given name. This practice, it appears is the result of the extensive influence of the Telugu culture in the south. A sample of such names is given as below:

Masculine Names	**Feminine Names**
Misra Bhudev	Behera Sarasvati
Sara Binod Kumar	Sitapur Vijay Lakshmi
Tripathy Vinaykumar	

However, if the migratee from the neighbourhood of Andhra Pradesh has settled down in the interior of the state, the normal pattern of his name becomes reversed with the surname rendered in the end. Thus, a change in structure of the name-of-person becomes evident over a period of time.

5.3.3 Surnames in Names

In Oriya culture, the practice of using surname as the end part of the name owe its origin to the profound influence of the Western culture. This had happened in the late nineteenth century (Ranganathan, 1953a), and is continuing. In this respect, it is observed that the relationship of the family names with in the prevailing caste groups has hopelessly been confusing, in many instances. Thus, a variety of surnames are used by a wider cross-section of the society belonging to different castes, and in all such names, it is generally not possible to know the caste background of the bearer. An illustration of such family names is given under :

Barik	Mahapatra	Roy or Ray
Behera	Nayak or Naik	Sahu
Das	Patra	

However, majority of the family names in the state, are representative in one way or the other, of the caste with which a person is associated. Sometimes family professions taken up in the past, are also used as surnames. Since professions were restricted to in the rigid social framework of the castes, it is quite possible to know the caste background from such surnames. Thus, among the Brahmin families, the following surnames are employed.

Surname	Meaning
Dikshit	Descendants of those who were imparting diksha i.e. higher education. Another view is that their ancestors had obtained higher education.
Dwivedy	Whose fore-fathers were proficient in at least two Vedas.
Hota	It is a distorted form of Hotri. Hotri is a short form of Agnihotri.
Mishra	Whose ancestors had been proficient in a variety of professions.
Pani	It is a short form of Panigrahi.
Panigrahi	Whose fore-fathers used to solemnize the marriages.
Pathi	Descendants of those performing puja once in a day. An other view point is that they were knowing at least one Veda.
Puja Panda	Descendants of the people wholly involved in the rituals of puja.
Satpathy	Belonging to those families who were experts in Shatapatha Bramhana of Yajurveda.
Tripathy	Whose ancestors were knowing at least three Vedas. Another legend believes that they were performing puja three times a day.
Upadhyaya	Descendants of teachers.

Surnames were also adopted from the official positions available in the state, in its feudal days. They denote the past status of the family. A sample of such surnames is given below:

Family Name	Meaning
Bada Jena	Chief Commander.
Choudhary	Village headman.
Hajari	An army position, possessing one thousand soldiers.
Jena	Army Commander.
Kanungo	Revenue officer.
Mullik	Conferred title on zamindars and jagirdars.
Sahani	Official in the inner court of the ruler.
Sarkar	Administrator.

Similarly, certain words normally employed as auxiliaries in masculine names, were used to denote family names. Initially, they might have originated from the part of the personal names of some ancestors, as had taken place in Bengal. An illustration of such family names is given as below:

Deb, Deo, Das, Dash, Nath, Pani, Pati, Singh

Kayastha known as Karan in the state, is an educationally forward caste. It had been the indigenous writer-caste. Patnaik, or the chief reader is often employed as their family name. Other surnames used by them are listed as under :

Bahidar	Mohanty
Das	Patra
Kanungo	Rai or Ray
Mahapatra	Rai Chaudhry or Ray Chaudhry

In the same way, every caste in the state, is possessing a set of the family names. For instance, a caste known as "Ganda" whose profession is beating the drums, during the marriages, is having the following family names (Senapati and Sahu, 1968):

Bagh	Dipak	Mahananda	Tandia
Banki	Jagdala	Nag	Varsagar
Bayana	Kumbhar	Ranbira	Versa

Bhibhar	Kusa	Sika
Chhatriya	Luha	Suna

Among the erstwhile Royal families, specific family names have been in use. A sample of the family names of different Royal families, is given as under :

Bhunj Deb or Bhunj Deo	Samant Singhar
Deo	Singh
Narsingh Deo	Singh Deo

Another source of obtaining the family names, was the titles, conferred by the local rulers, on certain natives. These titles or some of them are now being employed as surnames.

Surname	**Meaning**
Behera	Sweeper in the Lord Jagannath Temple.
Biswal	Feudal title. The headman of a village.
Bisi	Feudal title awarded to the soldiers.
Chaudhury	Head of a village.
Nayak	Community head.
Patel	Head of a cluster of a few villages.
Pradhan	Village head.
Rajguru	Royal priest.
Senapati	Commander in chief.

In addition, there are surnames denoting specific caste affiliations. The under-mentioned family names are used by the castes in the broader sense, mentioned against each one. In this category, surnames are used by different caste groups of an equal social standing. Hence, the illustration is only indicative.

Surname	**Caste**
Barik	Barber
Bhoi	Scavanger
Kundu	Potter
Maharana	Carpenter

Parida	Milk man
Raut	Fisherman
Raut Rai or Raut Ray	Kshatriya
Sahoo	Teli or Oil extractor
Swain	Related to Lord Jaghannath

It is interesting to note that certain names denoting animals are also employed as surnames. Initially, they might have formed part of the given names of some gods, or from their vernacular equivalents as had been the case in Bengal.

Examples:	**Surname**	**Meaning**
	Bagh	Tiger
	Hati	Elephant
	Nag	Cobra
	Sand	Bull
	Singh	Lion

Different surnames are used among the Rajputs of the state. They appear to be the given names of some ancestor. At the present, family members are not aware as to how the particular family name has come into use. A sample of such family names is listed below :

Family Name	**Other Form**
Baliarsingh	Baliar Singh
Bhujawal	
Jhabbarsingh	Jabbar Singh
Mansingh	Man Singh
Paharsingh	Pahar Singh
Sunder-rai	
Uttar Kapad	

In respect of the Oriya family names, it is observed that whatever may be its form, derivation or meaning, the family members as on date may generally not be indulged in the specific work, or occupation, as conveyed by the same. Similarly, if some academic achievement of the ancestors has been employed as the surname, it is very rare that any one of the family may be possessing that accomplishment, at present. In many situations, the family may not be in a position to convey as to how the same is being used as their family name. Hence, surnames in Oriya culture have lost their function. Yet, they denote the most important part of the names.

5.3.3.1 Change of surnames

In rare instances, surnames undergo change due to the desire of the family to replace their old fashioned family name with a modern one. Sometimes, it is just the whims and fancies of the family members which prompts such a change. Similarly some persons may like to gain social mileage, by using the caste names of the higher castes. A sample of the such surnames, along with their new form, is given as under :

Old surnames	**Changed surnames**
Bahidar	Patnaik
Mahanta	Mohanty
Mahapatra	Mohanty
Malla	Mahapatra
Patnaik	Rao Patnaik
Patsahani	Mahapatra

In the examples cited above, the family name Rao Patnaik was used only after the family shifted to another place, near the Andhra border.

5.3.3.2 Two-worded surnames

Some family names in the state are two worded, and hence, both the words have to be carried together in such a surname. An illustration of such family names is given as below :

Bada Panda	Bhunj Deo	Raut Rai
Baliar Singh	Puja Panda	Singh Dev
Bada Jana	Rai Chaudhury	

5.3.4 Prefixes

By and large, prefix titles are not used in the names-of-persons. Yet, specific prefixes denoting the status of the individuals are employed in some names. In the former Royal families, the undermentioned prefixes are in common usage :

Prefix Title	Meaning
Raja	King
Rani	Queen
Maharaja	Emperor
Yuvraj	Crown Prince
Yuvrani	Wife of the Crown Prince
Rajkumar	Prince
Rajkumari	King's daughter
Rajguru	Royal priest
Kunwar	Born in a Royal family

Along the border districts touching Bihar, employment of prefixes is quite common. A sample of such prefixes used in the names, is given as under:

Prefix	Meaning
Jamindar	Big land lord
Jyotisha	Astrologer
Kabi	Poet
Kabichandra	Distinguished poet
Kabi kabiraj	Highly distinguished poet
Kabiraj	Ayurvedic doctor
Kabiratan	Distinguished Ayurvedic doctor
Baidya	Ayurvedic doctor
Purohit	Priest

Since these prefixes do not form a part of the names, they are ignored in cataloguing. Strangely, caste denoting prefix titles are not generally employed in the state.

In the feminine names, prefix titles are not used except among the females belonging to the erstwhile Royal families.

5.3.5 Anglicised Surnames

As is the case in West Bengal, several family names, have been transformed into their anglicised version, and are used in the names-of-persons, on interchangeable basis. Thus, two forms of such family names are in existence. An illustrations of such family names, is given as under

Vernacular form	Anglicised form
Nayak	Naik
Rai	Ray
Rai Chaudhury	Ray Chaudhury
Rautrai	Rautray

5.3.6 Female name after marriage

Family names in the state are passed on through the male line. Hence, a woman carries the surname of her father till her marriage that gets replaced by the surname of her husband after marriage (Patnaik, 1994). In certain cases, if the name of a girl contains 'Kumari' as the auxiliary in her maiden name, the same is also changed to 'Devi' or 'Debi' after marriage.

Thus, a girl named Rama Kumari Mishra after her marriage to Bidhan Chandra Panda, may be known as Rama Devi Panda. On the other hand, a female with the name 'Puspa Rani Patnaik' after marriage with Bhudeo Das, would acquire the married name Puspa Rani Das.

It is also observed that several feminine names-of-persons do not include surname. Therefore, these names denote the personal names alone. There may not be any change in such a feminine name, after marriage. In such cases, the catalogue entry be made under the entire given name, without inverting the words.

Examples : Arati Dei

Gayatri Devi

Kamala Devi

5.3.7 Tribal Names

Several tribal communities inhabit in Orissa. Some of the well known of these tribal groups are Munda, Santal, etc. The naming pattern of the tribal persons is the same as is seen in the non- tribal community, with first part of a name-of-person being the given name followed by the surname. The given name here again, can be either single or double worded. The second word of a two worded given name is the auxiliary, invariably to be read along with the first word. A sample of the tribal names is given as under :

Masculine Names	**Feminine Names**
Chitaya Prasad Majhi	Basanti Dei
Jaminnikant Mallik	Maratic Murmu
Prafull Mansingh	Puspa Rani Hansdah
Ram Chand Kisku	Saraswati Hembran

5.3.7.1 Family Names

Each tribal family generally bears a surname. This is derived from the caste names, the name of the sub-caste, or some other feature of the family. Some of the tribal family names look like :

Behera	Kisku	Singh
Ghadel	Majhi	Tudu
Gomang	Mansingh	
Hembran	Nayak	

5.3.7.1.1 Change of surname

A solitary instance of change of family name into a totally a new one has been reported wherein the family name 'Tudu' has been changed to 'Majhi'.

5.3.7.2 Names without family names

Some women do not use family name in their names. Hence, their names denote the given names alone. An illustration of such names is given as under :

Basanti Devi

Marati Murmu

5.3.8 Muslim Names

Muslims constitute a small minority of less than 2% of the states population. They are lagging behind in education. There appears to be an acute shortage of the family names among the Muslims. Some of the important and commonly used surnames among the Muslims of Orissa are

Baig	Malik	Raja
Khan	Moulana	Shah

Three types of structures of the Muslim names-of-persons are existing, as described here under :

1. Names without surname

In some names, no surname is used, and the entire is the personal name. A name-of-person falling in this class, is generally consisting of two words, rendered separately. Such names should be retained in the natural sequence of the words. This structure is quite widely followed among the Muslims. An illustration of some of the names is given as under:

Masculine Names	Feminine Names
Idris Ali	Farida Khatun
Faruq Abdulla	Hasina Begum
Mansur Ali	Sabida Bibi

2. Names possessing prefix titles

Some persons may not use surname, and instead a prefix may be present, indicating their social status. It often remains common for all persons of a family. In the state, prefix to a Muslim name, is regarded as the family name. Yet, a feminine name does not possess the same. A sample of such names with prefixes is given as under :

Mir Kabir, Sheikh Hafijulla, Sk. Babuddin

3. Names possessing family names

The structure of the names-of-persons, is 'Given name - family name'. However, this pattern is confined to the masculine names, and feminine names may not bear the surname. A sample of the names falling in this category, is given as below :

Arkan Ali Khan	Hasan Ali Khan
Azad Shah	Zahir Baig
Azeem Ali Moulana	

5.3.8.1 Change of name after Marriage

In Oriya Muslims, an unmarried girl generally carries Khatun as the complementary part of her given name. Since the practice of employing the family name or the prefix title is not there in the feminine names, the entire name is regarded as the given name. After marriage, the auxiliary Khatun is replaced by Bibi or Begum. Thus, for example, a girl having the maiden name Ameena Khatun becomes Ameena Bibi after marriage.

5.3.9 Christian Names

Christians form a very small minority of about 2% of the state population. They are mostly converts or the descendants of the converts. A large number of them are from the tribal groups. Each Christian name-of-person bears a family name in the end. The personal name occurs at the beginning. The new formed religious zeal has not been able to affect the naming pattern. The surname is generally the tribal name, as was in usage, prior to the conversion. The given name may or may not be tribal in its form. Many of them are biblical names. As the Christian society in the state is very small in size, deep investigations on their names-of-persons have not been carried out in this study.

5.4 SIKKIMI NAMES

5.4.1 General

Sikkim is the only state in the country, which retained its sovereignty for more than two decades, after the British rule was ended in 1947. It was governed by a hereditary monarch, known as Chogyal. The meaning of Chogyal is Dharamraja (Singh, 1993c). He in fact, was the Maharaja of the state. As per the treaty of 1890, Sikkim became a protectorate of the then British India, and thereafter though with slight modifications, of the Republic of India. In September 1974, it was made an associate state of the country. On April 26, 1975, it became a full-fledged state of the Union of India, and with this development, the institution of Chogyal was abolished.

Sikkim lies on the eastern foot-hills of Himalayas. With Tibet on the north and north-east, Nepal on the west, Bhutan in the east and Darjeeling of West Bengal in the south of the state. Its geographic area is 7, 096 sq. km. and its population is slightly more than 4 lakh (Census of India 1991, 1995). It is the least populated state in the country.

5.4.2 Ethnic Composition

There are several communities inhabiting the state. Some of the important communities, as per the Census of 1981, are given as below (Singh, 1993c):

S.No.	Community	Origination	%of the population	Religion
1.	Bhutia	Tibet	6.8	Buddhism
2.	Lepcha	Aboriginal	7.0	Buddhism
3.	Nepali	Nepal	61.0	Hinduism
4.	Limbu	Nepal	5.0	Hinduism
5.	Sherpa	Nepal	3.4	Buddhism
6.	Tibetan	Tibet	1.3	Buddhism

In the present research work, Limbus are considered as part of the Nepali community as they possess a common culture. Similar is the case with Tibetans and Sherpas who are very close to Bhutias. Thus, there are three major ethnic entities, Viz, Nepalis, Bhutias and Lepchas. Each one is retaining its own identity.

In terms of religious following, 68.37% of the state population is Hindu and 27.15% human beings are Buddhists. About 3.3% belongs to Christianity (Census of India - 1991, 1995). In this context, it may be added that almost all the Nepalis are Hindus, though a very small proportion of them, such as Tamangs follow Buddhism (Singh, 1993c). The other two major communities namely Lepchas and Bhutias are mostly Buddhist. A microscopic proportion of Lepchas, believe in Christianity. Specific characteristic features associated with the religious followings, are enumerated below :

(1) Nepalis in general, follow Hindu religion. They all carry features associated with the caste structure.

(2) The surnames of the Nepalis, do not provide any sense of territorial belonging. In other words, place names are not used in their family names.

(3) Some Nepalis now follow Buddhism, have been identified with the Bhutia and Lepcha communities. Many among them have discarded their caste affiliations, and have instead adopted the territorial belongings to denote their family names.

(4) Lepcha persons do not have any family names. They derive the same from the divisions or sub-divisions of their tribe. The surnames so obtained are considered as part of their geneological belonging (Singh, 1993c).

(5) A Bhutia seldom employs his clan name, since he does not possess a strict social organization of the clans. Many Bhutia clan names are associated with locality names but there is no sense of genealogical identity involved. In other words, they do not regard the clan members as descendants from a common ancestor, as is the case of the Lepcha (Singh, 1993c).

5.4.3 Names-of-persons

Sikkimi names-of-persons are similar in structure, to the East Indian names. The surname wherever employed, is generally placed in the end. The personal name among the Bhutia and Lepcha tribals, usually consists of two names written separately. In the Nepali community, the practice of breaking the personal name is prevailing. An illustration of the Sikkimi names is as under :

Nepali Names

Masculine Names	**Feminine Names**
Bir Bahadur Dungyal	Asha Rai
Ganga Prasad Tewari	Chetan Pradhan
Man Bahadur Sharma	Dil Kumari
Vinod Kumar Rai	Phulmaya Tamang
Nar Bahadur Bhandari	
Ram Prasad Dhakal	

Lepcha Names

Masculine Names	Feminine Names
Dup Tshring	Angel Ruth Issac
Gautam Lepcha	Chewang Mith Lepcha
Kesang Saring Lepcha	Chungkit
Passang Namgyal Lukson	Dolma Raugamung
Robert Lepcha	Normit Marry Lepcha
Sonam Choda Lepcha	
Sonam Shipmo	
Tashi Rongkup	

Bhutia Names

Masculine Names	Feminine Names
Dorji Wanchuk	Karma Dolma
Jigma Lachungpa	Lobsang Choden
Jigme Dorji	Pema Choden Bhutia
Kunchok Norbu	Pema Lhamu Bhutia
Narmit Wazalingpa	Samten Dolma
Pemait Wazalingpa	Sonam Diki Lachungpa
Pema Wanchuk	Sonam Doma
Pema Wanchuk	Yancheng Bhutia
Sonam Choda Bhutia	

Tibetan Names

Masculine Names	Feminine Names
Gyalpo Dhundup	Sonam Chokyi
Tenzin Sangpo	Tenzing Dawa
Thupten Dorjee	Tsering Lhakey

Sherpa Names

Masculine Names	Feminine Names
Lhakpa Dorji	Nima Sherpa
Pemba Tshering	Purba Doma
Tenzing Sherpa	Tshring Phuti

5.4.4 Nepali Names

Nepali community is known in the state as Gorkhali. In their names-of-persons, caste denoting appellations do not provide any sense of territorial belonging (Singh, 1993c). On the other hand, characterization of social hierarchy based on caste system is reflected. Several castes exist in the Nepali society. Important among them are listed as under (Singh, 1993c):

Bhujel	Gurang	Rai
Brahmin	Limbu or Subba	Sherpa
Chettri	Newar	

The above mentioned nomenclature of the castes, are regularly employed as family names. Sometimes, a sub division of the caste, known as thar (i.e. clan name) can also be used as a surname. However, Limbu and Subba are synonyms to each other, and both are often employed in an interchangeable basis. In addition, a few occupational descriptors are also used as family names. An illustration of such family names based on the occupations, is given as below:

Surname	Caste Name	Occupation
Darjee	Damai	Tailoring
Pradhan	Newar	Trading
Saraki	Cobbler	Shoe making
Viswakarma	Blacksmith	Iron-working

The other form of surnames among the Nepalis comes from their clan names. For instance, in the Chhettris, the following are the names of the clans used as family names (Ghosal, 1993a):

Adhikari	Bista	Paural
Andari	Karki	Subedi

Basnet	Katwal	Thapa
Bhattarai	Nirula	

Likewise, the Damai caste which is traditionally involved in the occupation of tailoring, is segmented into the following thars (Ghatak, 1993b):

Bagdas	Dass	Maley	Sewa
Bardawa	Hingmang	Pariyar	Suji
Bhitrikoti	Karkidodli	Ranapaheli	Sundas
Darnal	Labar Sewa		

Every caste group of the Nepalis has its own social divisions based on thars. In the caste of Limbus, the following clan names (i.e. thars) are in usage (Ghosal, 1993b):

Laotti	Nambang	Phurumbo	Thaqim
Libang	Pandhak	Sering	
Muringla-Nugo	Phendua	Tamling	

In the structure of the component parts, Nepali names-of-persons are similar to the same of East India. As such, the first part is the personal name followed by the family name. The given name can either be single worded or double worded. The surname comes in the rear. It may generally represent the caste or the specific occupation of the individual, or of the fore-fathers, as per the Hindu varna system.

5.4.5 Lepcha Tribe

The principal tribal people of the state, the Lepchas are supposed to be the original inhabitants of Sikkim. They call themselves Rong-kup or Mutanchi Rongkup. Rong means both 'to wait' and 'peak'. Muntanchi Rongkup conveys 'mother's loved ones' (Ghatak 1993c).

Though Lepchas are distributed in all the four districts, they are mainly concentrated in the North. The Dzongu area, in the North District was treated as a Lepcha reserve for quite some time, and lies in the lower range of Kanchendzonga where the main river Teesta flows (Ghatak, 1993c).

5.4.5.1 Social Divisions

Lepchas are divided into groups by birth and marriage. These groups are a patrilineal clan or exogamous putse/ptso, which is believed to have originated from some supernatural or legendary ancestors. Some of the putse are listed as under (Ghatak, 1993c):

Karyakmoo	Lingsingmoo	Solongmoo
Limoo	Sangdenmoo	Thyungmen

The above listed clan names are employed more or less as surnames. Also, the names of community such as Lepcha and Rungkup are the generic family names, and are in usage.

5.4.6 Bhutia Community

Bhutia sometimes spelt and pronounced as Bhotia, is derived from their habitat 'Bhot'(Tibet). They claim their origin from Tibet, hundreds of years ago. The ruling dynasty of the state, had been a Bhutia. The community is preseving its own language, known as Bhutia language. It is written in the Tibetan script. The community is scattered all over the state, though its concentration is discernible in the North Sikkim.

5.4.6.1 Social Divisions

The Bhutias are divided into two broad groups. They are : (1) Tondu rus-shi, within which they have 4 rus; and (2) Beb tsengye which include 8 rus. The 4 sub-divisions of the former, and the 8 sub-divisions of the latter, are enumerated as under (Ghatak, 1993a) :

Chechuthapa,	Ithenpa	Namchangopa	Phenpunadik
Chungiopa	Kachopa	Namnakpa	Shandarpa
Gansapa	Nachangopa	Phenchungpa	Shengapa

5.4.6.2 Surnames

A Bhutia seldom uses his clan name as he does not possess a strict social organization of the clans. Many Bhutia clan names are in fact, associated with locality but there is no sense of the geneological identity involved. These social division terms based on territories or places are used as surnames. In order to differentiate a place or territory name from a family name, 'pa' is often added in the end, which means belonging to. A sample of such family names is given above under the social divisions. They segment the community socially as well as territorially. Further, the community name Bhutia is also used as a generic surname, by a few persons.

5.4.7 Prefixes in names

Prefix titles are not traditionally employed in the names in the state. Yet, a few ones are in usage in some of the names. An illustration of such prefixes is given below :

Prefix title	Meaning
Kazi	Head of a village.
Lama	Buddhist Monk.
Yapu	Royal priest.

Of late, some persons belonging to infuential big land holding families, have started suffixing 'Kazi' to their names. In this way, the prefix title has been hardened to become the family name.

5.4.8 Structure of the names

In the Nepali society, the structure of the names is the same as exists in the Hindu society of North India. Thus, there are two categories of the name. They are with surname and without surname.

Among the Bhutia and Lepcha tribes, again there are two broad categories of the names-of-persons. In the former one are included those names which have become Westernised. The last part of such a name is the family name. An illustration of such names is given as under

Lepcha Names	Bhutia Names
Gautam Lepcha	Jigme Lachungpa
Tashi Rongkup	Pema Choden Bhutia
Angel Ruth Lepcha	

In the latter category fall those names-of-persons not possessing any family name. The entire name is the personal name. A sample of such names is given as below :

Bhutia Names	Lepcha Names
Dorji Wanchuk	Dup Tshring
Kunchok Norbu	Chungkit
Samten Dolma	
Sonam Dolma	

5.4.9.1 Change of name after marriage

An unmarried girl is generally carrying in the last part of her name, the surname of her father. After her marriage, it is replaced by the surname of the husband. In case the husband or father is not employing any surname, it is observed that the last part of the name of the husband/ father is suffixed to her name.

Example: Sonam Wangchuk (daughter of Dorji Wangchuk). After her marriage with Jigme Dorji, her name has become Sonam Dorji.

5.4.9.2 Personal Names

It is surprising to find that in both the tribes, many of the words are common in masculine and feminine names. Thus, it may not generally be possible to know the sex from a given name. In some feminine names, the word Doma or Dolma is often suffixed. They can be termed as sex marker.

5.5 ANDAMAN AND NICOBARI NAMES

5.5.1 General

Andaman and Nicobar refers to a group of 204 islands in the Bay of Bengal. Out of these, only 38 are inhabited. The islands located in the north form the Andaman, and the ones situated in the south are called Nicobar. The entire area is administered by the Union of India, as it is designated a Union Territory. Its geographic area is 8,249 sq. km. and its population is about 2.8 lakhs (Census of India, 1991, 1995).

The ethnic composition of the demography of the Territory is a veritable 'Mini India' as people from different linguistic parts of the country are residing there (Singh, 1994a). Broadly, the inhabitants of the islands may be grouped in three categories described as under:

5.5.1.1 Aborigines

The original inhabitants of the Territory are basically the aborigines. In 1981, their number was 22, 361 which had constituted 11.85% of the population (Singh, 1994a). Several primitive tribes are existing, and some among them are hostile to the outside world. No serious study on their naming pattern has been carried out. Therefore, only a scanty information which is available has been utilized in this study.

Of late, some tribals particularly the ones from Nicobar group of islands, have come into the mainstream of the civilized life. Many of them have taken up jobs and other occupations. Individuals possess specific identity in the form of their names. There are three practices in vogue, described as under :

1. Some tribals have been named by the biblical names. By their appearance, they do not look different from other Christian names. Such a name-of-person is having two words, both denote the personal name. No surname occurs. However, in some of the feminine names, the second word represents the name of the father/husband. A sample of such names is given below :

Masculine Names	**Feminine Names**
Henry George	Cecily Richardson
John Richardson	Irish Abner
Leonard John	Nina David
Thompson Daniel	
Wilson George	

2. Some tribals have preserved their indigenous names, and also add (prefixed or suffixed) some specific biblical name. An illustration of such names is given below :

Masculine Names	**Feminine Names**
Abenezer Walter	Alizaba Abenezer
Aberdeen Edward	Barkara Rojeena
Abednego Michael	Nevė Marry
Marcus Barnabas	Perpitua Valentine
Valentine Ignatius	

3. Yet, as an exception, some persons have retained their tribal names alone. Such names are single worded. A few examples of such names are given below :

Masculine Names	**Feminine Names**
Chogegi	Barkura
Chui	Candova
Meo	Noo

Among the Nicobar tribals, Muslims who are the progeny of the Muslim traders from Minicoy and Gujarat, who had married local tribal girls, in the past, maintain their affiliation with their tuhet, kinem or miroottoo. They prefer to select names from the holy book, since they do not possess names of local origin (Justin, 1994). Their names are generally double worded, with no family name occurring. For the purpose of cataloguing both the words have to be retained in the same sequence as used in the name-of-person.

The tribal names-of-persons, in general possess the following characteristic features :

1. If a name is two worded, the entire denotes the personal name, or, the second word may denote the name of father or husband, as the case may be.

2. Feminine names-of-persons from Andaman, are generally derived from the names of flowers (Ranjit Danials, 1996).

3. Usage of family names in the names-of-persons, is not prevailing.

4. The identity of a person is established through his given name. Hence, the order of the words occurring in a name be not altered.

5. Muslim tribal names-of-persons have to be treated at par t with the Muslim names.

5.5.1.2 Locals

They are the decendants of the convicts brought in from different parts of the country to serve their punishment term at Port Blair during 1858 to 1942. After their term of sentence of more than 10 years was over, they were given the option to bring their families from the mainland and to settle down in different villages. They were provided agricultural land for cultivation. Their number in 1951 was about 10.000 (Sarkar, 1994).

The community of Locals is a casteless and hierarchy free society. It has only three religious groups - Hindus, Muslims and Christians. These religious divisions are not stratified and all are considered equal (Sarkar, 1994).

Among the Hindus, it is surprising to note that no caste system is existing. In fact, no body is aware of his caste or that of his ancestors. For this reason, the Locals do not employ any surname. Similarly, Muslims also do not give any importance to different divisions like

Shia, Pathan and Sunni. However, most of the Locals are Sunnis. Christian Locals mostly belong to the Anglican Church, but they are not socially segmented from the Roman Catholics. Although, there are a few religious divisions, they do not affect social interaction. There is absolutely no social hierarchy among the Locals, no concept of varna order. No one is considered superior or inferior at the social plane (Sarkar, 1994).

5.5.2.1 Names-of-persons

The names-of-persons of the Locals, generally consist of two words, both the words denote the personal name. Among the feminine names, the second word may sometimes, represent the name of the father/husband. A sample of such names has been provided in Hindi and Muslim names.

5.5.3 Migrants from the mainland

After the partition of the country in 1947, a large number of families from various parts of the country immigrated into Andaman and Nicobar. In particular, a heavy inflow of refugees from East Bengal (The present Bangladesh) came to settle down permanently. Similarly, Tamils, Keralites, Telugus, Punjabis and the persons from the Hindi speaking areas also migrated (Singh, 1994a). At present, the demographic picture is quite cosmopolitan, reflecting a miniature India.

As the population had emerged from different linguistic areas, it is observed that each group has preserved its own cultural identity. For instance, language used in a family is generally the same as that of its region in the mainland. In this way, a variety of languages exist in the Territory. However, for inter- communication across their community, Hindi is often used. As per the Census of 1971, Bengali was used by 24.42% followed by Hindi 16.07%, Tamil 12.61%, Malayalam (12.12%) and Telugu 8.12%. In addition, Nicobarese language was spoken by 15.60% of the people (Singh, 1994a).

Religion wise, Hindus form the most dominant group 67.53% followed by Christians (23.95%). Muslims constitute the least one with 7.61% of their population (Census of India 1991, 1995).

5.5.3.1 Names-of-persons

The pattern of the names-of-persons of the migrants, is the same as used in the linguistic part of the country from where the family had immigrated. Thus, a Bengali name is likely to have the Bengali pattern.

Similar is the case with other linguistic groups discussed in other sub-chapters.

5.6 EAST INDIAN NAMES IN AACR- 2

The above discussion on the sociological aspects of naming converges upon three broad systems of the names-of-persons as menifested in the three regions of East India, viz. West Bengal and Orissa; Sikkim; and Andaman and Nicobar Islands.

(a) West Bengal and Orissa

The structure of the names-of-persons is the same as it exists in North India. The first part of a name is the personal name followed by the family name. The given name is generally broken into two distinct component parts and both the parts are rendered as separate words. The second part is the complementary word employed as the decorative component. This has been in conformity to the North Indian practice. Yet, the personal names of recent times can be single worded, and it may not be possible to break them into two parts. Other features associated with the names- of-persons are:

1. Usage of two types of surname

In the Bengali and Oriya names-of-persons, some surnames have been anglicised. In this way two types of the family names have come into play, in a few instances. They are the vernacular and anglicised forms. Both of them are used in an interchangeable way.

2. Multi-worded surnames

Some family names are multi-worded. There may or may not be any connecting symbol that identifies them easily. The connecting symbol if used, is the hyphen. In rendering such surnames, all the words have to be taken together as one unit.

3. Prefix titles

In general, prefix titles are not employed in the names from West Bengal and Orissa. Yet, in a few names of some important persons, of the past, and in some names-of- persons of the Muslim, prefixes are used. They have to be treated as recommended in North India. Similar is the case with the Sikkimi names.

4. British culture - impact

In transforming the structure of the names-of-persons into a new one, persons generally convert their personal names into intial form. As the given name comprises two parts, there are two initials in a name. The family name is written in its full form, which establishes the identity of the person.

5. Surname in the end

Almost all the Hindu names-of-persons bear surname in the end. Among the names of the Muslims, family name may or may not occur. In some Muslim names, it can also form the first part of some of the names. If it so, it invariably remains subordinate to the given name.

6. Relation between surname and caste

In both the states, the relationship between the caste structure and the surnames, has been hopelessly confusing in many instances. Thus, different family names are used by a wide cross - section of the society, belonging to diversified caste groups.

7. Pen-names

Pen-names are not generally used. Yet, as an exception, a few Muslim names may bear such appellation, in the end. As the literary-name acquires a very important part of the name, the main entry is to be made under it. This is despite occurrance of surname in the name.

(b) Sikkim

Two types of persons are found in Sikkim and the hilly districts of West Bengal. They are described as under:

(i) Nepali persons

They generally follow Hindu religion. Their names are similar to those of the Hindi speaking persons. They have to be treated as recommended in North India.

(ii) Persons following Buddhism

Lepchas and Bhutias are the prominent communities, following Buddhism. They do not possess surname. However, they have now started deriving the same from the names of the territories and from their clans. If such a suffix occurs in a name, entry is to be prepared under it. Otherwise, the main entry is to be made in the natural sequence of the words of the name, under the given name. Yet, in some names, the second part may denote father's or husband's name. The prefix title, if appearing in the name is to be ignored.

(c) Andaman and Nicobar

Generally, a tribal name-of-person consists of a single word, or at the most two. If a name comprises two words the second word may denote the name of father or husband in a few cases. Hence, such a name does not pose any problem in cataloguing. In AACR 2, all the tribal names have to be rendered in their natural sequence. The names from other linguistic areas have to be treated as per the origin of the persons. Similarly, the names of the Locals have to be rendered in their own sequence.

In the light of the above analysis, the names-of-persons from East India zone, have to be rendered in accordance with the following cataloguing rules :

E.1 With the exception of E.2 to E.5, enter an East Indian name- of-person under its ultimate part if it has been used as the pen-name, or in its absence, under the family name. If no family name is employed, enter it in the straight order. If a prefix title is also used, it has to be omitted except in the following exceptional instances where it is needed to be preserved in an inverted order.

(a) If it has become the part of the name as is the case in the Muslims.

(b) If it has been bestowed by the British rulers.

Examples:

Names-of-persons	**Catalogue entry**
Aminul Haka	Aminula Haka
Anand Sankar	Anand Sankar
Bharti Kumari Shah	Shah, Bharti Kumari
Dilroba Begum	Dilroba Begum
Dorji Wangchuk	Dorji Wangchuk
Imadadula Hake Milana	Milana, Imadadula Haka
Kanhu Charan Lenka	Lenka, Kanhu Charan
Kesang Saring Lepcha	Lepcha, Kesang Saring

Mahasweta Debi	Mahasweta Debi
Marcus Barnabus	Marcus Barnabus
Utpal Kumar Das	Das, Utpal Kumar

E.1.1 Enter a Bengali or Oriya name under the multi-worded family name, provided the same has been used in its full form. The words occurring in such a surname have to be taken together in the same sequence as occurring in the surname. The family name in the Bengali and Oriya culture occupies the last part of a name. The connecting symbol if present, is the hyphen. In some double-worded family names, both the parts may also be written as one unit.

Examples:

Names-of-persons	**Catalogue entry**
Alok Ranjan Das Gupta	Das Gupta, Alok Ranjan
Mamata Rani Patsahani	Patsahani, Mamata Rani
Nand Gopal Sengupta	Sengupta, Nand Gopal
Raj Kishore Raut Ray	Raut Ray, Raj Kishore
Upendra Nath Ray Choudhury	Ray Chaudhury, Upendra Nath
Uttam Kumar Das-Gupta	Das-Gupta, Uttam Kumar

E.1.2 Enter a Bengali or Oriya name-of-person under that form of his surname in which the bearer has achieved his recognition among the readers, provided the surname is having two forms, namely the vernacular and the anglicised. If this can not be ascertained, enter it in the form appearing in the work. The other form not chosen in the entry, can be connected by a suitable cross-reference.

Examples:

Names-of-persons	**Catalogue entry**
Rabindra Nath Thakur	Tagore, Rabindra Nath
Jagdish Chandra Basu	Bose, Jagdish Chandra
Manohar Rai	Ray, Manohar
Rabi Ray	Rai, Rabi
Shyama Prasad Mukherjee	Mukherjee, Shyama Prasad

E.2 Enter a Bengali or Oriya Muslim name under the given name if no surname is employed in the end, provided the first few words are forming part of his family heritage. They may also include the family name. These words have be inverted. If family name is also used in the end, enter it under the surname.

Examples:

Names-of-persons	**Catalogue enries**
Abdul Burkat Ataul Ghani Khan Choudhury	Choudhury, Abdul Burkat Ataul Ghani Khan
Khan Ataur Rahman	Rahman, Khan Ataur
Khan Muhammad Saif-ul-Islam	Saif-ul-Islam, Khan Muhammad

E.3 Enter a Muslim name-of-person from West Bengal and Orissa, under the word other than Mohammad provided the name consists of more than two words, and the first word is Mohammad, and no surname is used. Similarly, Khan is to be treated as a part of the given name, if the personal name is of two words.

Example:

Name-of-person	**Catalogue entry**
Mohammad Akram Khan	Akram Khan, Mohammad
Mohammad Mosharraf Hossain	Mosharraf Hossain, Mohammad
Mohammad Zahirul Islam	Zahirul Islam, Mohammad

E.4 Enter a Muslim name-of-person under the last part of his name, provided the author has given clear cut indications to treat the last part of his name as the most important part. This is applicable if no family name is used, in the end.

Example: Mohammad Abdul Matin (Shortened Name M.A. Matin)
The main entry should be under Matin

E.5 Enter a East Indian female name under her given name, if the name of her father or husband has been suffixed to her name. This is relevant in such feminine names bearing no surnames.

Examples:

Names-of-persons	**Catalogue entries**
Cecily Richardson	Cecily Richardson
Sonam Dorji	Sonam Dorji
Fouzia Hossain	Fouzia Hossain
Mita Huq	Mita Huq
Nargis Zafar	Nargis Zafar
Nilufar Akhter	Nilufar Akhter

Chapter VI

SOUTH IINDIAN NAMES

6.1 SOUTH INDIA

6.1.1 General

Andhra Pradesh, Tamilnadu, Kerala and Karnataka, together with the Union Territories of Lakshadweep, and Pondicherry form South India. Several districts in the northern parts of Karnataka show a perceptible Marathi cultural influence. In the naming of persons, Marathi structure is closely followed. Hence, the prescriptions for cataloguing provided for the Marathi names of West India, are valid for such names too. The remaining area has a unique South Indian pattern of names-of-persons. Almost all the names from this zone, possess some prefix attachments such as the house/village name, father's or husband's name, and so on. In addition, usage of caste denoting family names is very low in their occurrance. In those names where caste appellations are employed, they remain subordinate to the personal names. Based on the languages, the entire South Indian zone can be divided into the following linguistic groups:

1. Telugu-Hindu, Muslims and Sikhs of Andhra Pradesh have been covered.

2. Tamil-Hindus, Muslims and Christians of Tamilnadu and Pondicherry have been studied.

3. Malayalam-Hindus, Muslims and Christians of Kerala and Muslims of Lakshwadeep have been included. The Union Territory Lakshwadeep is a Muslim dominated area with quite a different system of naming. Hence, their names have been adequately covered separately under the Malayalam names.

4. Kannada Hindus and Muslims of Karnataka have been included.

It may also be mentioned here that the Union Territory of Pondicherry had been a French colony and as such, the influence of the French culture on the names-of-persons is discernible. In the sub-chapter on Tamil names, this aspect has been included. In certain pockets of the country, Arabic settlements exist. The inhabitants claim their descent from the migrants of the Arab countries. Their naming pattern bears a strong Arabic influence. This has been discussed separately under the Telugu Names.

Important sociological factors that govern the name-of-persons of South India are as follows:

6.2 TELUGU NAMES

6.2.1 General

The recommendations of the States Reorganisation Commission, paved the way for the formation of the state of Andhra Pradesh in 1956, consolidating Telugu speaking regions together. Further readjustment of its boundaries had taken place with Tamilnadu in 1960. Now, its geographic area is about 2.75 lakh sq. km. and its population is around 66.5 million. Hindus constitute majority (about 89.14%) being followed by Muslims (8.91%) (Census of India 1991, 1995).

On the east of the state is the Bay of Bengal. The state has Orissa on its north-east. Madhya Pradesh in the north, Tamilnadu in the south, Karnataka in the south-west, and Maharashtra in the west.

6.2.2 Names-of-persons

A name-of-persons from Andhra Pradesh generally consists of two component parts. The first one is the house name followed by the personal name. The house name signifies the family and the given name identifies the person. In addition, some persons belonging to higher castes also add some attachments to their names indicating their caste or sect. (Viswanathan, 1965).

A sample of the Telugu names is given below:

Masculine Names	Feminine Names
Bezwada Gopal Reddy	Anumandla Rajeswari
Kasu Brahmanand Reddy	Kurapati Usha Rani
Nara Chandrababu Naidu	Nandmuri Lakshmi Parvati
Tanguturi Prakasham Pantulu	Sristu Subbalakshmi
Turlapati Narayana Rao	Somireddy Jamuna

6.2.3 House Names

Every Hindu family belonging to Telugu culture invariably possesses a distinct house name (Soni, 1992) through which the family is known all around. In Telugu circles, it is known as "intiperu" or the house name. It is an indispensable part of the names of all the persons in that family. It is passed on to the younger generation, through the male line. Females, on the other hand, employ the house name of their father till their marriage. Thereafter, it is replaced by the house name of the husband (Gupta, 1993). Hence, a house name denotes the family name or the surname. It generally consists of a single word.

The concept of house name, in Telugu family is very old and has been in usage from times immemorial. As such, it is difficult to know its origin, form or derivation. However, in its present composition, one can possibly trace its derivation. The channels of such derivation are:

(a) Residency of Ancestors

Often, house names are derived from the names of places, in a large number of families. Such places may or may not appear in the current political map of the state.

Examples: Gollapudi, Jalaguam, Nandendla, Nandamuri, Nellore, Ongole, Pamulaparti, Sarvepalli

(b) Names of Sacred Places

Certain families adopted names of specific holy places as their house names which may be within or out side the state.

Examples: Kasi, Tirupati, Prayaga, Varanasi

(c) Names of Animals, Fruits or Vegetables

A few house names are also carried out from the names of animals, flowers, vegetables, fruits, spices, trees and some edible products. An illustration of such family names is given below (Gupta, 1993):

House Names	Meaning
Allam	Ginger
Annam	Cooked Rice
Banthi	Marigold
Burela	A sweet dish
Cheraku	Sugarcane
Gurram	Horse
Kandula	Red gram
Kodi	Hen
Mallala	Jasmine
Nakka	Fox
Palakura	Green vegetable
Pappu	Daal
Pesala	Green gram
Pitta	Small bird
Ulligadda	Onion

(d) Names of Physical Objects

Certain house names denote the names of specific objects or items. A list of such family names is given below (Gupta,1993):

Family Names	Meaning
Bandi	Cart
Cheruvu	Public water tank
Gampala	Basket
Ghanta	Bell of a temple
Kattula	Sword
Koneru	Temple tank
Kota	Fort

(e) Personal Names as House Names

In certain families, specific personal names of their ancestors are employed as House Names.

Examples: Devireddy, Umareddy, Vasireddy

(f) Religious Accomplishment of the fore-fathers

Sometimes, it is the religious achievement of the fore-fathers which is employed as the house name.

Examples:	Family Names	Meaning
	Ayyalasomayajula	Senior of a team of yagan performer
	Bhagavatula	Mastery over Bhagavatam
	Chaturvedulu	Knowing all the four Vedas
	Puranam	Having full understanding of the Puranas
	Vedula	Specializes in the Vedas

(g) Physical characteristics of an ancestor

Example: Kappaganthula (=Leaping frog)

(H) Unintelligible House Names

In exceptional cases, family names were found to denote nothing, Perhaps, they might have been distorted in usage, over a long period of time into an unintelligible word.

Example: Tamana

6.2.3.1 Characteristics of House Names

There are several features associated with house names important among them are described as under:

1. House names are very old in origin. Perhaps, they were introduced more than a thousand years ago.

2. House name is the permanent part of a Telugu name-of-person. It is irremovable.

3. The family as on date, does not know as to how and when a particular word became their house name.

4. Even when a village from which the house name is derived, has vanished, its name change, or merged with a neighbouring bigger unit, the house name is continued in its original form, and is not affected by any of these factors.

5. Family member generally can not identify the location of the village whose name is being used as their house name except in a negligible number of instances.

6. Generally, the family may not have any ties with the village whose name is being employed to denote their family name.

7. House names are independent of the caste structure. Thus, it is usually not possible to know the caste of the bearer from a given house name.

8. Different families possessing a common surname, are generally believed to be related to each other, through a common male ancestor (Gupta, 1993).

9. A house name in a Telugu name-of-person, is generally denoted by its initial form, in an anglicised form. However, when rendered in the vernacular, it is written in full.

These characteristics are equally applicable to house names derived from other sources also. In other words, a person does not know the reasons for his having a particular house name.

6.2.3.2 Practices of house-name in names

Among the names of common persons, house are rendered in their full form, before the given names. However, in general, people are identified in the public, only by their personal names.

In the educated community, the house name is generally converted into its initial form and the given name is used is its full form. However, if a specific house name is such that is starts with the sound phonetically equal to bh, ch, or kh and can not be represented by a single alphabet of the English language, two letters, instead of one are used to contract the house name with the second letter in small case. Yet, the given name is employed in its full form.

The above mentioned practices suggest that a house name in Andhra Pradesh, is subordinate to the given name.

6.2.4 Given Names

Given names in Telugu culture, may be simple or complex. If a name is simple, it usually consists of a single word or at the most two words, written separately.

If a given name consists of two words, the second word, though written separately, has to be read, in the context of the first word.

Examples:	Ashok Babu	Appa Rao	Krishna Murthy
	Rama Rao	Ranga Chari	Uma Maheshwar

If a given name is complex, which many masculine names are, it is usual to have more component parts. In general, personal names of more than two words are in abundance. Yet a few given names may be of 5 or 6 words. If a name is having more than two words, it is generally required to know as to which particular part possesses the potency. In this respect, it has been observed that a person is generally known in public only by a small part of his given name. Hence, the foremost problem, in handling such a Telugu name-of-person, is to identify the specific portion of the given name, through which the individual is known in the wider circle. The following examples would help in illustrating the point:

Full Given Name	Shortened Given Name	Entry Element
Venkata Narasimha Rao	V. Narasimha Rao	Narasimha Rao
Taraka Rama Rao	T. Tama Rao	Rama Rao
Setu Rama Rao	S. Rama Rao	Rama Rao
Venkata Gopala Laxmi Narsimha Rao	V.G.L. Narsimha Rao	Narsimha Rao

From the illustrations of the sample of the names-of-persons given above, having more than two words, it appears that in general, the last two components of a masculine name are the potent part of a name-of -person, through which he establishes his identity. Hence, a catalogue entry is to be prepared under it. The remaining portion of the given name together with the house name, is to be inverted.

However, the process of shortening of the personal names is not common in the given names of females. A woman, in other words, is known through her given name, usually consisting of one or two words only, There are a few exceptions in which a given name of a female extends to more than two words, Here the process of shortening the name follows more or less the same way the masculine name do. An example of such a feminine name is given below.

Full Given Name	Shortened Personal Name
Veera Venkata Seetha Lakshmi	V.V Seetha Lakshmi or V.V. S.Lakshmi

6.2.4.1 Breaking of personal names

In Andhra Pradesh, in the educated society, there is evidence that several people, in order to be know by smaller names, are breaking their given names into smaller units, in rare instances, and prefer to be known widely by the last part of their names. As the process of breaking the given name, is based, in many cases, on the whims and fancies of the individual, there is no uniformity in the process. In addition, the net result of this exercise is sometimes very funny, in many instances. A sample of such names is given as below:

Given Name	Broken Name	Last part of name
Krishnaswamy	Krishna Swamy	Swamy
Krishnachelam	Krishna Chelam	Chelam
Rangachari	Ranga Chari	Chari
Venkateshwaru	Venkateshw Arlu or Venkateshwar Lu	Arlu Lu
Satyanarayanamurthy	Satyanarayana Murthy or Satya Narayanamurthy	Murthy Naryanamurthy

Similarly, in another process, if a name consists of more than one word, and the last word is an insignificant part of the given name (i.e. an auxiliary), it is observed that some persons, in rare instances, disclose only the last part of their names. The other parts are usually concealed under their initials. A sample of such names is given as under:

Given Name	Contracted Names	Recommended Entry words
Ravindra Prasad	R. Prasad	Prasad
Subba Rao	S. Rao	Rao
Venkatagiri	V. Giri	Giri

Venkatapati Rao	V. Rao	Rao
Vidyadhar Rao	V. Rao	Rao

The implications of the above described unusal practice, are that some women suffix the part of the name of their husband, as an attachment to their given names. It forms the end part of their names. Some examples of such a feminine names are:

Shanti Rao, Kanaklata Prasad

In feminine names-of-persons, breaking of personal names or reducing some part of the name into initial form is not resorted to. However, the house name represented by an initial, remains subordinate to the given name. In other words, a female continues to be known by her given name. Feminine given names in Telugu culture are often ending with any of the under-mentioned auxiliary words (Subba Rao, 1961a):

Akka, Amma, Bayi, Bi, Bibi, Sani

However, the trend is changing fast in favour of many new feminine given names. In such a name, the following auxiliaries are generally used:

Devi, Kumari, Lata, Rani

6.2.4.2 Imitation of the Names of other cultures

Certain persons in the state are named after the names of some prominent national heroes and heroines. If the distinguished personality is from some other linguistic region, and the last part of his name bears his surname, for instance, denoting his caste background, it is observed that the same is retained in the same sequence as it appears in the name of the hero. In other words, the entire name becomes the given name in Telugu culture. Thus, a peculiar class of the Telugu names has come into existence.

<u>Examples</u>:	**Masculine Given Name**	**Feminine Given Names**
	Bal Gangadhar Tilak	Indira Priyadarshini
	Jagdish Chandra Bose	Jhansi Lakshmi
	Jawahar Lal Nehru	
	Rabindra Nath Tagore	

Subhas Chandra Bose

Babu Rajendra Prasad

Some Telugus adopt the full name of prominent nationalist personality like Rabindra Nath Tagore, Subhash Chandra Bose and so on, preceded by their Telugu family name in full or shortened. Such names should not be mistaken but should be dealt as Telugu names and entered under the personal name in full.

Similarly, Telugu feminine given name like Jhansi Lakshmi should be taken as denoting the legendary Lakshmi Bai of Jhansi and should be rendered as such without dropping or altering the word Jhansi as a prefix denoting the place.

Another practice among the Telugu speaking persons which surfaced recently, is the adoption of the famous international surnames like Gandhi, Kennedy, Lenin, Nehru Stalin etc., as personal names with or without addition of the suffix 'Babu'. Such names should be taken as given names and entry should be made under the same.

6.2.5 Attachments in Names

Some among the forward castes attach some additional word denoting their caste affiliation, after the given name. In some others, the attached word represents the profession of the ancestors.

If a caste name attachment is also used, the name has three components. The sequence is "House Name-Given Name-Caste Name". As per Ranganathan (1953a), they are important attachments and hence, they need not be promoted to the level of the main entry. Examples of a few names having caste names are as given below:

House Name	Given Name	Caste Name
Mukurala	Ram	Reddy
Nara	Chandra Babu	Naidu
Gorantla	Buchaiah	Chowdary
Poknuri	Subramaniam	Sastry
Kandukuri	Vireshlingam	Pantulu
Bulusu	Venkata Ram	Sarma
Potti	Sriramulu	Shetty
Pampati	China Hanumantha	Gupta

In feminine names-of-persons, caste denoting attachments are not generally employed. Therefore, a female name-of-person is having only two component parts. They are "House name - Given name". Yet, as an exception, some women have used their caste names in their names. House name is such a name in generally abandoned.

Examples: Renuka Chaudary

Subhashini Reddy

However, in educated communities, some persons make use of the caste attachment, as if it were the family name. They convert all the other parts of their names into initials. This is another pattern of the Western transformation of the names. However, the process of contracting the names is not found in the feminine names-of-persons.

Example: V.L. Pantulu

C.V.K. Reddy

A.N.S.P. Sastry

6.2.5.1 Implication of caste attachments

It is also observed that several personal names in Andhra Pradesh are ending with iya or lu. If however, some specific feature like caste is added after the given name, iya or lu is generally dropped out.

Example:	Given Name	Given Name and Caste Name
	Kamaiya	Kama Reddy
	Ramulu	Ram Reddy
	Ramaiah	Ram Sharma
	Venkateshwarlu	Venkatesh Naidu

Hence, if a person decides to use his caste name in his name afterwards, an inevitable change may also occur in his name, in some instance.

6.2.5.2 Change of Given Name

Rare instances occur where in the personal names of some persons are changed, through the legal process, and the persons are known only by the new names, afterwards. It has been observed that generally old fashioned given names are dropped in favour of more fashioned names. The examples are given as below (Subba Rao, 1961a):

Feminine Names		Masculine Name	
New Name	Former Name	New Name	Earlier Name
Pushpavalli	Pullamma	Virabhadra Rao	Virayya
Suryakala	Suramma		

6.2.6. Female name change after marriage

Traditionally, Telugus subscribe to the patrilineal norms of kinship. It means that family names are passed on in the male line, from father to son. A girl retains the house name of her father until marriage. After getting married, it is replaced by surname of her husband.Thus, if Desiraju Saraswati Devi marries Yellapragada Dhananja Rao, her name after marriage becomes Yellapragada Saraswati Devi (Subba Rao, 1961 a).

6.2.7 Dropping of caste feature

Certain people in order to conceal their caste identity, may drop out such features from their names, at somewhat later stage of their life. Thus, a transformation in name takes place. Similarly, many persons do not prefer usage of the caste names in their names.

6.2.8 Telugu persons settled in other states

Several Telugu families immigrated to North India, have adopted the prevailing naming pattern in the linguistic belt. Five forms of structures have been found in such Telugu names-of-persons. They are in addition to the traditional pattern as used in Andhra Pradesh. The new structures of names are described as under:

(a) Dropping the house name and attaching caste feature word in the end.

Examples: Kausalya Sastry

Rama Devi Reddy

(b) Employing house name in the end.

Examples: Satyanarayana Golakota

Ramana Gutta

(c) Using last part of the husband's name, in the rear portion of a name. The house name may or may not be retained.

Examples: Sitadevi Govindraju

Sarda Ashokvardhan

Bhattu Susila Jayant

(d) Placing the house name in the middle. The person has been settled in the United States.

Example: Arvind Junuthala Reddy

(e) In Tamilnadu, some Telugu females are using the name of her father in between the house name and her name. After marriage, the name of the husband comes directly after her name. The structure is "House name - Given name - Husband's Name". (Sjoberg, 1994).

Example: Chitrala Rangnadham Hemalata (Unmarried name)

Gurram Hemalata Tirumurti (Married name)

6.2.9.1 Muslim Names

Muslims of the state generally follow the pattern of the names-of-persons as used in the northern parts of the country. Yet, in a few names particularly belonging to the rural belt, a component similar to the house name, is used. This component is either the name of village or caste/sect name.

Examples:

Masculine names	Feminine names
Auratkar Moinuddin	Marichpeth Mahabooba Bibi
Islampeth Yusuf Beg	Tangada Janbi
Karamtudi Janu	
Kottapeta Yusuf Hussain	
Pathan Subhan	
Sundaragiri Basha	

6.2.9.1.1 Arabic Names

In the city of Hyderabad, there are Arabic settlements in which families belonging originally to the Arab countries have been living for a very long period. Their names are different in their structure, than the same found in other Muslim names-of-persons. They generally carry the name of their father after their personal name. In between the two names a conjecture bin (meaning thereby son of), or bint (conveying the daughter of) is placed. This connecting word is helpful in identifying both the component parts of a name-of-persons. In rare instances, name of the father's father is also appearing. In a few exceptional instances, surname is also used.

Examples of such names are given as below:

Masculine Names	**Feminine Names**
Abdul bin Salam	Aiysha bint Yahiya
Addullah bin Saleh bin Mazi	Zainath bint Abdullah
Abdullah bin sayeed	
Ahmed bin Mohammad Ramzan	
Hamza bin Omer	
Hasan bin Sayeed Wahalan	
Mohammad Bin Abduallah Qureshi	
Yahiha bin Abdullah	

There are a few discernible features of the Arabic names of persons, described as under:

1. The name of the Qabila, through which an Arabic Muslim family is generally identified, is not used.

2. The given names are generally single worded.

3. Some names-of-persons contain prefix titles. If a prefix title is used in the name, it can be omitted, provided it is not forming part of the name. However, if such a title is employed in the name of the father, it is to be preserved.

6.2.9.2 Sikh Names

A macroscopic minority of the Sikhs live in and around Hyderabad. They are descendants of the Telugu speaking people, who got themselves converted into the Sikhism, several centuries ago. Their mother-tongue is Telugu and they generally follow the teachings of the Sikh Gurus, more rigidly as compared to their Punjabi counterparts. Their names are slightly different from the names of the Punjabi Sikhs. Examples of a few Telugu Sikh names-of-persons are given as under:

Masculine Names	**Feminine Names**
Sardar Davinder Singh	Sardarni Kailash Bai
Sardar Gobind Singh	Sardarni Tara Bai
Sardar Guru Singh	
Sardar Hari Har Singh	
Sardar Iqbal Singh	
Sardar Jaswant Singh	
Sardar Joga Singh	
Sardar Maha Gobind Singh	
Sardar Raja Singh	
Sardar Sardar Singh	

6.2.9.2.1 Characteristics of Sikh Names

In some respect, Telugu Sikh names-of-persons are quite different. Some specific characteristics of the names-of-persons are described as given below:

1. Sardar and Sardarni are used as prefixes in the masculine and feminine names-of-persons respectively. In North India, they are also used. But their usage is restricted to addressing, and therefore, they never form the part of the Punjabi names-of-persons. In Telugu Sikh names, they are somewhat akin to an intiperu (house name), and are to be preserved in a sub-ordinate manner.

2. Telugu Sikh names generally do not possess such specific features as caste names or the name of the village. Hence, Singh is the terminating word in such a name.

3. Feminine names generally possess "Bai" as the auxiliary. This is unlike a Punjabi name of a female, which has Kaur as the auxiliary.

4. Major sources of the names among the Telugu Sikhs, are the Hindu religious books. Hence, their names are very similar to the names of Telugu Hindus.

5. The personal names of Sikh Gurus are generally avoided in Punjab. However, in the names of the Telugu Sikhs, quite a large number of the names are formed on the names of the Gurus.

6. Shortening the names by abbreviating the initial parts of the names as generally resorted to in North India, is not done. Hence, Singh can not become the prominent part of any such a name-of-person.

6.3 TAMIL NAMES

6.3.1 General

Tamilnadu is the new name for the former state of Madras. In came into existence in 1956, when the Tamil speaking areas were consolidated together, and non-Tamil regions were separated out, from the then Presidency of Madras. Minor adjustments of borders were further made with the neighbouring states in 1960. As of now, the area of the state is about 130, 058 sq. km. and its population is approximately 55.85 million. Hindus are in vast majority (88.67%), followed by Christians (5,69%). Muslims are 5.47% (Census of India 1991, 1995). With Chennai (formerly Madras) as capital, the state has boundaries with Kerala in the west, and Andhra Pradesh and Karnataka in the north-east and north-west respectively. It opens in the east and south in the Bay of Bengal and Indian ocean respectively.

6.3.2 Names-of-persons

Several patterns of the names-of-persons are used in the state. However, almost all of them have the name of father, as an essential prefix (Ranganathan, 1969a). Females after marriage may use the name of the husband as the prefix. In some instances, name of the village of the ancestors, or the place of birth is also employed as an additional prefix (Sengupta, 1974b). Also, some names may possess specific title denoting some other features. Representative sample of the Tamil names-of-persons is given as below:

Hindu Names

Masculine Names	**Feminine Names**
Arcot Laxmanasamy Mudaliar	
Chanchipuram Nataraja Annadurai	Ganapathi Mallika
Muthuvel Karunanidhi	Jayaraman Jayalalitha
Ramaswamy Venkataraman	Rajendran Sulochana
Shiyali Ramamrita Ranganathan	Vijaylakshe Kalyan Sundaram

Subrahmanyan Anantharaman Ayyangar

Muslim Names

Masculine Names	Feminine names
Abdul Hasan Khasim	Abdul Khader Saleema
Abdul Jamal Mahamadu	Hasina Mohamad
Jaffar Syed Mohammad Ali	
Mohamad Jabbar Sayadu	

Christian Names

Masculine Names	Feminine Names
John Kenedy Gnana Kumar	Anthonydoss Dorathy
John Edmund Selvadory	Joseph Alphonsa Mary
Joseph Jayakumar	Robert Josophine Marry
	Samuel Josophine Kamala

6.3.3. Hindu Names

In Tamil culture, the personal name is generally preceded by the name of the father or husband as the case may be. Thus, most of the names, have general pattern "Father's Name-Personal Name" (Ranganathan, 1964). Among the educated persons, it is quite a common practice to contract the name of the father or the husband into its initial form.

Examples:

Masculine Names	Feminine Names
Krishnaswamy Srinivasan	Harihar Lalitha
Srinivasa Sampath	Kailasamiyer Kamakshi
Vaidyanathan Subramanian	Vaidyanathan Gowri
Venkataraman Ramamurti	Viswanathan Meenakshi

Some Tamil names-of-persons have, in addition to the name of the father, village name or the birth place name. Hence, the sequence is "Village Name-Father's Name-Given Name" (Sengupta, 1974b). However, this particular structure is found mostly in masculine names. Feminine names possess this pattern only rarely. Among the educated persons, the practice of converting both the attachments namely the place name and the father's name, into their initial form, is prevailing. Few examples of this pattern are given as below:

Masculine Names	Feminine Names
Madras Sundarramiyer Gopalkrishan	Chille Sekhar Uma
Kalanapuram Rangachari Parthasarathy	Tumuluri Seetharaman Lakshmi
Natuvilmatom Srinivasan Ramaswamy	
Tiruvadi Venkataraman Ramamurti	
Vallampadugal Srinivasa Arunachalam	

6.3.3.1 Anglicised Structure

Another pattern of the names in which the father's name or the name of the husband as the case may be, succeeds the given name, is also known in Tamilnadu. Here, the sequence of the words is "Given Name- Father's Name". In this context, it is observed that this pattern is employed only by those persons who are educated and have migrated to another linguistic belt. In a few instances of the feminine names, this pattern is observed even in respect of those who are staying in the state.

Examples:	Masculine Names	Feminine Names
	Ashok Parthasarathy	Janaki Ramachandran
	Jagdeesa Swaminathan	Kalyani Sethuraman
	Srinivasan Vardarajan	Minu Swaminathan
		Sujatha Viswanathan
		Usha Sundarrajan
		Vani Jayaraman

6.3.3.2 Names of Politicians and Musicians

Some distinguished and renowned personalities in politics and performance arts, have adopted unique pattern in which place or district name comes in the beginning. This is followed by the given name. Father's name, which forms an essential part of all the traditional names is absent. An illustration of such names is given in the following examples:

Masculine Names	**Feminine Names**
Arcot Veerasamy	Kovai Sarala
Ariyakudi Ramanuja Iyengar	Sulamangalam Rajalaxmi
Kaladipet Vardachariar	
Kumari Anandan	
Ramanathpuram Srinivasa Iyengar	
Vazapadi Ramamurthy	

Another variation in the structure of the names is that some specific characteristic feature of the person is prefixed or suffixed to his name. Of used attachments such as father's or the husband's name and the place name, etc. are discarded. A sample of such names-of-persons is given below:

Masculine Names	**Explanation**
Gemini Ganesan	Gemini is the name of the studio in which his first film was made
Kalki Krishnamurthy	Kalki is an adopted name, from the initials of his name coupled with a part of his given name.
Shivaji Ganesan	He had played the role of Shivaji in a drama.
Subrahmania Bharathi	Bharathi was a little bestowed by a local ruler. He had discarded his sect appellation Aiyer..

Feminine Name	**Explanation**
Sowcar Janaki	She acted in a film Sowcar.

In the above illustration, it is observed that the person gets public recognition by the coined word, which is prefixed or suffixed to his or her personal name. It is some what akin to a pen-name. Hence, the entry is to be made under this coined word. The personal name would become subordinate to this specific word. Similar is the case with the place name employed by some of the politicians, etc.

6.3.3.3 Tamilians in foreign lands

As already stated, many educated Tamilians have adopted the structure of names in which the name of the father or of the husband comes in the rear. After they migrate to other countries, they sometimes acquire recognition through the father's name. In such case, it so happens that the wife of such a person accepts the last part of the name of her husband (which is the name of his father) as the last part of her name. The name of her husband which normally comes in a female name, is not used at all. Hence, the structure of her name becomes "Given Name - Name of Father in law". Similarly, their children also employ the name in the end part of their names. Thus, the pattern of their names is "Given name - Grand Father's Name". In such a name-of-person, it appears as if the grand father's name has virtually become the family name.

Examples:	**Masculine Names**	**Feminine Names**
	Anand Amurtharaj	Padma Joseph
	Ramesh Krishnan	Nalini Sundaram
	Ravichandran Sethuraman	

It may be noted that the reservoir for obtaining the name of the father, grand father or the self is common. Therefore, it is difficult to recognise each component part of such a name. Yet, by observing the manner in which the person contracts his name, it can be understood as which part of the name is the most important. In a feminine name, husband's or father in law's name can be easily spotted.

6.3.3.4 Usage of Surname

As per one version, Tamilians don't need surname. "Our names, rugged and heavy in quality, are enough to sustain a person's dignity without the aid of a surname", observes Subhadra Krishnamurthy (1983). However, another view-point is that the civilization of the West has not been able to influence Tamil culture. The Western practice of using the family names, is not in vogue among the Tamils. Yet, Certain persons add after their name an irremovable patronymic word indicating ancestral features (Ranganathan, 1954c):

1. vocation such as Asari (=smith); Chettiar (=trader); Pattar (=priest);

2. office such as Mudaliar, Udayer;

3. attainment in learning such as Avadhani, Jatavallabhar, Sastri;
4. ritual standing such as Dikshita, Pandaram, Vajapeyar;
5. religious following such as Ayyar, Ayyangar;

These attachments have been wrongly understood to denote the generic "caste names" (Ranganathan, 1954b). They in fact, are impotent words, and as such are not qualified to be used as entry elements. Thus, if a Tamil name-of-person is ending with any such or a similar attachment, the preceding word representing the personal name together with the patronymic word form the entry element. In the absence of such an attachment suffix, given name is the only word appearing in the end part of a Tamil name, under which the catalogue heading is to be prepared.

Another observation in this context, is that these suffix attachments are not generally employed in the feminine names. A sample of such masculine names with the suffix, is given as below:

Names-of-persons	Catalogue entry
Ananthraman Srinivasa Iyer	Srinivasa Iyer, Ananthraman
Krishamurthy Anand Iyengar	Anand Iyengar, Krishamurthy

Yet, another important observation in this respect, is that the attachments may either appear as independent words or stand coalesced with the personal name (Ranganathan, 1954b). They are always treated as irremovable part of the names.

Examples: Namakkal Ramamalingapillai
Ramaliangadigal

However, in order to imitate the Western practices, certain Tamilians have started converting all the words in their names accept the last, into initial form. Though, the end word is an impotent attachment, it is observed that the person acquires prominence only through such a word. In many cases, he may not disclose other features of his name such as the personal name. In such a specific situation, there is no alternative but to prepare the entry under such impotent word.

Examples: A.S.P. Ayyer, J.S.M. Ali
S.S. Pillai
H.V.R. Iyengar

The above practice of shortening the names-of-persons does not generally prevail among the feminine names.

6.3.3.5 Given Names

Given names in Tamil culture are mostly single worded. They are drawn from several sources of which the following deserve mention:

1. Names of Hindu gods and goddesses, such as Kartikeyan, Krishnan, Natarajan, Ranganathan, Srinivasan, Subramanian, Vankataraman, etc. for masculine names, and Parvati, Radha, Seetha, etc. for feminine names.
2. Names of the rivers like Ganga, Godavari, Jamuna, Kaveri, Krishna, Mandakini and so on;
3. Holy place names such as Badri or Badrinarayana, Kashinathan or Kasipandyan, etc. ;
4. Names of some decorative flowers such as Kusuma, Mallika, Rosa, etc.;
5. Specific pleasing colours such as Manjalaghi;
6. Names of the precious stones such as Chintamani, Punmahl and so on;
7. Nomenclature of some birds like Kokila, Panchavarnakili, etc.

An important finding about the given names, is that many a masculine given names (not all) terminate with "an". This is a peculiarity of the southern states of Tamilnadu and Kerala, and constitutes a feature of easy identification of the southern names. However, when such a personal name appears in combination with other name or with some other patronymic attachment word, it is observed that "an" is generally dropped. With the father's name usually prefixed to the personal name, chances are that 'an' if appearing in the given name of the father or husband, may be ignored while writing the full name of the son/daughter/wife. Similarly, while adding an attachment after the personal name, the same change may occur.

Examples: Nagarajan may become Nagaraja when prefixed to the given name Krishaswamy.

Sriraman becomes Sriram when the attachment Nadar is suffixed to the given name.

6.3.3.6 Use of Sri and Thiru

Certain personal names may begin with Sri and in such a name, "Sri" is an integral part. Therefore, it is to be retained. Though, in a normal situation, it is merely an honourable word of addressing. An illustration of such names in which Sri is forming an inseparable part, is given below:

Srikrishnan Srinivasa Srishah
Srilakshmi Sriraman

In this respect, it can be added that "Sri" is generally employed only in those specific names derived from the names of gods, like Rama, Krishna, etc. Its equivalent in Tamil "Thiru" is used as an irremovable feature, in a number of the names.

Examples: Thirumahl, Thirumahan, Thiruvalluvar, Thiruvengadam

In all such names"Thiru" is to be retained. However, Thiru and its feminine "Thirumati" when employed in respectfully addressing others, do not form part of such names. These epithets are ignored for the purposes of cataloguing.

Personal names of individuals in Tamilnadu are generally single worded, though, some of then may be compound. All compound names are rendered as if they were single worded personal names. In other words, the so called auxiliary undergoes complete amalgamation with the name, giving no scope for confusion in dealing with such a name.

6.3.3.7 Imitation of the names of national heroes

Some persons are named after prominent national heroes and leaders using only a part of the name, by which the important personality is known. A sample of such names is given as under:

Masculine Given Names	Feminine Given Names
Bose	Jhansi
Gandhi	Jhansi Lakshmi
Nehru	
Patel	

Sometimes, the full name of the personality is also used in forming a given name. If the same includes specific features as the name of his father or his caste denoting feature, etc., it is observed that the same are retained in the name. Similarly, if a prefix title is employed in the name of the hero, the same is also imitated. The following are some masculine given names formulated in this way:

Babu Rajendra Prasad

Bal Gangadhar Tilak

Netaji Subhash Chandra Bose

In naming of persons in exceptional instances, names of a few international personalities are also employed, as the given names. A sample of such masculine personal is given as below:

Kennedy, Lenin, Stalin, Tito

6.3.3.8 Breaking of the personal name

Tamil names-of-persons are lengthy in form. In an effort to shorten them to smaller size, some persons break their given names into two or more parts. Sometimes, even father's name is rendered in a split from. Few examples are:

Name-of-person	Shortened Name	Entry word
Jagdeesan Krishna Murthy	J.K. Murthy	Murthy
Chandrasekhar Venkata Raman	C.V. Raman	Raman
Sitaraman Satya Narayana	S.S. Narayana	Narayana

As seen in the above examples, all the words in the full name are converted into their initials except the last word. Though, the last word is the result of splitting the given name, and as such is considered impotent, the cataloguer has no choice and is bound to abide by the unsual choice of the author.

6.3.4 Muslim Names

Muslims in Tamilnadu form a small minority. They also have different structures of the names-of-persons. Broadly, there are three structures in the Muslim names-of-persons, as listed under:

(a) Father's Name -Given Name

Like the Hindus, several Muslims have the structure in which the name of the father precedes the given name. Among the educated communities, it is quite a common practice to reduce the name of father into its initial form. Examples of such Tamil Muslim names are:

Masculine Names	**Feminine Names**
Abdul Hasan Khasim	Aeyiaz Fathima
Gaffar Allah Pichai	Akbar Noorjahan Beevi
Imamudeen Mohammad Moinuddin	Ibrahim Tajnisha
Jamaludeen Noordeen	Jaffar Mujeebunissa
Jaffar Hameed	Mohamad Ahmad Kabilabibi
Nawabali Fakruddinali	Mohamad Hameed Jameela

(b) Village Name-Father's Name-Given Name

In another pattern, village name is added before the name of father and the given name. It is customary to abbreviate both the parts of a name. In this respect, it is observed that if the name of the father is a compound word, the practice is to write it in two separate words. This pattern is however, confined to masculine names. A sample of such names is given as under:

Avul Pakir Jainulabdeen Abdul Kalam :- Pakir Jainulabdeen is the name of his father. It bears Pakir meaning a saint as the prefix. His shortened name is A.P.J. Abdul Kalam.

Nagoore Mohamed Peeran Hanifa:- Nagoore is the place name, and Mohamed Peeran is the father's name. His short name is N.M. Hanifa

Trichy Khader Javed Basha:- Trichy is the place name. Khader is the father's name His contracted name is T.K. Javed Basha.

In addition, some families adopt a word, generally the name of some of their ancestor, or some other patronymic word, and employ consistently as the first part of their names. It is followed by the name of the father or husband. The given name is the last part of the name. In some names, father's name is not used. A sample of the names is given as under:

Masculine Name	**Feminine Name**
Abbas Ibrahim Shahjahan	Abbas Shahjaha Norjaha
Annaikar Obaidulla	Odham Afthunisa

Giramani Abdul Haq

Natamakar Habibula

Vijayan Mohamad Nainar Kader Meera Pillai

The patronymic words convey specific family background. Some of the words have been explained as under:

Annai= Elephant

Girmani= Chief of a tribe

Natam= Head of a village

Odham= Near sea shore

(c) Husband's name as suffix

Among the educated females, some suffix the name of the husband to their personal names. A sample of such names is given as under:

Ayeesha Ghalib; Fatima Shiraj; Shajida Thajudeen; Vahida Sharief

6.3.4.1 Attachments in Tamil Muslim names

In general, other than the father's or husband's name and the place name prefixed to the Tamil Muslim name, suffixes are not used. However, as an exception, some names may add some suffix words denoting some profession of the ancestors. It appears that in recent years, the trend is changing, with the usage of such suffixes on the decline. Some examples of the suffixes are:

Suffix title	**Meaning**
Labbai	A Tamil Muslim
Maraikayar	Trader
Rowther	Boatman
Sarkari	Sugar producer

As per Naidu (1994), the term Maraikayar is derived from the Tamil word mara = wood and rayar = owner indicating that they were owners of wooden boats. Similarly, Labbai denotes that the person is a desendant of the Arabs who came to trade in India in the 11th and 12th centuries. However, it is now a term of respect among the Muslims of Tamilnadu.

If any such attachment word appears in a name, it is to be taken along with the given name. Entry should be avoided under such an attachment word.

In addition, to the suffixes described above, some names-of-persons do also carry some other suffix words such as the following denoting some specific features.

Suffix word	Meaning
Meeran	Respectful word
Pichai	Blessings

Similarly, some given name could be like Mohamad Meeran, in which the second word is only a decorative compliment to the name. It is some what akin to an auxiliary.

6.3.5 Christian Names

The religious minority group belonging to Christianity is a very small one. The names-of-persons bear the same structures as used by the Hindus. Even many of the words used in the names of Christians are common. The following patterns of Tamil Christian names are widely followed:

(a) Father's Name - Given Name

In this pattern, girls after marriage may use the name of the husband as the prefix. Examples of the names are:

Masculine Names	Feminine Names
Devaraj Rayappan	Joe Ponamma
David John Das	Solomon Juliet
Johnson Francis	
Selvaraj Ponuraj	

(b) Given Name - Father's name

Among the feminine names, this pattern is more popular. After marriage, a female carries the same of her husband instead of her father. Some examples are:

Masculine name	Feminine Names
Thomas Jayaseelan	Lucyamma Lazurus
	Roseline Arulappan

6.3.5.1 Surnames

In the Corromandal coast in the southern most region of the state, many family names are used among the Christians. Yet, the status of the family names is the same as it exists among the Hindus. The personal name together with the surname should be used as the entry elements. Some of the examples of the Christian surnames are as under:

D' Costa	Fernandez	Machado
D' Cruz	Fernando	Queriera
D' Cunha	Kagoo	Wilvarayr

6.3.5.2 Given names

Personal names can either be biblical, modified biblical Tamil names, or purely Tamil names. Sometimes, they are suffixed with such attachments as Babu, Das, Sami, Amma, etc. A sample of the names with their Tamil equivalents, is given below:

Biblical Name	Tamil Conversion
Anthony	Anthonysami
Francis	Francisco or Francisca
Joseph	Joe
Lazurus	Lazar
Lucy	Lucyamma
Mariam	Mariamma
Paul	Chinappan
Pauline	Chinamma
Peter	Arulappan
Rosa	Rosamma

6.3.6 French influence on Tamil Names

Pondicherry, a small union territory on the east coast, south of

Chennai city, is a predominantly Tamil speaking region. It observes the same naming patterns as are seen in Tamilnadu. Having remained for a couple of centuries under the French rule, a strong influence of the phonetics of the French language (the official language of the area for a considerable period of time) could be described in the rendering of Tamil names. The following are the examples of such aberrations:

Tamil Masculine Name	**French transformation**
Bhaskaradas	Bascaradasse
Jeyaraj	Djearadjou
Kandasamy	Candsamy
Palani	Pajani
Sundaram	Soundarame
Ulaganathan	Ulaganathane
Tamil Feminine Name	**French Version**
Jothi	Goti
Lalitha	Lalida

6.4 MALAYALAM NAMES

6.4.1 General

The State of Kerala, created under the provisions of the States Reoganisation Act of 1956, consists of the previous state of Travancore-Cochin, barring four Talukas of the Trivandram district and a part of the Shencottah taluk of the district of Quilon. In addition, Malabar district of the erstwhile Madras Presidency was merged into it. At present, its geographic area is 38, 863 sq. km. and its population is about 29 million. Hindus constitute the majority of 57.28% followed by Muslims (23.33%). Christians comprise about 19.32% of the state population (Census of India 1991, 1995).

A noticeable feature of the state demography has been that Hindus, Christians, and Muslims have specific pockets of concentration. In the northern part of the state, for instance, Muslims are in overwhelming majority. The central portion has Christian domination, whereas Hindus are in vast majority in the southern districts.

With the highest literacy rate in the country, people are highly mobile, and are generally found in all the major cities of the country. Many Keralites are also serving foreign countries more so in the Gulf. Prosperity of the families in the state is quite high. It is the southern most state situated between Tamilnadu in the south-east, Karnataka in the north and a long coast line in the west with palm plantations aplenty.

6.4.2 Names-of-persons

The names-of-persons from the state possess several structures, with hardly any uniformity in the pattern of the names. Sometimes, even the structure of the names of two brothers may differ. However, as in other parts of the South India, caste denoting attachments are not generally used. Yet, wherever they are employed in the names, they remain sub-ordinate to the given names. A sample of the names is given as under:

<u>Examples</u>: Hindu Names:

Masculine Names	**Feminine Names**
Adoor Gopalakrishnan	Kakkat Sarojini Amma
Chettur Sankaran Nair	Nalapat Balamani Amma
Mechettu Gopalan	Punneth Radha
Nair Gopalakrishnan	
Puthoyodavan Somachandran	

Muslim Names

Masculine Names	**Feminine Names**
Erachithod Hasan	Aiysha Hassan
Hassanu Kunju	Hajara Beevi
M.M. Shahul Hameed	Laila Shahul
Noohu Kannu Rawther	
Vatanapalli Kasim	

Christian Names

Masculine Names	**Feminine Names**
Akanad Mathai Issac	Aleyamma Thomas

Alapat Verghese Poulose	Baby John
John Mathai	Moolamattom Verkey Pyle
Oommen Chandy	Sara Kutty
Palathinal Joseph Joseph	Sharly Issac
	Thevareeth Saramma Abraham

6.4.2.1 House Names

Every family belonging to Malayalam culture, invariably possesses a unique house name, which has been in usage for many generations, in the past. This house name is employed as an essential feature in the names by a very large number of persons (Ranganathan, 1964). Its major characteristics are described as under:

1. A house name is merely a word usually describing some noticeable context of the location, surrounding, or some characteristics of the ancestral house.

2. The family in the present context, may not know the exact location of the ancestral house whose features have been deployed to represent the house name.

3. Since the house names were introduced into the families many generations ago, it might be quite possible that the house whose specific characteristics have been used, might have disappeared or its particular features might have vanished by now.

4. Its concept is so much deep rooted that the family is generally identified in the social circles by the house name. Therefore, the house name at the social plane is the surname of the family.

5. In rare instances, some families may bring a change in their house name, which may occur when a new house is constructed. In such a situation, the house name is matched with the characteristics of the new family home. Among the Muslims, quite a few educated persons have changed their house names.

6. There is no correlation between the house name and the specific profession in which the family has been traditionally engaged. In other words house names and caste names have no relationship among each other.

7. In some exceptional cases, house names may not convey any meaning as the same might have been deformed over a long period of time.

8. House names of the Christians convey prosperity, during the far-off

days. They still continue to be ahead in prosperity and well being.

An illustration of the house names used in the state, is given as under:

House Name	Meaning
Alumudu	Opposite of a peepul tree
Ambalamukhu	Corner of a temple
Kandathil	Paddy field
Mangtu	Mango forest
Mullankuzhilili	Small portion of a big house
Puttenangadi	New small town
Thudabarambil	Combination of multiple house site plots

The following house names have becomes unintelligible:

Chembakassery Kochiparambill Vellodi

House names in Muslim families, are similar to those used by the Hindus. However, during the recent decades, several educated families changed their house names. The Malayalam words hitherto denoting their house names were replaced by Persian and Arabic words. Such house names may generally be of two words. The first one is the personal name of a family member followed by a generic word Manzil which means a mansion. Some examples of a few new house names of the Muslims, are given as under:

Aisha Manzil Fathima Manzil Laila Manzil
Aji Manzil Habib Manzil

6.4.3 Structure of Names

(a) House Name - Father's/Husband's Name -Given Name

Several structures of the names-of-persons exist in the state. The age old tradition, which is still followed by a very large number of families, is to use the house name as the first part of a name-of-person, which is ordinarily followed by the name of the father (or husband in case of a married female). The personal name comes only after the name of the father or husband, and is usually the end part of the name. This pattern more or less conforms to the one obtained among the Tamils.

Examples: Hindu Names:

Masculine Names	**Feminine name**
Kambanthodath Kunhan Viswanathan	Chagayil Narayanan Sarojini
Thettalli Sankaran Vinodkumar	
Velliayanpalli Parmeswaran Sreenivasan	

Muslim Names

Masculine Names

Mattapallil Mohammad Kunjurawther Shahul Hussain

Punathil Kunju Abdullah

Feminine Name

Tharakanveedu Mohammad Hameed Lailamma

Christian Names

Masculine Names	**Feminine Names**
Akanad Mathai Issac	Moolamattom Verkey Pyle
Kumbakattu Thomas Samuel Kutty	Poikaiyil George Sosamma
Vedakevilla Chandy Poulose	

(b) House Name -Given Name

Another structure of the names-of-persons also exists in which the name of father/husband does not appear at all. The structure of such a name, is the house name succeeded by the given name (Balasubramanyan, 1961).

Examples: **Hindu names**

Masculine Names	**Feminine Names**
Kodikunnil Suresh	Neinakalathi Saraswathi
Malyatoor Ramakrishnan	Nalapat Balamani Amma
Mullapally Ramchandran	
Parakat Unnikrishnan	

Muslim Names

Masculine Names	**Feminine Name**
Erachithod Hassan	Kallummootil Majitha
Hidur Mohammad	
Panakkad Shihab Thangal	
Pulakkara Muhammad	

Christian Names

Masculine Names	**Feminine Name**
Palathinkal Francis	Puttenvedu Annamma
Paravur George	
Valiathothathil Philip	

(C) Father's Name - Given Name

Likewise, there are some other individuals not employing their house names and the names of such persons simply include the father's name or the name of the husband, as the case may be, followed by the given name.

<u>Examples</u>: **Hindu Name**

Masculine Names	**Feminine Name**
Mangtu Keshav Nair	Parmeswaran Janaki
Neelakanta Padmanabhan	
Sankarpillai Gopinath	

Muslim Names

Masculine Names	**Feminine Names**
Abdul Rahim Baiju	Abdul Karim Sahada
Kunhiloyanutty Avukaderkutty Naha	Abdul Rahman Aisha Beevi
Mohammad Sharef Shahjahan	

Christian Names

Masculine Names	**Feminine Name**
John Mathai	David Baby

Joseph Joseph

Ooman Chandy

(d) Village Name - Given Name

Some well-known artists, politicians, writers, etc. have used another pattern of their names, in which they employ the name of their village followed by their name. The features such as house name and the name of the father, are discarded by them.

Examples: Hindu Names

Masculine Names	**Feminine Name**
Adoor Gopalakrishnan	Pattan Saraswathi
Malyatoor Ramakrishnan	
Pankonnam Verkey	
Pattam Thanu Pillai	
Vayalar Ravi	

Muslim Name: Vaikom Muhammad Basheer

(e) Given Name - Father's/Husband's Name

Yet, another pattern of the names also exists, in which the name of father or husband as the case may be, is suffixed to the given names. Some names are:

Hindu Names:	**Masculine Name**	**Feminine Name**
	Bipin Chandra Narayana Kurup	Shobha Narayanan
Muslim Names:	**Masculine Names**	**Feminine Name**
	Salim Abdul Karim	Soja Abdul Ali
	Sharmad Mohammad Haniffa	
Christian Names:	**Masculine Names**	**Feminine Names**
	George Thomas	Mary Verges
	Mathai Poulose	Saramma Abraham
		Sharly Issac

(f) Given Names - Father's Name - House Name

In some names of the Christians, the order of different parts has been changed. The solitary example given below is of such a name:

Augustine Kurian Chalil
[The order is "Given Name-Father's Name- House Name"]

(g) Other Structures

Some persons brought other variations in their names by changing the position of several parts. Some examples of such names are given as below:

House Name in the end	**Village Name in the end**
Akbar Aikara	George Irumpayam
James Arampulickal	George Onakkur

Among the educated class, names of individuals are often shortened, by abbreviating all the parts of the name accept the personal name. This practice leads to the conclusion that the house or village name, and the name of the father are both subordinate to the given name.

In some cases, persons belonging to the forward castes, also employ their caste representing names as the end part after their personal name. The names in such situations become four worded. An illustration of popular attachments used in Nairs, Brahmins, and Muslims is given below:

Among Nairs	**Among Brahmins**	**Among Muslims**
Kurup	Battahthirpad	Haji
Menon	Iyer	Koya
Nair	Iyengar	Rowther
Nambiar	Namboodiri	Sait
Nambissan	Namboodiripad	Thangal
Panikkar	Sarma	
Pillai	Sastry	
Warrier		

Iyers and Iyengars are believed to be the descendents of the immigrants from Tamilnadu, many of whom live in Palkkad. As these families have continued to live in Kerala for a very long period of time, they have adopted the Malayalam culture. However, the occurrence of Sastry is very rare. Further, Panikkar is used as a suffix in some Christian names also.

The suffix Haji is also used as a prefix in some Muslim names. It is not required to be retained in cataloguing, as it is not the part of the names. The other suffix be treated as essential but impotent attachments. In addition, in all the three religious groups, suffixes such as Amma, Babu, Kutty, etc. are used as auxiliary words to the personal names.

6.4.4 Implications of caste names

As explained while discussing Tamil names earlier, quite a large number of masculine given names end with 'an'. However, if in such a name the caste representing name is used, it is noted that 'an' is dropped as a matter of convention.

Examples: Parmeshwaran becomes Parmeshwara Kurup. Krishnan has become Krishna Menon. Narayanan may become Narayan Nair.

6.4.5 Social Practices

Nairs form a prominent and influencing Hindu community of Kerala with a strong martial tradition. They along with some other communities follow the matrilineal system of kinship. Under this system, the property, office and the house name are all transmitted through the female line from the mother or mother's brother (Jayaraman, 1989). Hence, the house name and the caste denoting names, wherever employed, in these communities, pertain to the mother's family and not of the family of the father.

Example: Mullankuzhirn Kesavpillai Murlidhar Nair

In some names instead of the given name of the father, personal name of the mother is employed in the names of the members. The house name and the caste surname if also used are drawn from the mother's family. Hence, all the components of such a name, are from the mother's family.

Masculine Names	**Feminine Name**
Chakyat Narayini Amma Surendran	Kalappurackal Meenuamma Sarasa
Madhavi Amma Unikrishnan	

Names of females among Nairs, and in those other castes, deriving parentage from mother's side are not changed at all as a consequence of marriage. They continue to use the same house name which was in usage at their maiden stage. In their caste denoting names too, if employed, no change is discernible. Yet, in the recent times, the system of matriliny has declined, and with this female names are changed after marriage in a few instances.

In Brahmins particularly, as the lineage is derived from the paternal side, changes take place in the house name and the name of father which are replaced by the same of her husband. If caste denoting name is also employed, after her marriage the same of her husband is used.

6.4.6 Prefixes

In the state of Kerala, prefix titles are not employed in the names. This is contrary to the North Indian practice wherein a variety of caste, professional, religious, social or educational prefixes are in vogue. However, as an exception, Sardar K.M. Panikkar, a renowned historian from Kerala, was using "Sardar" as the prefix to his name. This on investigation, has been found as an exception, and is due to a predominant influence of the Hindi culture in which he had lived for a very long period of time.

6.4.7 Christian Society

Kerala Christians are essentially Hindu in culture, Christian in religion and Oriental in worship (Sreedhara Menon, 1979). They perform several ceremonies which bear resemblance to those of the Hindus. For instance, corresponding to the namakaranan ceremony, is the Baptism of the Christians. The names given to the children are mostly Biblical names. However, several among them have their counterparts in the Malayalam language. A sample of such names along with their vernacular equivalents is given below (Anantha Krishna Iyer, 1912):

Vernacular form	Biblical form
Chacko	Jacob
Johny	John
Mariam	Mary
Mathai	Mathew

Paily	Paul
Patros	Peter

Kerala Christians are divided into several sects. Chief among them is the Syrian Christians. They are descendants of the converts from high caste Hindus. They form a forward looking community. Their educational attainment is quite high. They speak Malayalam, and have been identified with the mainstream of Kerala culture.

6.4.7.1 Strange practice

In many of the Christian families, as a social practice, the given name of the grand father (from father's side in respect of the eldest male child, and from the mother's side for the second male child) is repeated. Thus, if the name of the grand father (i.e. mother's father) and the personal name of the father are exactly same, it is observed that a peculiar name comes into being, in the anglicised form. An illustration of such names is given as under:

George Geroge   Thomas Thomas

6.4.8 Lakshadweep

Lakshadweep comprises a group of 27 islands, in the Arabian Sea. Prior to November 1973, these islands were known as Laccadive, Minicoy and Amindivi. At present, they form a Union Territory. The area of all the islands, is about 32 sq. km. and their population is about 51, 700. The northern group of islands are called Amindivi. The remaining group including Minicoy islands are known as Laccadives. The nearest state in the mainland is Kerala, situated about 300 km. away. Muslims are in vast majority (94%) (Census of India 1991, 1995).

6.4.8.1 Names-of-persons

The structure of the names-of-persons is the house name, followed by the personal name. In some specific masculine names, caste name or a similar appellation is also suffixed. A sample of the names is given as below:

Masculine Names	**Feminine Names**
Kandeth Shaik Koya	Komalam Amina Manika
Neelathupure Ali Manikfan	Puradam Hawwa Bifan
Padannatha Mohammad Sayeed	

6.4.8.2 Caste structure

There are three broad caste like ethnic groups existing among the Muslims of these islands. They are described as under (Singh, 1993b):

Caste	Meaning
Koya	Land-owning aristocratic caste. During the far-off days, almost all the shipping vessels were owned by their an cestors, In addition, the entire trade was under their con trol.
Malmi	Served as navigators in the sailing vessels owned by the Koya during the distant days.
Melacheri	Belonged to the labour class. Their traditional occupa tion was climbing coconut trees, for plucking the nuts, tapping neera/ meera, processing coir and rope making.

The Minicoy society is also stratified and arranged into the hierarchy of four groups. The Manikfan are equivalent to Koya, Thakrufan are believed to be higher in social status than Thakru. During the far-off-days, Thakru used to work in the sailing ships. The lowest class Raveri corresponds to Malacheri of the other islands (Singh, 1993b).

6.4.8.3 Family Name

Similar to the house name in Kerala, every family in the islands has a permanent house name. This comes in the beginning of every name. However, it differs from a Malayali house name in one respect that it generally conveys no meaning. An illustration of some house names is given as below:

Komalam	Neelathupure	Puradam
Nalakam	Padannatha	

6.4.8.4 Suffixes

In the feminine names-of-persons, specific suffix titles are used. They generally denote the caste background of the bearer. The following suffixes are used in the names of women:

Ethnic group	Suffix
Manikfan	Manika (Tandan, 1993a)

Thakrufan	Bifan (Tandan, 1993d)
Thakru	Bi-bi (Tandan, 1993c)
Raveri	Kambilo or Manja (Tandan, 1993b)

A person in the islands is known by his personal name. It is generally the last portion of the name. However, if a caste type suffix is also used, the given name would appear one word before the last. In such a name, the last two words taken together form the entry.

6.5 KANNADA NAMES

6.5.1 General

The present state of Karnataka was constituted as Mysore, under the States Reorganisation Act, 1956. Renamed as Karnataka in 1973, it includes the territories of the erstwhile states of Mysore and Coorg, the districts of Belgaum, Bijapur, Dharwar and Uttar Kannada, of the erstwhile Bombay Presidency; Raichur, Gulbarga, and Bidar districts from the former Hyderabad state; and Bellary district alongwith the Dakshin Kannada district of the Coimbatore district in the then Madras Presidency. Spread over an area of 191,791 sq. km., it has a population of about 44.98 million. Hindus are in overwhelming majority (85.45%), followed by Muslims having 11.64% of the population of the state (Census of India 1991, 1995).

Karnataka is situated on the western edge of the Deccan plateau and is bounded by Maharashtra and Goa in the North, and north-west, Kerala and Tamilnadu in the south, and south-east; Andhra Pradesh in the east and the Arabian Sea in the west. It is one of the four states of South India. Standing in proximity to Maharashtra, and yet closely linked to the southern parts of the country, Karnataka represents a rare blend of the Tamil, Telugu and Marathi cultures with Bangalore, the cosmopolitan metropolis as its capital.

6.5.2 Names-of-persons

From the stand point of the names-of-persons, Karnataka is among the few states in the country, displaying a variety of patterns. The impact of Marathi culture is more visible as compared to other cultures of the south (Mrigeppa, 1994).

Muslims of the state generally have the same structure of their names as do the Hindus. However , among the educated persons, a simplified model of the names, is used. This conforms to the patterns discussed in the Muslim names under the North India. As the literacy among the Muslims is comparatively low, not many names-of-persons could be obtained for the present work.

An illustration of the Hindu names-of-persons from the state is given as under:

Masculine Names	**Feminine Names**
Jagannath Rao Joshi	Balaganchi Chandrasekhar Sandhya
Masti Venkatesh Iyengar	Sarojini Mahishi
Menta Sathyanarayana Shetty Venkatesh	Uma Jagannath
Siddavanahalli Nijalingappa	
Tonse Ramesh Pai	

In pursuing different names-of-persons from the state, it is observed that the specific pattern of the names, is very much dependent on the historical association of the region. Also, the proximity to the other linguistic belt is found to have been influencing the naming pattern. Based on the existing structures, the names-of-persons can be grouped into the following classes:

(a) Names from the erstwhile Mysore state.

(b) Names from Coorg.

(c) Names from the area with prominent Marathi influence.

(d Names from the regions with Telugu influence.

(a) Mysore region

There are five practices being followed in the names-of-persons of the Mysore region. They are described as under:

(i) Place Name- Given name

This is the popular most form of the names-of-persons. In this practice, the name of the village is prefixed to the given name (Krishan Kumar, 1993). The village name generally pertains to the original native place of the family. In recent times, some persons employ the present place name, and in this way a change is brought in such names. In some specific names, persons also suffix a common noun, denoting their caste.

Among the names of the educated persons, the place name is converted into its initial form. An illustration of such Hindu names is given as below:

Masculine Names	**Feminine Names**
Baglodi Devarao	Bangalore Rajlakshmi
Begur Rudramoorthy	Gorur Seshamma
Kengal Hanumanthaiah	Kittur Rani Chennamma
Mokshagundam Visveswaryya	Mysore Thirumalamma
Moddabirdi Veerappa Moily	
Tumkur Kasinath	

An illustration of the Muslim names-of-persons, using the above pattern is given as under:

Masculine Names	**Feminine Names**
Allapalli Syed Umar Farooq	Chinnapatna Ayeesha Banu
Cherkalam Abdulla	Mysore Akeela Begum
Jagalur Mohammad Imam	
Neelamangala Ibrahim	

(ii) Village Name-Father's Name -Given Name

In another pattern, persons are also adding the name of the father in between the two parts. Therefore, the pattern of such a name is Place Name-Father's Name-Personal name (Balasubramanyan, 1961). In this category of the names, some persons are also attaching their caste name. An illustration of the Hindu names is given as below:

Masculine Names:

Bellary Shamanna Kesavan

Kulkunda Shivarao Niranjana

Malangi Shivalingadevaru Gurupadaswamy

Salagame Venkatasubbiah Ranganna

Somanahally Malliah Krishna

Feminine Names: Balanganchi Chandrasekhar Sandhya

Basovapura Jaikrishnareddy Jyothi

Palangala Anatharama Nagaveni

Among the Muslims, the under-mentioned names-of-persons are falling into the above category:

Masculine Names	**Feminine Name**
Challakere Kareem Jaffar Sharief	Srirangapatna Kareem Nazma Bano
Sindhgatta Gaffar Anwar Pasha	Kowdenahali Chotu Bhai Firoza
Tumkur Sirajuddin Gaffur	Tiptur Ahmed Nasreen
Yellapuri Rafiq Ahmed	

(iii) Father's Name - Given Name

In yet another category, a slightly different pattern is discernible. In such a name-of-person, no place name occurs and hence, the structure is Father's name - Given Name (Balasubramanyan, 1961). In addition, a few names-of-persons may also bear caste name in the end. A sample of the names is given as under:

Masculine Names	**Feminine Names**
Basavaiah Rachaiah	Arun Kasturi Naik
Chowdacharya Parmeshwarachar	Malikarjun Sharda
Devagouda Javare Gouda	Rangraj Shalini Urs
Ramnath Vasudeva	Subbaiah Sampurna
Sannanjappa Sivappa	
Srinivasa Sampath	
Yellappa Ramakrishna	

(iv) Given Name - husband's name

In the names of the married educated women, a simplified model is also in vogue. Under this pattern, the name of the husband either in full form, or in part, is suffixed to the personal name of the female. An illustration of such names is given as below:

Hindu Names:	Arunadhati Ramesh	Prema Venkatesh
	Kalpana Jayaprakash	Santosh Venugopal
	Lalitha Murthy	Sujatha Somesekhar Reddy
Muslim Names:	Khatunisa Akhtar	
	Rafikha Rahim Khan	
	Yasmeen Nissar Ahmed	

(v) Transformed structure

Some persons, in order to bring some novelty in their names have suffixed the name of the village. In shortening their names, they contract the village name into its initial form. Some examples of such names are:

Masculine Names	**Feminine Name**
Rajasekhar M	Nirmala V
Srinivasa Rao Savur	

In the context of potency, it is observed that whatever may be the structure of a name, the personal name is the most important in establishing the identity. If caste name is also suffixed, given name together with the caste attachment form the entry element. Similar is the case of the place name.

(b) Names-of -persons from Coorg

Coorg is a district in Karnataka. During the British time it was a separate entity, and after the independence its status was changed to a "C" category state. However, the entire area was merged in 1956, into the then Mysore state (i.e. the present day Karnataka). It is known as Kodagu. It possesses its own individuality. The structure of the names-of-persons is found to be different from the other areas of the state. Every name has three component parts. They are the house name, the name of the father or husband, and the given name (Subbakrishna, 1994). An illustration of some Coorgi names-of-persons is given as under:

Masculine Names	**Feminine Names**
Chekkara Thimmiah Bopanna	Malettira Naniah Thangamma

Cheppudire Muthanna Poonacha Manepanda Appiah Ponnamma

Cheranda Chengappa Bopiah Pattada Uthiah Saroja

Kodendera Madappa Carriappa

Muddura Kariappa Belliappa

Napaneravanda Karumbaya Medappa

House Name

Every family possesses a distinct house name, which is akin to a vernacular surname in Telugu or Malayalam speaking region. The family is identified in the social circles by it. It is generally employed as the first part of a name-of-person. It is also known as the family name or the surname, in the district. Yet, it is different from a Western surname. Some of the important features of the house name are described as below:

1. Every Coorgi family is having a specific house name. It remains a permanent part of the names-of-persons, in a family.

2. Family names have been in usage for a long period of time and therefore, their origin can not be ascertained.

3. The words denoting house names in Coorg, are generally unintelligeble and hence, their form or derivation can not be known.

4. A house name is generally a single worded entity. Among the educated persons, it is contracted into initial.

5. A house name is sub-ordinate to the given name in status. In fact, it is the least important but essential part of a name-of-person.

(c) Marathi influenced names

It may be recalled here that before the formation of the state, several districts situated in the northern parts of the state, were forming part of the Bombay presidency. They include Belgaum, Bijapur, Dharwar, and North Kanara. In these districts, prominent Marathi cultural influence is perceptible. The structure of the names-of-persons in this area, corresponds to the one used in Maharashtra.

In the north eastern side of the state lies two districts. They are Bidar and Gulbarga. Both of them were part of the erstwhile Hyderabad state. Because their location is being in proximity to the Marathi speaking districts, a dominant Marathi influence is discernible. In the names-of-persons, the Marathi traditions are being followed (Sengupta, 1974b). Hence, the structure of the component parts of these names is the same as employed in the Marathi culture. Therefore, the analysis presented for the Marathi names is also applicable to the names-of-persons from the Marathi influenced region. However, a brief description of such names is given here.

A names-of-persons possesses three distinct components. The sequence is "Given Name - Father's Name - Surname". In the name of a married woman, husband's name, instead of the father's name is used. This uniformity in the structure of the names-of-persons is contrasted to the lack of uniformity in the southern part of the state (Mrigeppa 1994). Some examples of the names are given below:

Masculine Names	**Feminine Names**
Ashok Devraj Bagmar	Neela Chandrasekhar Patil
Basappa Danappa Jatti	Radhabai Raghunath Deshpande
Devendrappa Shankarappa Masudi	Sumatidevi Rudrayya Hiremath
Ranganatha Ramachandra Divakar	
Shivanand Basappa Ganagi	
Somappa Golappa Hadimani	

Muslim Names

Masculine Names	**Feminine Names**
Habiburrehman Abdulkarim Khan	Mehmooda Mohammadibrahim Pathan
Mohammadali Ahmedali Kittur	Nasimabano Ismail Khan
Najirahmad Mohammadhusain Malwad	Seema Mohammadibrahim Hublikar
Sajidkhan Inayat Khan	

Surnames

Similar to the state of Maharashtra, surnames are drawn from several sources. Important ones are:

(i) Place names as Family Names

This category of the surnames is most popular. There are two practices in vogue. In the first one, the place name is use as such, where as in the other practice, " kar" meaning there by resident of is added.

Examples:	Place Name	Modified Place Names
	Hittangi	Hublikar
	Hubli	Hulsurkar
	Jatti	Kakatkar
		Kelkar

(ii) Names of Eatables as Family names

Certain, families in the region employ the names of some eatables, as their surnames, and strangely the persons are not aware as to how and why the specific word is being used as their family name:

Examples:	Family Names	Meaning
	Akki	Rice
	Menasinakayi	Chilly
	Roti	Indian made bread
	Ullegaddi	Onion

(iii) Temple Names as Surnames

This category of the family names is found only among the Brahmin families. Some specific families have been identified with certain Hindu temples, and the same features are use to denote their surnames. Some examples of such family names are given as under:

Family Name	Meaning
Bhavmath	Temple possessing an attached well
Geddaimath	Winning temple or the leading prestigious temple
Hiremath	Old temple
Hosamath	New temple
Tambrallimath	Copper bearing temple
Tippimath	Garbage temple

(iv) Social status as the surname

In some families, specific surnames indicating social status or prosperity of the fore-fathers are in use. Sometimes, locational feature of the house of the ancestors is also used to denote the surname. A list of such family names is given as under:

Family Name	Meaning
Chikkamani	Small house
Doddamani	Big house
Hadimani	Road-side house
Katthi	Donkey owner
Kudari	Horse owner
Menasinakayi	Chilli grower
Moolmani	Corner house
Tenginakayi	Coconut grower

(v) Position denoting surnames

Such as Deshpande, Kamat, Kulkarni, Patil, etc. Their explanations have been covered under Marathi names.

(vi) Caste derived family names

Such as Joshi, Pujari, Kumbhar, and so on.

In this respect, it is observed that whatever may be the form, meaning or derivation of a family name, it has no bearing on the current situation. Generally it had come into usage many years ago, and is continuing since then.

Peculiar Marathi influenced Muslim names

In addition to the description of the names-of-persons, given above, another unusual practice is followed in the Marathi influenced region in the eastern parts of the state. The relevant observation of Hussain Khan (1994) is reproduced as under:

"Typically a male has four names, lineage name, personal name, a title depending upon the political office with which the lineage is vested with, and the father's name is also suffixed to specify clearly the identification of the person. A typical full name of a member of

Mali Patel biraderi might therefore be 'Khasim Patel Lalba Patel Mali Birader.' Here the suffix 'Mali - Birader' refers to his biraderi of which he is a member agnate (birader). However, if one is the son of the Mali Patel of the village, he carries instead the suffix 'Pattedar Mali Patel' which indicates not only the membership but also his position of being the rightful (pattedar) successor (sic) to his father's position of Mali Patel. Save for the direct line of Mali Patel, all other agnate of the biraderi are considered as biraders. If one belongs to Mullani sect, his personal name would be suffixed with his father's name and then with his biraderi, as for instance, 'Dasthageersab Fakeersab Kondgoli'.

The depth of biraderis in Gulwar ranges from three to seven or even more generations. Some of the biraderis in the village are known by the name of their common ancestor as 'Meera Patil biraderi', 'Khond Patel biraderi' or by the place from which they have migrated to the present village and established their residence, as Bhogsa Patel biraderi (immigrants from the village called Bhogsa), 'Chigaralli Patel biraderi' (immigrant from the vilage called Chiragalli). The prefixes indicate the village from where their first ancestor came and from whom they have descended.

Mullanis are politically inferior and are considered as servicing people. Their lineages are known by the place of their origin or from the place where they have migrated here as Khondgoli, Tumkur, or in some other cases by their traditional occupation like awati (measure keepers), mulla (who offer ritual service at mosque), etc.

The political office of Mali Patel and Police Patel are considered to be of high social prestige in the village context. The members of the biraderis whose ancestors have had held one of these offices get the title'Patel' suffixed to their individual names. The term Patel with which all the members of the biraderi are addressed is not merely a form of courtesy but manifests the distinguished political status.

Those members of the Mali Patel and Police Patel lineages who do not directly hold the office but are Patels by virtue of being members of such lineages are distinguished by a suffix as had already been mentioned as 'Mali-Birader' or 'Police-Birader' as the case may be. Where as the person who holds the office and his incumbent who is no other than his own eldest son are called as' Pattedar Mali Patel' or 'Pattedar Police Patel' respectively."

Though the structure of the names-of-persons, is a Marathi one, the family name may consist of one, two, or sometimes even three words. Hence, the catalogue entry has to be prepared under the full form of the family name. In addition, it can be inferred that the surname can differ from one member of a family with the other.

In the feminine names, generally the usage of surname is not prevailing. A female name-of-person generally comprises two parts. Personal name followed by the father's or husband's name. In such a name, the entry has to be prescribed under its natural sequence.

(d) Telugu influenced names

Situated in the eastern parts of Karnataka, are the Kolar and Raichur districts. Their location being in close proximity to Andhra Pradesh, Telugu influence can vividly be seen. In the names-of-persons, there is a similarity in the structure with the same of Andhra Pradesh. Some examples of the names are given as under:

Masculine Names	**Feminine Names**
Bhat Sheshu	Karnam Suguna Pushpa
Chintarevula Gopinath Joshi	Kolahina Seetha
Joshi Murlidhar	Potturu Rangamma
Kolar Jayathirath Rao	Pujari Sudha
Lakha Shivappa	

The first part of such a name is the house name. It is followed by the personal name. In some rare instances, caste name is also added.

In a large number of cases, house name is denoted by the village name though in some others, caste name may also be used. The house name is a permanent part of the name-of-person, but is subordinate to the personal name. Among the educated persons, it is generally shortened into its initial form. Therefore, for the purposes of cataloguing, entry has to be perpared under the given name or the personal name together with the caste name, if used.

6.5.3 Prefixes

Among the Hindus, prefix titles are not in common usage. However, a prominent politician of the state, is found to possess specific prefix. This title was bestowed affectionately by the people. It has been observed that it is used in addressing, and is not employed in writing. Hence, it deserves to be excluded in cataloguing.

Example: Karnatakaputra Jagannath Rao Joshi

But, in the names-of-persons of Muslims several prefixes are used. In general, they are required to be dropped at the time of cataloguing. The guidelines given in the Muslim names under the North Indian Names are valid, in deciding the issue.

However, a complication can arise when one observes the fact that in some of the Muslim names, prefix title may be present in the name of the father or husband. As the name of the father or husband forms an integral part of the name-of-person in many cases, it is desirable that such prefix titles have to be preserved.

Examples: Mohammad Dastigir Haji Mohammad Ibrahim Shaikh
Mumtaz Begum Hakim Abdulla Sayed

6.5.4 Simplified Model

Some persons have discarded the usage of the name of the father and the village name, etc. in their names. Their names are reduced to the given names followed by the caste name. Some examples of such names are given as under:

Masculine Names	**Feminine Names**
Divaspati Hegde	Chandraprabha Urs
Jagannath Rao Joshi	Sarojini Mahishi
Ram Krishna Hegde	

If such a name-of-person belongs to the Mysore region, the caste name is to be considered subordinate with the given name, but retained in the entry. In the Marathi influenced region, the caste name is the most important part of such a name. In other words, there is a change in the potency of the words, on account of its shifting to an unconventional position.

6.5.5. Kannada names in cataloguing

Based on the above discussion, Kannada names can broadly be classified into two categories. Their description is given as under:

(i) Marathi dominated belt

It is generally the family name, employed in the end part of the name, under which the main entry has to be prepared. This is similar to the treatment given to Marathi names. However, there is an exception to it, described as under:

If a name is consisting of only two components, namely the personal name followed by the father's or husband's name, the catalogue entry has to be made under the first component, i.e. the personal name.

(ii) Non-Marathi regions

Rest of the state generally has one or the other patterns of village name-father's name-personal name or father's name-personal name or given name-caste name. In each of these cases, entry is recommended under the given name with other elements inverted in their sequence.

6.5.5.1 Problem in cataloguing

It is observed that the village name in the non-Marathi area of the state remains secondary to the names. Yet, it becomes the surname in the Marathi dominated area. Here, it is the most important part of the name-of-person. This matter can be resolved from the placement of the name of the village. If it is prefixed, it remains secondary. If it is suffixed, it acquires a very important part of the names. In most cases, the matter can be resolved. However, some persons in order to bring novelty in their names, may use the village name in the end. Similarly, migration of one part to another within the state, can bring a change in the structure of some names-of-persons. In case of any doubt, a cross-reference entry is recommended.

6.6. SOUTH INDIAN NAMES IN AACR- 2

There are a few prominent features associated with South Indian names-of-persons. Their description is given below:

(a) Use of house name

In the name of Telugu and Malayalam speaking persons, along with the inhabitants of Coorg district in Karnataka, usage of house name is prevailing. Thus, each family has a distinct house name which is used as the first component part of the names-of-persons. It is found subordinate to the other parts.

(b) Usage of village name

In the old Mysore districts of Karnataka, and Tamilnadu, usage of place name as an essential part of many names is prevailing. In Kerala, in a few names-of-persons, the name of the village is used. In

Telugu culture, many house names are the village names. Generally, the village name comes as the first part of a name and remains secondary to the other parts of the name. Yet, some persons may employ the name of their nativity in the end part of their names. Wherever may be its position, it remains subordinate to the other component parts of the names-of-persons. On the other hand, in North Karnataka, a village name is used as the surname under which the entry is to be prepared. Thus, if the name of a place is suffixed to a name, it can either be the surname as is the case in North Karnataka, or it may denote a secondary part of the name as is often the case in the other parts of Karnataka. This can cause confusion. In order to resolve the conflict, the following points be kept in view:

(i) If a shortened form of the name can be obtained, it can always be known whether the village name is used as the family name or a secondary part of the name.

(ii) If a village name is used as the surname, as is the case in the Marathi influenced region of Karnataka, father's name is also used before it. However, such a simple mechanical method of dealing with such names, may not yield correct result in all the names. For instance, if an author has dropped the name of his father, the prescription may fail. In any doubtful situation, the cataloguer is advised to prepare a cross-reference entry.

(c) Usage of father's name

In the old Mysore region of Karnataka, Tamilnadu, and Kerala, father's name is also used. If it occurs along with the place name, it generally comes in between the place name and the personal name. If no place name is used, it preceds the personal name. Yet, in some of the names of the educated persons, and in the names-of-persons from North Karnataka, the name of the father or husband succeeds the personal name. This can become a source of confusion. To resolve the conflict, the following clues can be quite effective :

(i) If the contracted name of the author can be known, either from the publication or otherwise, the name of the father or husband and other secondary parts, can be identified.

(ii) A feminine name-of-person may easily reveal the masculine personal name, denoting the name of her father or husband.

(iii) If the name of father is prefixed to a given name, it is generally abbreviated into its initial. If it is suffixed, it is often written in its full form.

(v) In the names-of-persons from northern Karnataka, family name component occurs after the name of the father or husband. As surname is the most important part of a name, entry is to be prepared under it.

(d) Use of caste surname

Family names in the entire South India, are employed very sparingly.In specific names-of-persons where they are in use, they remain subordinate to the personal names. They occupy the last position of a name. Some persons may use the caste denoting family name, prominently. If it is so, the entry has to be prepared under the surname. This is to be treated as the preference of the author. Otherwise, the given name together with the surname form the main entry elements. Yet, in the names from North Karnataka the treatment has to be different.

(e) Breaking of the personal names

In some names-of-persons, particularly belonging to the educated community, splitting the given names is resorted to. The intention is to use the last part of the personal name prominently. If the preference of the author can be known, the last part has to become the entry element. Similarly, some persons may use the last two parts of their names, prominently. In general, the author provides his preference to treat some part of his name, as the most important part. In the absence of such a preference, the entire given name is to be used as the main entry element.

(f) Use of prefix titles

Prefixes in the names are not generally used in South India. Among the Muslims, they are in use in a few names. They have to be treated in the same manner as recommended in North India. Yet, they have to be preserved if they occur in the name of father or husband, as the case may be.

(g) Arabic influened names

Names-of-persons claiming their descent from the Arab countries, make use of the conjuctures bin and bint in between their names and the name of the father. In such names, surnames may also be used, though rarely. If a surname is in use, entry is to be made under it. Otherwise, the entire name is to be rendered as such.

The following cataloguing rules have been prescribed:

S.1 With the exception of S.2 to S.6 enter a South Indian name-of-person, under the given name. The given name generally occurs in the ultimate or penultimate part of the name. If any prefix title occurs in the name, it is generally dropped except in a rare instances as described in North India. Yet, if it is employed in the name of father or husband, as the case may be, the same has to be preserved.

Examples :

Names-of-persons	**Catalogue entry**
Avul Pakir Jainulabdeen Abdul Kalam	Abdul Kalam, Avul Pakir Jainulabdeen
Chamarajanagar Subbarao Chandrasekhara	Chandrasekhara, Chamarajanagar Subbarao
Kandathil Mamman Philip	Philip, Kandathil Mamman
Shiyali Ramamrita Ranganathan	Ranganathan, Shiyali Ramamrita
Trichy Viswanathan Kartikeyan	Kartikeyan, Trichy Viswanathan

S.2 Enter a South Indian name under the combination of the personal name and the family name taken together as the entry element. The other parts of the name have to be inverted. This is valid only in respect of the names bearing surname in the end.

Examples :

Names-of-persons	**Catalogue entry**
Marri Channa Reddy	Channa Reddy, Marri
Ramakrishnan Rabindranath Menon	Rabindranath Menon, Ramakrishna
Ram Krishna Hegde	Ram Krishna Hegde

S.3 Enter a South Indian name-of-person under the last part of the name, if it forms the prominent part of the name as per the preference of the author.

Examples:

Names-of-persons	**Contracted Names**	**Entry words**
Chandrasekhar Venkata Raman	C.V. Raman	Raman
Krishna Iyer Kalyan Raman	K.K. Raman	Raman

Venkate Kurupath Narayana Menon	V.K.N. Menon	Menon

S.4 Enter a name-of-person from the southern parts of the country, under the personal name in the normal sequence if the name of his/her father or husband as the case may be, is suffixed to the personal name.

Examples :

Names-of-persons	Catalogue entry
George Jacob	George Jacob
Manorama Madhuraj	Manorama Madhuraj
Saraswathi Narayanaswami	Saraswathi Narayanaswami

S.5 Enter a South Indian name-of-person under his or her coined word, used as the pen-name, provided the person has gained his or her identity through the pen-name. The other parts of the name have to be inverted.

Examples:

Names-of-persons	Catalogue entry
Gemini Ganesan	Gemini Ganesan
Sowcar Janaki	Sowcar Janaki
Subrahmania Bharathi	Bharathi, Subrahmania

S.6 Enter a name-of-person from the Marathi influenced region of Karnataka, as per the rules of cataloguing framed for West Indian names.

Names-of-persons	Catalogue Words
Habiburrehman Abdulkarim Khan	Khan
Najirahmad Mohammadkarim Malwad	Malwad
Neela Chandrasekhar Patil	Patil
Ranganatha Ramachandra Divakar	Divakar

S.7 Enter an Arabic name-of-person under the surname if used in the end. In the absence of the family name, the entire name is to be rendered as such.

Name-of-persons	**Catalogue Entry**
Ahmed bin Mohammad Ramzan	Ahmed bin Mohammad Ramzan
Mohammad bin Abdullah Qureshi	Qureshi, Mohammad bin Abdullah
Zainath bint Abdullah	Zainath bint Abdullah

S.8 Enter a Sikh name-of-person from Andhra Pradesh into his/her personal name. The prefix title such as Sardar or Sardarni, is to be inverted.

Name-of-persons	**Catalogue Entry**
Sardar Nanak Singh	Nanak Singh, Sardar
Sardarni Hira Bai	Hira Bai, Sardarni

Chapter VII

West Indian Names

7.1 WEST INDIA

7.1.1 General

Goa, Gujarat and Maharashtra constitute West India. In addition, two union territories namely Daman and Diu, and Dadra and Nagar Haveli being situated in close proximity to Gujarat form a part of West India. The northern districts of Karnataka, by virtue of being in the vicinity of Maharashtra, are also profoundly influenced by the Marathi culture. Here, the names-of-persons, bear a close resemblence to those of the Marathis.

This demographic picture of the zone has under gone a remarkable change with a large number of Sindhis from Pakistan migrating and settling down in this part of the country. Sindhis possess a separare culture of their own, and so is their naming pattern. In addition, Parsees are also a minority group of West India.

Linguistically, West Indian zone can be divided, into the following groups :

1. Marathi - Hindus and Muslims of Maharashtra, speaking Marathi.

2. Gujarati - Hindus and Muslims of Gujarat, Dadra and Nagar Haveli and Daman and Diu, speaking Gujarati.

3. Konkani - Hindus, Muslims and Christians of Goa, speaking Konkani.

4. Sindhi - Mostly Hindus of Maharashtra and Gujarat, and nearby states speaking Sindhi.

Names-of-persons belonging to Parsee community, have been separately dealt with, although they more or less conform to the Gujarati pattern. In addition, in Goa, Daman and Diu, and Dadra and Nagar Haveli, because of a long spell of the Portuguese rule some changes have been noticed in the names-of-persons. In specific, the basis structure of the names has remained unchanged but certain words have been transformed into their Portuguese formats. Such names have been discussed under Konkani Names. Sociological investigation of the names-of-persons belonging to West India, is as follows:

7.2 MARATHI NAMES

7.2.1 General

Linguistic reorganisation of states led to the formation of the state of Maharashtra comprising Marathwada (Marathi speaking area of the former Hyderabad state), Vidarbha region of the Central Provinces and the Marathi speaking districts of the erstwhile Bombay state. Encircled by Madhya Pradesh in the north and east; Andhra Pradesh, Karnataka and Goa in the south-east, south and south-east respectively; Gujarat in the north-west and Arabian Sea in the west of the state, it sprawls over 307, 690 Sq. km. with a population of nearly 78.9 million. Religious break up of the population is 81.12% Hindus, 9.67% Muslims, 6.39% Buddhists and 1.22% Jains (Census of India 1991, 1995). Marathi is the official language of the state.

7.2.2 Names-of-persons

A Marathi name-of-person is generally made of three component parts. They appear in the sequence of given name, 'name of the father' (or husband, as the case may be), and the family name (Ranganathan, 1964). Though Buddhists and Jains of the state are separate religious groups, they too follow the culture of the Hindus besides their naming practices. In the present sub-chapter discussion of Hindu names-of-persons also includes Buddhists and Jains. Therefore, all Marathi names-of-persons, irrespective of their religious affiliations conform to the 'personal name', 'father's/husband's name' and the 'family name' structure. Some examples, to illustrate are :

Hindu Names

Masculine Names	**Feminine Names**
Atmaram Sridhar Naik	Chhaya Narayanrao Kokate
Nishikant Dhondapani Mirajkar	Nanda Shankarrao Vaidya
Manohar Sridhar Vaidya	Sunita Vitthalrao Thawre
Parsuram Krishnaji Savant	Usha Prakash Chowdhary
Purushottam Jaikrishna Deoras	
Yashwantrao Balwantrao Chavan	

Muslim Names

Masculine Names	**Feminine Names**
Abdulrazzak Mohammadshafi Punekar	Maqbool Fida Hussain
Abdul Rehman Antulay	Mehrunissa Mohammadkhalid Kotwal
Abdulsattar Muhammadismail Dalvı	Swaleha Abubakr Shaikh
Haroon Iqbal Mulegaonkar	Tahirabanoi Mohammadismail Inamdar
Kazi Tanveer Mohammad Ahmad Fakir	Tanveen Begum Haji Mohammad Mistry
Khalid Abdulhamid Ansari	Zubedakhatun Shirajuddin Parlekar
Rafiq Balumiya Zakaria	
Shahin Abdulrazzak Karmawala	

7.2.3 Use of Surnames

Family names among the Maharashtrians had perhaps existed earlier to the founding of the British rule in the country. Hundreds of years ago, several distinguished family names such as Bhosle, Gaikwad, Gokhle, Hegde, Shinde, etc. were in existence and specific Maratha families were identified by such surnames in the country.

Archaeological excavation in the state had revealed that family names such as Bhanu, Ghaisas, Pathak, and Prabhudesai were in use during the 12th century (Ketkar, 1924). However, the usage of these surnames in the names-of-persons was not seen on a large scale. During the British rule, their employment in names had picked up momentum and became popular in due course. Now, the situation is that there is hardly any Marathi family not having a surname. British influence in transforming the structure of Marathi names-of-persons, has been felt quite early. An important observation (Book review, 1887) that "as it is a fact, all over India, especially amongst the Marathas,... to make hereditary and distinctive the third appellation, and to all intents and purposes to convert it into a regular surname of European style", is quite relevant.

Though the usage of family names has increased to such an extent that almost all the Maharashtrian names-of-persons carry the same, in the intimate and close circles, persons are generally addressed and known only by their personal names. In the villages particularly, individuals are identified by their given names (Soni, 1992). However, in public life, people are usually referred to by their family names. Hence, the catalogue entry has to be made under a surname.

7.2.3.1 Types of surnames

There is a wide range of family names in Marathi culture. Compared to the number of surnames used in the Hindi speaking states such as Uttar Pradesh, Bihar, and Madhya Pradesh, Marathi family names are in abundance. As per Soni (1992), they reflect the dynamic nature of the Maharashtrian society. A Marathi family name may be denoting any one of the following features:

(a) Name of the clan;

(b) Genealogical name;

(c) Caste name;

(d) Sub-caste name;

(e) Gotra name;

(f) Profession of the ancestors;

(g) Village name;

(h) Any other quality of the ancestors (good or bad), etc.

1. Village Name as Surname

The usage of village name as a family name, had come only after facilities for mass-transportation were developed and enlarged. This resulted in increasing the mobility of the common men to other areas. People were generally recognised by their territorial origin and subsequently, the names of those places had taken the shape of their family names. There are three practices of forming the surnames. They are described as under (Soni, 1992):

(a) 'kar' implying 'resident of' is added to a village name to form the surname;

(b) Place names are used as such, without any change; and

(c) 'e' is added at the end to form the surname.

This category of Marathi surnames derived from nativity, is very widely employed. A sample of such family names is given below :

Akolkar	Khandekar	Nagpurkar
Ambedkar	Laturkar	Narlikar
Aurangabadkar	Mumbaikar	Punekar

There are several classes of family names derived from the place names. They are described as under (Soni, 1992) :

(a) Names of the disappeared villages - such as Ajramkar;

(b) Surnames derived from the obsolete place names.

Some names of the places have undergone change over a long period of time, and now they are known by their new names. Yet, the family names denoting the old place names are continuing, and are not affected by the change in their nomenclature. Some examples of such surnames are:

Name of the place	**New place name**	**Surname**
Devgiri	Daultabad	Devgirikar
Khadgicha	Aurangabad	Khadgikar

(c) Present place names used as family names

<u>Examples</u>: Kolhapurkar, Nagarkar, Nagpurkar or Nagpure

(d) Pilgrimage place names used as surnames

It has been presumed that some ancestor of the bearer might have undertaken pilgrimage to a particular holy place and in this way, the name of the religious place has come to be associated with the family name. In some instances, the holy city may be located outside the state.

Examples: Kashikar, Paithankar, Ramteke

(e) Province names as family names

Examples : Bangale, Kanade, Maharashtre

(f) Names of places situated outside the state are also used as family names. Their examples are given as under:

Ahmedabadkar, Dehlikar, Indorekar, Kanpurkar, Mysorekar

2. Gotra name as surname (Soni, 1992)

Examples : Atri, Bharadwaj, Kashyap, Viswamitra

Some gotra names have been suitably converted into regular surnames. Examples are given as under :

Gotra Name	**Surname**
Akashayeya	Akashe
Bhabhravya	Barve
Chaitra	Chitre
Devadatya	Dev
Fanta	Phatak
Gokali	Gokhale
Kapura	Kapre
Kauravya	Karve
Pingal	Pingale
Somyani	Soman
Vyghra	Wagh

3. Community denoting surnames

Some surnames denoting caste affiliations of the persons are also used. For instance, the following are a few such family names used among the Brahmins:

Bhatt, Joshi, Pandit

In addition, there are some family names denoting the royal background of the bearer. The royal status of the family may be real or other wise. Similarly, it may represent the present status, immediate past one or sometimes, even earlier. A sample of such surnames is given as under (Soni, 1992):

Bhosle	Kadam	Shalivahan
Baghel	Kalchuri	Shilahar or Rathod
Bundela or Bundele	Maurya	Shishodia
Chandel	Palve	Solanki
Chavan	Parmar	Tanwar
Gaikwad	Peshwe or Peshwa	Yadav or Jadhav
Gehlot	Pritihar	
Holkar	Rastrakut or Rathod	

4. Profession representing surnames

Sometimes, family names denoting occupation or profession of one's ancestors, are also used. There are several classes of this category of the family names, described as under (Soni, 1992):

(a) Surnames denoting agricultural occupations such as

Family Name	**Other form**	**Meaning**
Kapase	Kapuskar	Cotton grower
Mali		Gardener
Phulkar	Phulare	Flower grower
Phulmali		Gardener dealing in flower growing

(b) Caste representing occupations

Surname	Other form	Meaning
Bhandekar		Copper vessel maker
Chambhare		Cobbler
Dhangare	Mendhe	Goat rearing
Gandhe		Perfume dealer
Gavali		Milkman
Kumbhare		Earthen pot maker
Maske		Buffalo rearing
Nakshine		Art work
Nahvi		Barber
Wadhai	Sutar	Carpenter
Vani		General merchant

(c) Precision professions

Family Name	Meaning
Dalal	Commission agent
Nanavati	Precious coin examiner
Parkhi	Precious ornament evaluator
Ratnaparekh	Evaluator of precious stones
Saroff	Gold and silver ornament dealer
Simpi	Tailor
Sonare	Goldsmith
Tambat	Coppersmith

5. Surnames denoting official positions of the ancestors

They are grouped in the following classes (Soni, 1992):

(a) Military positions

Family Name	Meaning
Gadkari	Security personnel of a fort.
Gadnis	Fort inspector.
Hazare	Incharge of one thousand personnel.
Killedar	Chief officer of a fort.
Kotwal	Officer in a fort.
Sardar	Senior Military officer.
Surnobat	Commander in chief.
Subhedar	Equivalent of the present Major General.
Topkhane	Ammunition store incharge.

(b) Administrative positions

Family Name	Meaning
Khagasiwale	Personal Secretary.
Samant	Chief of administration.
Vyavahare	Business-man of high reputation.

(c) Economic positions

The following family names denoting specific economic positions, during the far-off days, are in usage:

Amin	Jamdar	Potnis
Bakshi	Khazindar	Sarpotdar
Dange	Majumdar	Tankhiwale
Jakatkar	Potdar	

(d) Judicial positions such as Adalatwale, Dandadhikari, Lalkacheriwale, and so on.

(e) Clerical positions as family names. An illustration of the same is given as under:

Chitnis	Hasnavis	Kotnis	Sabnis
Daftardar	Kalamdane	Moharrir	Surnis

Hajarnavis	Karkhanis	Parasnis	Vakenavis
Harkare	Khasnavis	Peshkar	Vakil

(f) Village positions

Surname	**Meaning**
Choudhury	Helper to a Patil.
Desai	Deputy collector.
Deshmukh	Deputy collector.
Deshpande	Senior accountant in a village.
Ghatpande	Incharge of highways.
Grampande	Chief priest.
Inamdar	Recipient of a land-revenue free land.
Jahagirdar	Having major land-holdings in a village.
Jamindar	Land lord.
Kulkarni	Village accountant.
Mirasdar	Person who has inherited lot of land.
Pande	Learned and respected Brahmin.
Patil	Village head.
Sardesai	Collector.
Sardeshmukh	Collector.

6. Surnames denoting religious, superstitious, and other rituals (Soni, 1992):

Surname	**Meaning**
Acharya	A teacher in Vedas.
Agnihotri	Expert in performing yagna.
Avadhani	Specialist in meditation.
Chobey	Full command over all the four Vedas.
Dubey	Knowing at least two Vedas.
Dikshit	One who has received higher education.

Kshottriya	One who is well versed in Vedas.
Mahamuni	Chief of a group of Sadhus.
Maheshkar	Priest in a Shiva temple.
Muni	Another name for a Sadhu.
Pandit	Euridite Brahmin.
Paranjapaye	Expert in Japa.
Pathak	One who recites religious texts.
Puranik	Specialist in Puranas.
Purohit	One who performs religious rituals.
Rishi	First person who had recited Mantras.
Sadhu	One who has renounced the world.
Sant	Gentle person.
Shastri	Expert in the Hindu Shashtras.
Tapas	Shorter form of Tapasavi.
Tapasavi	Who has performed penance.
Tatvagyani	Expert in logic.
Upadhyaya	Teacher.
Vedanti	Specialist in Vedas.
Vedpathak	Teacher in Vedas.
Yagye or Yagnik	Specialist in performing yagna.
Yogeshwar	Expert in Yoga.

7. In addition, the following features or words are employed as family names (Soni, 1992)

(a) Title denoting such as Chakravorty, Chhatrapati, Samant, Rao or Rawat, etc.

(b) Words denoting bravery and valour such as Atulbali, Bahadure, Bhujaval, Mahabale, Randhir, Randive, Ranjit, Rânpise, Ranvagure, etc.

(c) Educational attainments such a Buddhisagar, Pandit, Sahastrabudhe, Vachaspati, Vidyasagar, and so on.

(d) Literary, arts and science related features such as Chitre, Gayak, Natake, Vignyane, etc.

(e) Names of trees, and plants such as Bhajikhaye, Gajare, Parole, Vange, and so on.

(f) Animal names such as Belle, Dhore, Ghode, Harne, Kesari, Singh, Wagh, etc.

(g) Names of birds such as Baghle, Hansraj, Popate, Rajhans, and so on.

(h) Words denoting emotions such as Date, Dheryawan, Vinod and so on (Ketkar, 1924).

(i) Words denoting colours such as Gore, Hirve, Kale, Karde, and Pivale.

(j) Vulgar words such as Hagware, Jhavakire, Lavde, Nalwade, and so on (Ketkar, 1924).

7.2.3.2 Double-worded surnames

In addition to the family names described above, there are some double worded family names used in the state (Belsare, 1960). A sample of such surnames is given as under :

S. No.	Description	Example(s)
(a)	Surname prefixed by the gotra	Vatsa-Joshi
(b)	Family names prefixed by the village name	Jatkar-Kulkarni Nagpurkar-Deshpande Tokekar-Joshi
(c)	Surname prefixed by the hereditary title	Naik-Nimbalkar
(d)	Family name suffixed by the place name	Joshi-Kharshikar Peth-Guhagarkar Shah-Wagdarikar
(e)	Surname suffixed by a word/title such as buva, ji, or Shastri	Aphlebuva Bhatkhandeshastri Khuperkarshastri Kohhatkarbuva Pathakji Sharmaji

In the above category of the surnames, generally both the words have to be taken as the entry words. However, buva, or ji if occurring in a family name, has to be ignored as it denotes a courtesy term. Shastri should be considered as an essential and irremovable word.

7.2.3.3 Anglicised family names

The British rule in the country has affected a few family names in the state. A sample of such surnames is given below:

Vernacular family name	**Anglicised surname**
Nayak	Naik
Shinde	Sindia

7.2.3.4 Change of surname

In exceptional cases, specific family names are changed. Generally, there are two main reasons for doing so, described as under :

(a) If the surname is conveying a bad or vulgar meaning, it can be changed to a new form, and the new form is used afterwards.

(b) If the family has shifted to some other village, a surname denoting the new place name is used, and in this way, a new family name is emerged.

7.2.4 Muslim Names

Muslims form the minority in the state. They however, have the same structure of names as do the Hindus viz, first is the 'given name', followed by the 'father's or the husband's name'. Family name comes last, and is the most important component, that establishes his identity

7.2.4.1 Surnames

As in the Hindu society, there are also several sources of obtaining the surnames among the Marathi Muslims. Important among them are described as under :

(a) Village name as surname

Among the Marathi Muslims, quite a few family names are derived from the place names but, on a lessor scale, compared to the Hindus. An illustration of such family names is given under :

Malegaonkar, Parkar, Punekar, Surve or Survekar

(b) Position titles such as Desai, Hakim, Inamdar, Jamadar, Tehsildar, etc.

(c) Occupational descriptors

Some family names are denoting the occupational names. There are two broad classes of this category, as enumerated below :

(i) Commercial occupations representing terms such as Attar (i.e. Perfume seller), Baghwan (Gardener), Maniyar (Glass bangle merchant), Tamboli (Betal leaves dealer), and so on

(ii) Religious profession terms: such as Imam (i.e. the person administering the holy prayer), Mulla (Person having lower status than Imam), Kazi (A judicial person), etc.

(iii) Terms denoting the family background: like Sayyid, Shaikh, Khan, Pathan, etc.

7.2.4.2 Prefixes

Prefix titles in the Muslim names-of-persons are not in wide usage. If they are used, they are to be dropped in rendering or preserved as recommended in Muslim names. However, if a prefix occurs in the name of father or husband, the same be retained. The examples are :

Names-of-person	**Catalogue entry**
Kazi Tanveer Murad Fakir	Fakir, Tanveer Murad
Razia Begum Haji Hasan Lonawala	Lonawala, Razia Begum Haji Hasan

7.2.4.3 Change of Female name after marriage

Total change of a name of a female may occur in a large number of cases as a consequence of marriage. Thus, a Muslim girl with the maiden name 'Sayyara Mohammadhussain Sayyid' after marriage with Dilshad Omar Inamdar, has become 'Suraiyya Dilshad Inamdar'.

7.3 GUJARATI NAMES

7.3.1 General

The present state of Gujarat has been carved out of the composite Bombay state on May 1, 1960 as a result of implementing the Bombay Reorganisation Act, 1960. It includes all the Gujarati speaking districts. The residual portion of the then Bombay state was renamed as Maharashtra. Extending over an area of about 1.96,024 sq. kms., Gujarat has a population of approximately 41.3 million. Hindus are in overwhelming majority (89.48%) followed by Muslims (8.73%). Jains are about 1.19%. In addition, 12, 924 Parsees also live in the state (Census of India 1991, 1995).

Located on the west coast, the state has a frontier with Pakistan in the north-west and is adjoined by Rajasthan, M.P and Maharashtra in the north-east, south and south-east respectively. The Arabian Sea lies in the West and South of Gujarat. Gujarati is the official language of the state.

7.3.2 Names-of persons

In the names-of-persons from Gujarat, father's name or the name of husband, in case of a married woman, always succeeds the given name. Usage of family names on the pattern of Western surnames, as the last part of the name is very much in vogue. Thus, the structure of a Gujarati name is 'Given Name - Father's Name - Family Name' (Sengupta, 1974b).

Examples : **Hindu Names:**

Masculine Names	**Feminine Names**
Bhabubhai Jethabhai Patel	Haku Vajubhai Shah
Chandrakant Maganlal Mehta	Hansa Jivraj Mehta
Gautam Shantilal Nanavaty	Leena Ambalal Sarabhai
Harindra Jayant Dave	Maniben Vallabhbhai Patel
Mohanlal Lalloobhai Dantwale	Mrinalini Vikram Sarabhai
Satishchandra Virchand Ghatalia	

Muslim Names

Masculine Names	**Feminine Names**
Ahmed Mohammadbhai Patal	Aminabano Mohmedamin Bhagar
Ameerkhan Sherkhan Patel	Laduben Mohame dkareem Jhaveri
Dostmohmed Hasanali Merchant	Rashidabai Abdulkhaleel Gandhi
Gulanabi Fatehbhai Momen	Shafiabai Abdulrahim Bohra

Halmohmed Vallmohmed Ngorwala

Mohmadirfan Yusufbhai Pocha

Mohmedramjanbhai Abdul Rehman

Ramzanali Noormohmed Momin

Yahya Abdulhussain Gandhi

7.3.2.1 Hindu Surname

There are several sources of Gujarati family names. Some of them are common with the same of Marathis (Soni, 1992). In specific, different surnames were drawn from the under-mentioned sources :

(a) Official position occupied by the ancestors;

(b) Mughul title conferred on some ancestor;

(c) Occupational descriptor of the fore-fathers;

(d) Names of birds, insects and animals;

(e) Given names of ancestors;

(f) Village or locality name;

(g) Caste/profession names.

(a) Official position as surname

A variety of positions occupied by individuals, a couple of centuries ago, have become a source of family names. However, it is surprising that many of these positions do not exist now, the surnames derived from them are still continued. A sample of such surnames is given given here.

Surname	**Meaning**
Amin	Land revenue inspector
Chaudhury	Big landlord
Desai	Head of a Pargana
Diwan	Minister or an administrator
Kamdar	Government official
Kothari	Grain and food store keeper
Mehta	Document writer/clerk

Mazumdar	Accountant in the Revenue Department
Mody	Grain store-keeper
Patel	Village headman
Patwari	Land revenue clerk

(b) Mughul title as family name

Mughul titles bestowed on distinguished persons, many years ago, are no longer used as surnames. However, as an exception only one such title is found to be employed as a family name.

Example : Badshah

c) Occupational descriptors as surnames

In addition, several occupation descriptors are employed to denote some family names. It is amusing to note that these occupations undertaken by the fore-fathers of the bearer, do not generally represent the current occupation of the family. Some such surnames are:

Surname	Short/other form	Meaning
Bari	Banker	Money lender
Dalal	Broker	Commission agent
Doshi		Cloth merchant
Gajjar		Meson
Gandhi		General merchant
Jhaveri		Gem and jewellery dealèr
Kanvi		Farmer
Kapadia		Cloth merchant
Lokhandwala	Lohana	Iron merchant
Parekh		Gold purety evaluator
Shah		Petty money lender
Sheth		Big businessman
Sharoff		Precious metal orna ments dealer
Vora		Oil merchant

(d) Animal, bird, and insect names as surnames

Another category of surnames is one in which names of certain animals, birds or insects are adopted as family names. Some examples of such surnames are given below:

Surname	Meaning
Ghoda	Horse
Hathi	Elephant
Popat	Parrot
Makkad	Insect

(e) Caste denoting surnames

Certain surnames denoting the caste affiliations of the bearer, are also in use. A sample of such family names used by Brahmins is given below :

Audicha	Dikshit	Padhya	Trivedi
Bhatt	Doshi	Pandya	Upadhyaya
Chaturvedi	Dwivedi	Purohit	Vyas
Dave	Joshi	Tripathy	

(f) Place name used as surname

Place names, with or without modifications are used to a limited extent, as surnames in the state. Investigations reveal that it is only after a family has moved out to a new place, the name of the earlier village or locality is used as the family name, discarding the original surname of the family.

Examples:	Surname	Derivation
	Betal	Migrating from Bet
	Jamkhambia	Belonging to Jhamkhamba
	Joshipura	Name of a locality
	Miroliwala	Resident of Miroli
	Surati	Originating from Surat

(g) Given name of a forefather as surname

In some specific families, if a member has excelled in his performance in a particular area, the personal name of such a person is adopted as the surname by his family. In such families, a change in surname may take place, if the event has occurred in recent times. A sample of such family names is given below :

Family Name	Explanation
Lalbhai	A short form of Ambalal
Sarabhai	Name of an ancestor

Official positions, occupation descriptors, village names or the personal names of the fore-fathers wherever used as family names are very generic in nature. Therefore, many families even unrelated and often unknown to each other, have common surnames. Sometimes, families adhering to different religious sects may be employing the same set of surnames. Hence, in many instances, it is not possible to determine the caste or even the religion of the bearer from a family name.

Further, most of the families today, may not be engaged in the specific profession or the occupation as represented by the family name. Similarly, if the family name is based on the official position, a family member seldom occupies that particular position at present.

7.3.2.2 Change of Surname

It is observed that in most of the families, surnames remain unchanged in spite of a change in occupation, profession or residence, etc. However, in rare instances, surnames are changed so as to represent the present scenerio. For example, specific occupational descriptors in the English language, became recently, surnames and their earlier family names were abandoned.

Examples :	Banker	Contractor	Engineer
	Broker	Doctor	Merchant

7.3.2.3 Shortening of Surnames

A solitary instance has come to our notice in which the family name was shortened. It is listed as under :

Zoon

7.3.2.4 Double worded surnames

Ranganathan (1964) has described the existence of several double worded family names in Gujarat. listed as below :

Abhang Homji	Kashi Parekh	Vaidya Shastri
Bhrugu Shastri	Kathiavad Divanji	Varmani Thanki
Jhaver Laxmichandvala	Pestan Jampsa	
Kankani Thanki	Shamal Becharvala	
Kara Kalyanavala	Vachchha Gandhi	

In this context, it is observed that the practice of using two worded family names is perhaps not in vogue now, as not even a single double worded surname was obtained from a sample of more than 1000 Gujarati names-of-persons, collected for the present work. Hence it may be concluded that either the double worded surnames have now been given up or their usage might be negligible.

7.3.3 Given names

A personal name in Gujarat is rendered as a single word entity. In the earlier times, most of the personal names were compound, which were terminating with -chand, -das, -lal, -mal, etc. The present generation names are simple and may not contain the auxiliary. Hence, from the placement, each component can be ascertained easily.

7.3.3.1 Usage of bhai, ben, and ji

It is observed that quite a few given names of men and women in Gujarat terminate at bhai or its feminine ben meaning brother and sister. Though similar suffixes of respect are also used in several other parts of the country, their use is confined to only in addressing others. In Gujarati culture, these suffixes form an integral part of the personal names, in many instances. Hence they can not be omitted. Similarly, many given names are ending with 'ji' which is again, to be retained as it forms an inseparable part of some Gujarati names.

7.3.4 Structure of names

Apart from the normal structure of 'Given name - Father's name Surname' among the Gujaratis, some persons have discarded the use of family name in their names. Such names bear only two parts namely the given name and the father's name (Ranganathan, 1964)

Examples: Chinubhai Chimanbhai

Jayakrishna Harivallabhdas

Shitanshu Yashaschandra

Family names were not in popular use in Gujarat before the turn of the century. The names-of-persons during that period had only two component parts. They were "Given Name - Father's Name". Another pattern also exists which is due to Tamil influence, under which the name of the father is preceded by the given name and no family name is used. As the name of the father and the given name are drawn from the same reservoir, it is difficult for a cataloguer to identify each component, correctly.

Example: Kailachand Ambalal

7.3.4.1 Dropping of father's name

In certain names of educated persons, the usage of the name of father (or husband) in their names has been discarded, retaining the surname. Thus, the sequence of their names become 'Given name - Surname'.

Examples:	**Masculine Names**	**Feminine Names**
	Ashok Mehta	Naina Dalal
	Shivkumar Joshi	Premlabai Chavan

7.3.5 Use of Takhallus

In addition to the usual three parts in a name-of-person, certain educated persons employ some literary name under which all their writings are published. It is observed that the pen-name on account of popularity, becomes a very important part of the name. Hence, the cataloguer is compelled to choose the same for main entry. A sample of such names is given below :

Name-of-person	**Catalogue entry**
Tribhuvandas Purushottamdas Luhar Sundaram	Sundaram
Junabhai Ratanji Desai Snharashmi	Snharashmi

7.3.6 Employment of prefixes

It is surprising to note that caste or profession derived prefixes often used in the neighbouring states, are not in wide usage in the names-of-persons. However, in rare instances, some prefixes are used. A sample of such titles is given as under:

Mahajan, Nagarsheth, Sresti

As the usage of the prefixes is restricted in addressing others, they do not form part of the names. Hence they deserve to be ignored at the time of cataloguing.

7.3.7 Western Transformed Names

Among some educated persons, it has virtually become a common practice to contract the personal and/or father's names into initials leaving the last part alone in full. This is to be taken as the author's preference by the cataloguer in deciding the entry word. Such names-of-persons have been grouped under the Western transformed category. Examples of such names are given below :

M.K. Gandhi, K.M. Munshi

7.3.8 Muslim Names

Gujarati Muslims have been classified into several sects. Prominent among them are Bohra, Khoja and Momin. Khoja in fact is a Sindhi word which has originated from Khwajah. Its meaning is a trader. They are believed to be converts from the Hindu Caste, Bhatia (Sinha, 1994a). Similarly, Momin is another business community. It is also known as Meman. They are converts to Islam from the Multani Hindu castes (Sinha, 1994b).

7.3.8.1 Names-of-persons

Gujarati Muslim names-of-persons, have the same structure as those of the Hindus. The usual sequence again is 'Given Name - Father's Name - Surname". Similarly, a female carries the name and surname of her father till her marriage. Thereafter, both of them are replaced by their equivalents in the husband's name.

7.3.8.2 Muslim Surnames

There are several types of surnames employed in Muslim families, described as under:

(1) Surnames denoting sect or sub-sect such as Bohra, Momin (or Memon), Khoja

(2) Official positions occupied by the fore-fathers such as Amin, Patel, etc.

(3) Occupation names of the ancestors such as Dalal, Gandhi, Jhaveri, Kapadia, and so on.

(4) Family names derived from place names such as Dahudwala, Madraswala, Nagori, Nagpurwala;

(5) Surnames representing the present occupation such as Bandookwala, Chattaiwala, Hingwala, Panwala;

(6) Their family names before conversion such as Chauhan, Makwana, Mansuri, Solanki (Sinha, 1994b).

(7) Nick name of an ancestor such as Chagla.

7.3.8.3 Given Names

Given names of Muslims are single worded. This has been despite two or more different words put together to form compound names. Most of the personal names are religious, and are drawn from the 99 names of God, another 99 names of the Prophet, and some other names described in the Holy books.

Several Muslim names in Gujarat may also include bhai or bhai or ji as integral part of the personal name. This is due to the influence of the Hindu culture. As they are permanent parts of the names, they have to be retained.

7.3.8.4 Change of name after marriage

Similar to the practice prevailing among the Gujarati Hindus, a female generally carries her father's name and the surname of her family. After her marriage, the name and surname of the father are replaced by those of the husband. However, her personal name, unlike in the Hindu society, is not changed as a consequence of marriage, in most of the cases.

7.3.8.5 Names without surname

In addition to the pattern of names described above, there exists another pattern among the Muslims in which no surname is used. These names are usually belonging to those people whose families have migrated from Hindi or Punjabi speaking area, in recent times. The sequence in such a name is "Given Name - Father's Name". Further, the name of the father is broken into two parts, and the second part, a resultant of the split, is used as if it were a family name, though it is only an insignificant part of the father's name. However, usage of this word is confined to the name of his wife and children. In the names of grand children, or of the wives of sons, it is never used.

Example: Muhemedahmed Abdul Rasheed

7.3.8.6 Prefixes in Names

Muslim names in Gujarat, sometimes, carry specific prefix titles. These titles usually pertain to a religious function such as completion of Haj. Such prefix titles are generally ignored. Yet, if such a prefix is used in the name of the father or husband (the middle part), it has to be preserved.

7.3.8.7 Hindu practices in Muslim names

As the name of the father is present in a traditional Gujarati name, it is observed that in the name-of-person who is a late convert to Islam, carries the name of his father (which is a Hindu name), as such. Thus, to a layman, it may look ridiculous, as one part of such a name is a pure Islamic name, whereas the other part is a Hindu component.

Example : Ahmed Haridas Solanki (Sinha, 1994d).

7.4 KONKANI NAMES

7.4.1 General

Goa, a tiny emerald land on the West Coast, is the 25th state of the Union of India. In December 1961, it along with Daman and Diu, was liberated from 451 years of colonial rule of the Portuguese. In May 1987, it was made a separate state, and with this, its over land districts of Daman and Diu were delinked to form a separate Union Territory. Konkani is the official language of the state, though Marathi is also used quite extensively. The state occupies an area of 3702 sq. km. with a population of 11.70 lakhs. Hindus constitute the majority (64.68%) followed by the Catholic Christians (29.86%), and the remaining are mostly Muslims (5.25 %) (Census of India 1991, 1995).

7.4.2 Names-of-persons

Persons of Goa generally follow the structure of their names belonging to West India. In specific, there is a similarity with the Marathi names-of-persons. The first component of a name is the personal name. It is followed by the the name of father or husband in respect of a married female. The family name which is common to all the members of a family is denoted in the end (Shirodkar, et. al., 1993). In terms of potency, surname is the most important component part of any name. An illustration of the names-of-persons is given as under :

Hindu Names

Masculine Names	Feminine Names
Caxiram Raghunta Swar	
Chanrakant Anil Naik	Shashikala Gurudutt Kakodkar
Laxman Ganpat Gaonkar	Shobha Vasant Kaneker

Christian Names

Masculine Names	Feminine Names
Franscisco Xavier Cardozo	Amelina D'Souza
Frollano Carmelino Machado	Clara Amelia Nunes Fernandes
Luis Alex d'Fernandes	Jane Cynthia de Souza
Oscar Oliver Dias	Lavina Maria Coelha

Muslim Names

Masculine Names	Feminine Names
Budan Ashraf Shaikh	Razia Khatun Abdul Majid Shaikh
Janoddin Mohammad Dossa	Syed Aminabee Abdul Hafiz
Mohammad Ahmad Khan	
Shaik Faquir Abdul Ahmad	

7.4.3 Surnames

There is a variety of family names employed in the state. For instance, many surnames are the modified form of the village names (Supner, 1993b). They generally end with 'kar'. In this respect, it is observed that family names were introduced many years ago, and the villages whose names were employed to form the surnames, may not exist now, or their names might have gone through a change over a long period of time. Still, the surnames derived from the village names are continued. Enquiry revealed that many of the persons do not have any ties with the village. An illustrative sample of such family names is given as under :

Azgaonkar	Halankar	Lotlikar	Setkar
Bandekar	Harmalkar	Palienkar	Setkar
Bandodkar	Kalekar	Pednekar	Shirodkar
Borkar	Kakodkar	Potkar	Tirodkar
Chodankar	Kerkar	Siolkar	Vernekar
Coingotkar	Kudaskar	Salgaonkar	Uskaikar

Specific surnames may also represent specific positions, occupied by the ancestors, hundreds of years ago. Though some of these have become obsolete now, they are still being employed as surnames. The following family names are quite popular among the Hindus. Their connotations as understood at the time of their origin, have been provided.

Family Names	**Meaning**
Dessai	Head of a Pargana
Kamat	Agriculture supervisor
Kulkarni	Land record clerk
Nayak or Naik	Head of a caste group
Patil	Village headman
Sardessai	Higher official than Dessai

The above listed family names denote the official status of the fore-fathers, and in the present context, they may not carry any such importance.

In addition, some family names were also derived from the caste affiliations of the Hindus. A sample of the surnames used by the Brahmins, is given as under :

Acharya	Parajpe	Shivasharma
Barve	Phadke	Sidhye
Devasharma	Prabhu	Sihastrabudhe
Gokhle	Sane	Umariye
Lomasharma	Shenai	Vaze

In the above list of the family names of the Brahmins, Devasharma, Lomasharma, and Shivasharma are used as family names by Saraswat Brahmins. Similarly, among the Chitpavan Brahmins, surnames such as Barve, Gokhle, Parajpe, Phadke, Sane, Sidhaye, Sahastrabudhe, and Vaze are in popular use (Periera, 1940).

Surnames may also be connected with specific interesting past anecdotes. For instance, in the Velip caste, several family names and their origin are given as below (Biswas, 1993) :

Velip:-Those people whose ancestors worshiped in the temple (of Mallikarjun) in the early period.

Gaonkar:- Those people whose ancestors settled in Gaon (village).

Vaiz:- Means a medicine man. The ancestors of these were Vaidyas.

Zarkar:- Zara means a fountain. The ancestors of these people lived near a fountain.

Maulikar:- Mauli is a tree. Plates for taking food are made of Mauli leaves. The ancestors of these people lived near a Mauli tree.

Kankar:- It is believed that once a person caught a specific variety of the fish which was known as Kanaro. A passer by asked, "who caught Kanaro?" The person answered that it was his and since then his descendants are known as Kankar.

Ghataukar:- Cattles are taken to the pasture and assembled in a shady place where there is water. Such a place is called Ghatau in Konkani. Ghataukar originated from that situation.

Dahikar:- The word was probably derived from those who prepared curds (dahi) from milk.

Ramudkar:- These people had come from a place called Ramud, about 70 kms away from Shristhal.

Sometimes, a conferred royal title on some natives by the earlier Muslim rulers is also used as a family name. The title is purely Indian in its appearance, and is not found in any other part of the country. It is used independently, as well as in combination to the local surname.

Examples: Prataprao or Pratap Rao

Prataprao Sardessai or Pratap Rao Sar Dessai

There exists a few multi-worded family names. A sample of such surnames is given as under :

Sinai Borker

Sinai Bhobe Cacule

7.4.4 Portuguese impact

More than 451 years of the Portuguese rule over the state has influenced a few Hindu names. In this process, some specific words are found to have been transformed into their new formats. These forms are employed with their vernacular equivalents almost in an interchangeable basis. An illustration of such names is given as under :

Vernacular word	Portuguese transformation
Kamat	Camolin
Kashiram	Caxiram
Sawant	Sawal

7.4.5 Christian surnames

Because of the long spell of the colonial rule of the Portuguese, conversion on a massive scale, from various castes of Hindus including Saraswat Brahmins, had taken place in the state. Since the Portuguese belonged to the Roman Catholic Church, the converted families also belonged to the same Church. Therefore, almost all Christians in the state are Roman Catholics. In this context it may be mentioned that though the process of conversion had occurred several hundred years ago, the caste status of the families as it had existed in the Hindu society before conversion has continued unchanged even afterwards (Rao, 1993c). Thus, a variety of occupational groups known in the Hindu society, by their castes, like Carpenters, Fishermen, Mahars, Washermen, and so on, are also found among the Catholic Christians of Goa. They mostly carry their Portuguese surnames given to their fore- fathers at the time of conversion, by the missionaries (Rao, 1993a). The surnames were adopted irrespective of the original caste affiliations, occupations, or places of residence, etc. Therefore caste association can not be identified from a Catholic surname. An illustration of the Portuguese surnames are given below :

Albuquerque	Coutinho	Lobo	Rebello
Alemao	Cunha	Lopes	Rodrigues
Alvares	Dias	Martins	Sa
Barbosa	Faleiro	Mascarenhas	Saldanha

Cabral	Fernandes	Mello	Sequeira
Carvalho	Furtado	Mendonca	Silva
Cardozo	Gaude	Mendes	Silveria
Coelho	Goes	Nogueira	Souza
Colaco	Godinho	Noronha	Velho
Correia	Gomes	Pereira	
Costa	Gonsalves	Rato	

In the above category of the Portuguese family names, it is observed that very often a prefix "de" is also used before a Christian surname. In usage, it conveys belonging to. Yet, as its consequence, the surname becomes double worded and both the parts are used. However, the prefix title does not have a place value, and hence at the time of filing, its existence is ignored.

After liberation of Goa, another trend has emerged in which many persons are employing d' in place of de. In this way, de Souza and d'Souza are the variants of Soza, and they are in usage in an interchangeable basis.

Another category of the surnames of the Catholics is the one in which the family has retained its old vernacular surname and in addition, a Portuguese surname has been added. In this way, two worded surnames exist in the Catholics of Goa.

e.g. Lobo-Prabhu or Lobo Prabhu

Sequeira-Shenoy or Sequeira Shenoy

De Souza-Kamath or D'Souza Kamath

Apart from the above categories of the Christian family names, some families in rare cases, preferred to continue with their original vernacular surnames. Such surnames, in other words have not been affected by the conversion into Christianity. In this context, it is observed that such surnames are generally derived from the village names.

Examples : Borkar, Gaunekar, Goankar

7.4.6 Change of a Female Name after Marriage

As a matter of tradition, family names in Goa including those of the Christians, are passed on the male line, from father to sons (Rao,

1993c). Females on the other hand, employ their father's family name till their marriage. After marriage, it is replaced by the same of her husband and her maiden surname is abandoned. In this respect, it may be stated that in a two worded surname in usage, its full form is employed as the surname in the name of daughter or wife, as the case may be. If the name of a female contains the name of the father also, it is noted that even that is also generally replaced by the personal name of the husband or, in a few cases, it is completely abandoned.

In addition to the prevailing practices described above, which are widely employed in a very large number of females, there exists yet another practice, though seen sparingly in which a female retains her maiden name in full measures and also adds the surname of her husband in the end. In order to do so, a conjecture "E" is used between the two surnames. Two examples found are given below :

Cynthia D'Souza E Nogueira

Enna Emerda Afonsa e Desa

7.4.7 Structure of Names

Among the Catholics too, the name of the father may be used as the middle component part of a name (Shirodkar, et. al., 1993). The element before it is the given name and the element following it is the surname. The under-mentioned examples are pertaining to such names:

Masculine Names	**Feminine Name**
Franscisco Luis Gomes	Maria Jou Fernandes
Jose Custodio de Faria	

However, during the last few decades, the practice of using the name of the father or husband, as the case may be, in the Christian names-of-persons is declining. The new practice is to employ two names for a person. They are generally known as first and the second names. Both of them appear in successive sequence, and in any single personal name, the sequence is fixed. In the educated persons, the middle part is very often converted into its initial form. In this respect, it is observed that the second name though employed in subordination to the first name, there are several names where reverse order is discernible. In other words, names with either of the two in any order can be formed.

e.g. Franscisco Xavier Cardozo
Xavier Franscisco Fernandes

7.4.8 Muslim Names

Muslims form a small minority. They are educationally less advanced as compared to the other two religious groups. Two sects of them are found in the state. They are Sunni and Shia. Sunnis constitute the bulk majority of the Muslims. There are seven endogamous subdivisions used to denote family names. They are listed as under (Supner, 1993a):

Aga, Baig, Fakir, Khan, Khwaja, Mirza, and Syed

The structure of the Muslim names-of-persons is however, the same as existing in the Hindu names. The first component part is the given name followed by the father's name and the family name in that order. The surname may represent the sect or the group in some cases, whereas village names are also employed in others. An illustration of a few names is given as under :

Masculine Names	**Feminine Name**
Budan Ashraf Shaikh	Razia Khatun Abdul Majid Shaikh
Mohammad Ahmed Khan	
Janoddin Mohammad Dossa	

7.4.8.1 Portuguese influences

Portuguese influence on Muslim names-of-persons can also be noticed from the fact that a few prominently employed words have been transformed into Portuguese form. An illustration of such words, is given as under :

Vernacular Words	**Portuguese equivalents**
Syed	Soid
Khan	Can
Shaik	Xec

7.4.9.1 Names without surname

There are names-of-persons not having the family names. Yet. as an exception, some persons disect the name of their father and use the second part of the personal name of the father as if it were a family name.

Examples: Shaik Faquir Shaik Adam

Sayed Aminabee Abdul Hafiz

Sayed Kasim Abdul Hafiz

Muslims of Goa also possess a variety of caste groups based on occupations. However, a few among them are open ones and the same can be adopted or acquired by any one. Hakim (means a medical doctor) is such a profession. Based on their vocations, different surnames have emerged. The examples of a few of them are as given below (Periera, 1940):

Caste	**Surname**	**Remarks**
Sayed	Shah	Sayed or Mir as prefix title, and the women use the suffix Begum or Bibi.
Shaik		Xec or Shaik as prefix title. Their females may use Bibi as the suffix.
Pathan	Khan	Their women employ Khatun or Bibi as suffix.
Khoja	Aga	Their spiritual leader is Agha Khan
Meman	Haji	They are highly religious people and would invariably go in for Haj

In females, bee, begum, bibi, khatun, and kahtu are often employed as auxiliaries in the personal names (Periera, 1940). In masculine names, auxiliaries are generally absent.

7.4.9.2 Prefixes

In some Muslim names, prefix titles are also used. Their treatment has been discussed under the Marathi Names.

7.5 SINDHI NAMES

7.5.1 General

Sindhis of India are the immigrants or the descendants of immigrants from Sindh province, now a part of Pakistan. They migrated to India after the partition of the country in 1947 and permanently settled down in different parts of the country. They follow Hinduism and speak Sindhi language. About 75% Sindhis live in urban areas (Census of India 1981). Business and service are the major occupations in which most of them are engaged. The Sindhi population of about 21 lakhs in 1981, might have grown by 1991, to nearly 26 lakh.

Historically, the present province of Sindh had a bondage with the Western India as it was a part of the then Bombay Presidency till April 1, 1936 when the Sindhi speaking area was separated into a new province. Perhaps, because of its past association with the Presidency of Bombay, that a large number of Sindhi refugees preferred to settle down in the present day states of Maharashtra and Gujarat. In 1981, Maharashtra and Gujarat accounted for nearly 6.5 and 9 Lakh Sindhis respectively. In Rajasthan, there were about 3.5 Lakh Sindhis. Delhi had nearly 55,800 (Census of India 1981).

7.5.2 Structure of Names

A Sindhi name-of-person has three components. The name of the father succeeds the given name. The family name comes in the end (Ranganathan, 1964). The sequence of all the three parts is fixed, and conforms to the Marathi or Gujarati pattern. A sample of Sindhi names is given as below :

Masculine Names	**Feminine Names**
Gopaldas Ramchand Bhatia	Bharati Ramesh Chothani
Goverdhan Assoomal Mahboobani	Papibai Khatwani
Kirat Chiothram Babani	Popati Ramchand Mirchandani
Komal Laxman Bhati	Sundri Assandas Uttamchandani
Lalchand Krishnachand Advani	Vimla Ashokkumar Asnani
Naraindas Chandumal Sippy	

In public usage, particularly in the educated community, surname is generally employed for addressing. Hence, the entry is to be prepared under the family name.

7.5.3 Surnames

Prior to conquering of Sindh by the British, in 1843, the practice of using surnames was not in vogue among the Sindhis. A name-of-person then was consisting of the given name, followed by the name of the father. The maiden name of a girl, carried her father's name while after marriage, got replaced by the same of the husband. All these practices were in conformity with the prevailing traditions of naming in Western India.

Those who were in direct contacts with the British, either by virtue of their employment in the government service, or otherwise, started employing surnames as integral part of their names. Thus, family names gradually grew popular to the extent that now, it is rather difficult to find a Sindhi family without a surname.

Many Sindhi families derived their surnames from the given names of their ancestors. As the given name of self and of the father were both forming integral parts of the name-of-person, generally the name of the grand father or some other ancestor was chosen to denote the family name. In such a name 'ani' was added to denote the family (Gauba, 1969a). A sample of such family names is given as below :

Surname	Name of the ancestor
Gyanchandani	Gyanchand
Karamchandani	Karamchand
Mirchandani	Mirchand
Ramchandani	Ramchand
Sadarangani	Sadarang
Tekchandani	Tekchand
Tolamalani	Tolamal
Uttamchandani	Uttamchand

The termination 'ani' in Sindhi language conveys no meaning. In fact, it is not a Sindhi word. In common usage, particularly in the names-of-persons, it is often understood to mean 'descendant of'. Virmani a Punjabi sub-caste and employed as a family name, though ending with 'ani' is not a Sindhi surname.

7.5.3.1 Shortening of Surnames

The above method of arriving at surnames by employing the given name of some fore-father made some of the Sindhi family names quite complicated and lengthy. As per Gauba (1969a), many Sindhi families shortened their surnames. Yet, some families are still using the full form of their family names. A sample of contracted surnames along with their original family names is given below :

Original Form	Contracted Form
Choithramani	Choithani
Kewalramani	Ramani
Mangharamalani	Malani, Mani or Vani (Gauba, 1969a)
Sipahimalani	Sippy
Tolamalani	Tolani
Vasumalani	Vaswani

7.5.3.2 Other Sources of Surnames

Apart from the above described category of persons who had come in direct contact with the British, there was existing another influential class of people who were in business. These people also started employing surnames in their names. However, unlike the other Sindhis, they used their sub-caste names to denote their family names. Such surnames are named after certain species of animals, birds, objects of the vegetable kingdom, inanimate objects or gods and semi-gods. Examples of such family names along with the meanings of some of them, are given as below (Thakur, 1959) :

Surnames	Meaning	Surnames	Meaning
Ahuja		Kailiri	
Asar-pota		Kataria	Dagger
Bajaj		Khathuria	Musk
Bathija		Kukreja	Hen
Bedija		Lakhanpota	
Chawla	Rice	Lota	Water pot
Chhabra	A kind of weed	Lulla	
Chhapru		Lund	
Chichria		Makhija	Honey
Chugh		Mamtora	
Dahira		Manchandia	
Dariri		Mohan-pota	

Dhamija		Nangdev	Serpent
Dhaneja		Nangpal	
Dhanija		Ram Rakhia	
Dhingra	Mushrooms	Rohra	
Dodeja	Date	Ruprel	
Dusya		Sachdeo	
Gera	Dive	Sonpar	
Harchpal		Thath Thakur	
Hinduja		Tulreja	
Joneja		Tuneja	
		Wadhwa	

Some families belonging to Hyderabad (Sindh) who migrated many years ago (for business purposes) to different parts of the world, deviated from this practice. They often derived their surnames from the personal names of their fore-fathers, and not from their sub-castes as was being done by some Sindhi business houses.

Even though a total change in profession has taken place, over a period of time, in many Sindhi families particularly after settling down in different non-Sindhi speaking areas, the usage of surnames has continued in the same way as had existed earlier in the erstwhile Sindh. In other words, people from both the categories are deploying either forms of their family names, and there is hardly any standardization left now as was being known in the earlier period, based on their occupation. Thus, it may not be easy to identify the present day occupation of a person from a Sindhi surname.

7.5.4 Takhallus or literary name

In some Sindhi names of men of letters, literary names are employed in the end. As the person generally establishes his identity through the literary name, main entry is to be prepared under it even when the family name is also used. A sample of such names is given as below :

Name-of-person	Entry word
Bhagwan Si. Thadhani Pushpu	Pushpu
Santdas Punhunmal Kishinani Santal	Santal

7.5.5 Change of name of a female after marriage

At the time of marriage, a majority of the given names of Sindhi females undergo change, in accordance with the choice of the husband's family. Once, her personal name is changed, the new name becomes her name, thereafter, allowing her maiden name to die. In addition, the name and surname of the husband replace those of the father. In other words, each and every part of the name of a girl is changed in many families, after marriage. This practice, it appears, is in conformity with the existing practice in some parts of Western India.

7.5.6 Given Names

Personal names are always rendered as a single word. The practice of breaking the given names, as resorted to in Punjabi and Hindi speaking belts, is not in evidence.

7.5.7 Shortening of Names

Of late, some persons for apparent reasons of brevity, and case of utterance, are shortening their names by discarding the auxiliary present in the name of their father as well as in their names. A solitary example found, of such a transformed name is given as below :

Original Name	Shortened Name
Lalchand Krishnachand Advani	Lal Krishna Advani

7.5.8 Sindhi Sikhs

Sikhs of the former Sindh Province form a small minority. They had also migrated from Sindh after 1947 and are now living in different parts of the country.

A Sikh name-of-person of Sindh origin, usually includes the name of father or husband, as the case may be. The family name generally comes at the end of a name. In addition, prefix title "Sardar" for masculine names and "Sardarni" for female names are also employed in the names-of-persons. An illustration of Sindhi Sikh names is given below:

7.5.8.1 Masculine Names

Sardar Tejasingh Bhagwansingh Jethra

Sardar Indersingh Harbhajansingh Lund

Sardar Hotusingh Dayasingh Labana

7.5.8.2 Feminine Names

Sardani Jodhabai Meharbansingh Guliar

Sardarni Monabai Nanaksingh Nagpal

7.5.8.3 Surnames

There is a variety of family names, among the Sindhi Sikhs. However in recent times, true to their creed to treat all the persons equally, family names hitherto employed by them have been replaced by a generic word "Khalsa" which is now suffixed to the names. This practice, it now appears is fast becoming popular and is used almost by all the persons of the current generation. As this word is not a family name, it can only be treated as an added common name. Entry has to be preferred under the personal name, by ignoring the prefix.

7.5.8.4 Change in the structure

Several Sindhi families who have settled down permanently in the northern parts of the country, have started abandoning the usage of their father's or husband's names. Such people are now writing their names followed by their surnames. This is perhaps a result of the influence of the surrounding culture.

Examples: Ramesh Choithani, Nirmal Bhatia

Several prominent Sindhis in their drive to abolish the caste pattern of the Hindu society, discarded the usage of their family names during the 1950s. The names of such persons thus got reduced to their names followed by the father's name. In other words, the process of naming in such a case has completed a full circle and has gone back to the pre-British time. A sample of such names is given under :

Jairamadas Daulatram, Pratap Dialdas, Dayaram Gidumal

7.6 PARSEE NAMES

7.6.1 General

Parsees are the descendants of immigrants from Persia (i.e. Iran) who fled their motherland during the seventh century, resisting conversion to Islam by force. Since then, they have been living in different parts of the country. They constitute a very small community, having a population of 76, 382. Gujarat and Maharashtra account for 12, 924 and 60, 501 Parsees respectively (Census of India 1991, 1995). Almost, 96% of the Parsees live in urban areas.

Initially, Parsees landed at Diu bringing their holy fire with them. They gradually moved to different villages and towns of Gujarat. Some of their strong holds had been Navsari, Ankleshwar, Broach, Surat and the surrounding villages. After several centuries, they moved to Bombay and other urban areas of Maharashtra. Their contribution to the nation in many fields of human endeavour, have been substantial. Many Parsees like Homi J. Bhabha, Piloo Mody, Nani A. Palkiwala, J.R.D. Tata, etc. have excelled in their performance.

As per Jal F. Bulsara (1969), Parsees, by virtue of their resilience, had adapted themselves to Hindu beliefs, customs and even to Indian dress. They learnt the Gujarati language which gradually became their mother tongue-of course, inescapably with a heavy mixture of Persian vocabulary making their adapted language "Parsee Gujarati". Yet they produced in course of time a poet of the calibre of Ardeshir Khabardar, whom K.M. Munshi extolled "the first poet of the community, who could rank among the best in Gujarati literature" (Bulsara, 1969). In other words, Parsees have accepted Indian culture in general, and Gujarati in particular.

7.6.2 Name-of-Person

Parsee names-of-persons adhereto the sequence of "Personal Name - Father's Name - Surname" (Sengupta, 1961). This sequence is in conformity with those of Gujarati or Marathi names. A few examples of the Parsee names are given below :

Masculine Name	**Feminine Names**
Homi Jehangir Bhabha	Alamai Piloo Dadiseth
Jamshetji Nusserwanji Tata	Cooverbai Ardaiveraf Irani
Khurshid Framji Nariman	Jerabai Khurshid Mehta
Minoo Rustom Masani	Ratamai Homi Indorewala
Nani Ardeshir Palkivala	Shirinbai Farrokhbhai Bandwala
Piloo Homi Mody	
Shahrukh Behram Mody	

7.6.3 Family names

Parsee surnames are largely drawn from the occupations of their ancestors. They are also based on the territorial residency (i.e. the names of places) of their fore-fathers (Sinha, 1994c). Describing how an occupational descriptor had become a surname, it has been reported that Sir Jamshetji Jejeebhoy (1783 - 1859) had migrated from Navsari to Bombay in the prime of his youth, and having little education, began his career as a vendor of bottles, slowly - he built up the business almost into a monopoly which enabled him to earn the family name "Batliwala" (Kanga, 1969).

An illustration of Parsee family names, derived from the occupation of their ancestors, is given as under :

Agboatwala	Fanaswala	Lilaowala	Pithawala
Bandwala	Fatakia	Machliwala	Roowala
Bonesetter	Ghaswala	Makhanwala	Rumwala
Cardmaster	Ghodkhoda	Masalawala	Sodawaterbottlewala
Chaiwala	Ginwala	Motaseth	Sonawala
Chhapgarwala	Hodiwala	Nalaseth	Sopariwala
Chhatriwala	Hathikhanawala	Nanporia	Tarmaster
Dadiseth	Junglewala	Narielwala	Tobaccowala
Daruwala	Kandawala	Presswala	Toddywala
Darukhanawala	Kapaswala	Palkiwala	Topmaster
Eendawala	Lakdawala	Paowala	Topiwala

The other major source of obtaining Parsee surnames has been from the territorial residency of the ancestors. Sometimes, family names are derived from the names of the countries, and at times, from the place name.

<u>Examples</u> : Canadawala, Irani, Zanzibarwala
Indorewala, Udwadis

Certain Parsee families have also coined their surnames from the personal names of their fore-fathers. Such family names generally end with ji, a respectful suffix in the Gujarati culture. If such a surname is in usage, all the three component parts of a name-of-person, denote only given names. The source of deriving all the personal names being common, it may become difficult for a cataloguer for not being familiar with the Parsee culture, to identify all the components, correctly. However, from the placement of the position of each part, one can easily identify each unit part. A few examples of such family names are given below:

Dadachanji, Sorabji

In addition, there are several surnames denoting specific occupations (or the official positions) of the ancestors. They are identical with the same in Gujarati culture. A sample of such surnames is given as under :

Gandhi, Kapadia, Mehta, Mody, Patel

7.6.3.1 Change of Surname

Several surnames in the Parsee community have been found to have undergone change. The usual logic of changing a family name has been a tasteless meaning associated with the word used as the family name. In the present survey only one such change in the surname, could be obtained, described as under (Kanga, 1969):

Bumlakhao (literal meaning : eater of Bombay ducks). It is changed to Bomanji or cursetji

7.6.4 Given Names

It is quite surprising that despite their stay for more than a thousand years in India, and their absorption of Indian culture in its totality, most of the personal names of Parsees still remain to be of Persian origin. The community being a closed one, it has preserved its unique identity in given names. However, in some masculine given names, terminations as bhai, ji, etc., and bai, mai, and so on in feminine names, are a result of the prominent Gujarati cultural influence. As these suffixes form integral part of the names, they have to be retained.

7.6.5 Shortening of names

It is observed that some Parsees contract their names and or the name of their father into shorter form.

Examples:- Sir Homi P. Mody's name was Hormuzi P. Mody. Here, P is the first letter of his father's name. However, he shortened his name into Homi. Similarly, Filoo and Noshir are the contracted form of Firoze and Noshirwan respectively.

7.6.6 Dropping the name of the father

There are several Parsees living in North India, who do not employ father's name in their names. Thus, their names would have two components namely the given name and the surname.

Examples : Firoze Gandhi, Piloo Mody, Ratan Tata

Piloo Mody was born in an influential Parsee family of Bombay. His father was a nationalist leader, and had been the Governor of Uttar Pradesh and Maharashtra. Piloo's original name was Piloo Homi Mody. The middle component represents his father's personal name. However, in later part of his life, he dropped the name of his father. Once, the present author happened to interact with Mody, while he was a Member of the Indian Parliament. On enquiry about the dropping of the given name of his father, Piloo informed that in his youthful period, he had gone in for education, to the United States. His father was a very well known personality then, as he was occupying the seat of Governor of Uttar Pradesh. Wherever Mody had gone, he was introduced as son of Sir Homi Mody. This was not liked by him, and hence, he dropped that part of his name which denoted his father's name.

7.6.7 Prefix Title

Similar to the practice prevailing in West India, prefix titles are not generally used in Parsee names. However, as an exception, only one prefix is used in a few Parsee names.

Example : Dastur (= priest)

In this context, it is observed that Dastur is also used as a surname in some families. Enquiries revealed that the family name is adopted in those families whose ancestors were performing the priesthood. Yet, in many names people who are priests, it is used as a prefix title. As this titles is not part of the name, it is ignored at the time of rendering.

7.6.8 Anglicised format

As has been the case with many names-of-persons from various regions of the country, the Parsee names too have under gone a transformation due to influence of English education, with the result that many Parsees started replacing the personal and the father's name components of their names with initials.

Examples: D.N. Wadia, J.R.D. Tata

7.6.9 Pen-name or takhallus

Among the Parsees, pen-names are rarely employed. In one case, a writer used it at the end of his name. Since he had dropped his family name, the catalogue entry in such a name be prepared under his pen-name.

Example : Ardesir Pharamaji Khabardar

7.6.10 Change of female name after marriage

Parsee community like any other community in West India, follows the patrilineal norms. Under this system, the surname is passed on to the next generation, through the male line. A girl employs the family name (and the name) of her father till she is married. Thereafter, both are replaced by those of her husband.

Example : If a Parsee female having her name Nerges Hormusji Bhethna marries Jehangir Boman Patel, her married name becomes Nerges Jehangir Patel.

7.7 WEST INDIAN NAMES IN AACR- 2

Names-of-persons from the zone of West India, possess the following prominent features:

(i) The usage of surname in the names-of-persons is almost universal, the exceptions being the names-of-persons during the beginning of this century, and a few persons presently. The surname occurs in the end part of a name and constitutes the most important part, through which the person establishes his identity.

(ii) In names where no family name is used, the sequence is 'Given Name - Father's or Husband's Name'. The entry has to be prepared in that order. Yet, some persons, in rare cases, have dissected their father's name, and used the second part of the dissected parental name as a surname. This being the case, the entry is to be made under that part for which preference has been expressed by the author.

(iii) Most of the surnames are single worded, though in a few instances, multi - worded surnames are also in use. If a multi-worded family name has been used, all the words have to be taken together as one single unit. However, if one word denotes a term of respect, it has to be ignored. In such a surname, the entry would be under the other word.

(iv) The structure of a name-of-person, is 'Personal Name - Father's/ Husband's Name - Surname'.

(v) Usage of prefix titles in the names is not common in the West zone. However, in some Muslim names, they are used, though rarely. If they are present, they have to be treated as the prefixes in the North Indian names. Yet, if a prefix is used in the middle component of a name, denoting the name of father or husband, it is to be retained.

(vi) Given names are rendered as single worded. This aspect is helpful in identifying a Western Indian name.

(vii) Usage of pen-name, though rare, is not very uncommon. If a literary name is used, entry has to be made under it.

Formulation of Rules

The discussion presented above, leads to the conclusion that the usage of family name in the names-of-person of West zone of the country, is very extensive. Barring a few Muslim names-of-persons and a few ones of other communities, almost all the names carry the surname in the end. Hence, the catalogue entry is to be made under the family name. If the surname is multi-worded, all the words taken together would be rendered as a single surname. Yet, there are exceptions described as under:

1. Some names may not possess the surname. A name falling in this category may consist of the given name followed by the father's or husband's name. Among the Muslims, such names are quite a few. During the beginning of this century, a large number of Hindu and other names were falling in this category. In such a name, the entry should be in the given name, i.e. the first part of the name.

2. Some names-of-persons may also include prefix titles. Among the Muslims usage of prefix titles in the names is fairly high. They are to be generally ignored except when they are:

(a) British titles;

(b) Titles which have become part of the names; and

(c) Titles used before the name of father or husband, as the case may be.

3. Takhallus or the literary name if used as a suffix to a name-of-person,

becomes the most important part of the name. The catalogue entry has to be prepared under it, even when the surname is also used.

The cataloguing rules in conformity to the AACR 2 can be prescribed, as follows :

W.1 Not withstanding the exception of W.2 to W.6 enter a name from West India under the surname. Any prefix used in the name has to be ignored, except where :

(a) it has been bestowed by the British rulers;

(b) it has become part of the name; and

(c) it is employed in the name of the father or husband, as the case may be.

Names-of-persons	**Catalogue Entry**
Abdulrazzak Mohemadshafi Punekar	Punekar, Abdulrazzak Mohemadshafi
Chaya Narayanrao Kokate	Kokate, Chaya Narayanrao
Homi Jehangir Bhabha	Bhabha, Homi Jehangir
Lokamanya Bal Gangadhar Tilak	Tilak, Bal Gangadhar
Lal Krishna Advani	Advani, Lal Krishna
Leena Ambalal Sarabhai	Sarabhai, Leena Ambalal
Vimla Ashokkumar Asnani	Asnani, Vimla Ashokkumar

W.1.1 If the name-of-person includes the literary-name or pen-name popularly called takhallus, with or without the surname, enter the name under the takhallus with the rest of the name inverted in the same order.

Examples

Names-of-persons	**Entry-word**
Ardeshir Pharamji Khabardar	Khabardar
Bhagvan Si. Thadhani Pushpu	Pushpu
Tribhuvandas Purshottamdas Luhar Sunderam	Sunderam

W.2 If a name-of-person from the West zone does not include the family name (and/or takhallus), enter it under the given name, in straight order. The prefix title if used can be removed or retained as per W.1. There is yet another exception described as below :

W.2.1 If the name of the father or husband has been broken into two parts and the last part employed distinctly as a surname, enter under that part, with all other parts inverted in the same order.

Examples :

Names-of-persons	Catalogue entry
Isamaile Abadulla	Isamaile Abdulla
Jairamdas Daulatram	Jairamdas Daulatram
Maqbool Fida Hussain	Hussain, Maqbool Fida
Muhammmedahmed Abdul Rashid	Rashid, Muhammedahmed Abdul
Narayana Hemacandra	Narayana Hemacandra

W.3 Enter a name from West India, under the multi-worded family name, by taking all the words together as one unit, provided any of the word is not denoting respect or affection. If so, such attachments have to be removed.

Examples :

Names-of-persons	Catalogue entry
Atmaram Sridhar Vats Joshi	Vats Joshi, Atmaram Sridhar
Chandrakanta Pabhudayal Sinai Borkar	Sinai Borkar, Chandrakanta Pabhudayal
Vyomesacandra Janardana Pathakji	Pathak, Vyomesacandra Janardana

W.4 Enter a name-of-person from the West zone, under the combination of a two worded family names, one pertains to the father and the other of the husband, taken together as one unit.

Example:

Name-of-person	Catalogue entry
Cynthia D'Souza e Nogueira	D'Souza e Nogueira, Cynthia
Nirmala Samant Prabhavalkar	Samant Prabhavalkar, Nirmala

Chapter VIII

EVALUATION OF THE ACCESSION LIST

8.1 GENERAL

Accessions List: South Asia is a monthly record (now, bimonthly) of all publications catalogued by the Library of Congress offices at New Delhi and Karachi. A cummulative index of author/title of the documents covered in all the 12 issues of the Accessions List is published in the December issue of this List. It is an indexing bulletin providing bibliographic details of monographs, serials and also documents in non-print media from the South Asian countries, procured for addition to the Library of Congress, in Washington, D.C. and some other participating libraries in the United States. Though, the majority of the documents included in the Accessions List are the printed books, released in recent times, it also lists such old titles in manuscript form, which were written, many years ago. Few manuscripts, several centuries old are also found in the List. These precious manuscripts are generally obtained in microfilm form. Publications in English language as well as in several other languages of South Asia, are indexed with the bibliographic details rendered only in Roman script. Entries of the publications are arranged alphabetically first by the country of origin, and within a country, under the languages. In the second section, non-print documents are listed country wise, disregarding the language aspect. Further, both the Library of Congress offices make efforts to obtain almost all the titles published during a given period in a country, the bulletin constitutes quite a comprehensive source of information, on new books and other documents, from South Asia.

The volume of the 'Accessions List' for the year 1995 is chosen for the purpose of this research study, viz. evaluating the rendering of

Indic names-of-persons, for the simple reason that almost all titles indexed therein are available for scrutiny the details, if so needed. The broad classification of the documents, by the compilers on the basis of the languages, is of great help in ascertaining the cultural background of most of the authors. Another clue to the linguistic background of an author, is the place of publication. Cases of authors not writing in their own language, works translated from other language and works published in places alien to the authors are small in number. By examining the parts of a name-of-person falling in such exceptional categories, one can always configure how it should be treated in a cataloguing system. Similar is the case of monographs in English and Sanskrit languages, where the authors could be from any part of the country. All such authors need to be identified first with a specific linguistic region, before examining whether their names have been rendered, correctly in the List. Where the cultural background is not apparent, help from the specialists was sought in resolving the confusion. In addition, bio-graphical year-books were also consulted. In case an author has more than one publication to his credit, only one of them has been considered for purposes of the evaluation.

A careful perusal of the rendering of the Indic names-of-persons in the 'Accessions List' has revealed that some are not entered correctly. Consistency has not been maintained in many instances. The Accessions List has been critically examined vis-a-vis the findings and recommendations of this research and cases where the rendering has not taken place in conformity with these recommendations have been considered, and highlighted in this evaluation. Some classes of the names-of-persons were excluded as they fall outside of the scope of this research. They are :

1. Persons who had flourished before the twentieth century.
2. Persons from the North - Eastern parts of the country.
3. Persons not disclosing their real names, but are using pseudonyms.
4. British nationals serving in India, before independence.
5. Anglo - Indians and Indian Christians bearing names of European structure.
6. Persons from Pakistan, Bangladesh, Nepal, and Bhutan.

The broad findings of this research work, the guidelines and the rules of the cataloguing framed therein, were applied to examine the correctness of the rendered entries of the Indic names-of- persons in the List and appropriate corrections where necessary, have been prescribed with suitable explanation in defence of the corrections.

8.2 NORTH INDIAN NAMES

The following names-of-persons, from North India have been found to have been rendered incorrectly, in the Accessions List. Entry number as appearing in the Accessions List has been mentioned against each. If an entry has been prepared under the title of the publication, name in the index corresponding to the entry, has been taken as the prescribed form of the heading.

S.No.	Name as rendered in Accession List	Correct prescribed Entry	Entry number in Accessions List
1.	Amrita Pritam	Pritam, Amrita	781
2.	Anand, Kumar	Kumar Anand	6432
3.	Attar Chand	Chand, Attar	3018
4.	Bala, Suman	Suman Bala	297
5.	Balraj Komal	Komal, Balraj	1521
6.	Bedi, Sohindara Singha Wanjara	Wanjara Bedi, Sohindara Singha	4790
7.	Bhanudatta Misra	Misra, Bhanudatta	1266
8.	Bhushan, Indu	Indu Bhushan	4795
9.	Brahmachary, Om Prakash	Om Prakash Brahmachary	375
10.	Candra, Dipaka	Dipaka Candra	2929
11.	Chadha, Rajni, Dr.	Chadha, Rajni	6505
12.	Chand, Amir	Amir Chand	3085
13.	Chandar, Krishan	Krishan Chandar	11792
14.	Chander, Harish	Harish Chander	7468
15.	Chandrika, Tara	Tara Chandrika	464
16.	Das, Babu Nemi	Nemi Das	1526
17.	Das, Shiva Tosh	Shiva Tosh Das	7471
18.	Dayal, Ishwar	Ishwar Dayal	9830
19.	Devi, Swapna	Swapna Devi	6568
20.	Giri, Narottam, Swamy	Narottam Giri, Swamy	10253

21.	Gopal, Jai	Jai Gopal	6793
22.	Gopal,,Neeraj	Neeraj Gopal	9883
23.	Gupta, Deepak, Dr.	Gupta, Deepak	9889
24.	Gupta, S.P., Dr.	Gupta, S.P.	366
25.	Gurmukh Singh, Major	Gurmukh Singh	9893
26.	Harbamsa Singha, Giani	Harbamsa Singha	1168
27.	Himmat Singh, Dr.	Himmat Singh	426
28.	Kanta, Mira	Mira Kanta	816
29.	Kishore, Adarsh	Adarsh Kishore	9972
30.	Krishna, Devyani	Devyani Krishna	453
31.	Krishna, Kanwal	Kanwal Krishna	453
32.	Kumar, Ajai	Ajai Kumar	9980
33.	Kumar, Anand	Anand Kumar	623
34.	Kumar, Deepak	Deepak Kumar	6836
35.	Kumar, Madhurendra	Madhurendra Kumar	9981
36.	Kumar, Ravindra	Ravindra Kumar	10073
37.	Kumar, Sanjeev	Sanjeev Kumar	9849
38.	Kumar, Satish	Satish Kumar	10239
39.	Kumar, Shailendra	Shailendra Kumar	3342
40.	Kumar, Shashi	Shashi Kumar	3343
41.	Kumar, Sushil	Sushil Kumar	511
42.	Kumar, Yogesh	Yogesh Kumar	3589
43.	Kumara, Brija Bihari	Brija Bihari Kumara	3344
44.	Lal, Rangi	Rangi Lal	9264
45.	Lal, Ranjit	Ranjit Lal	6843
46.	Maharshi, Hari	Hari Maharshi	7525
47.	Mathur, O.P., Dr.	Mathur, O.P.	10011
48.	Mishra, Harish Chandra Advocate	Mishra, Harish Chandra	10019
49.	Mohan, Chandra	Chandra Mohan	7055
50.	Mohana, Indira	Indira Mohana	7546
51.	Mukta, Parita	Parita Mukta	492
52.	Nanda, K.K.., Lieut. Gen.	Nanda, K.K.	3414
53.	Narain, Iqbal	Iqbal Narain	10157
54.	Pal, Jogindar	Jogindar Pal	1579
55.	Pala, Amara	Amara Pala	2330
56.	Pandey, Gyanendra, Dr.	Pandey, Gyanendra	10070
57.	Prabhakar, Vishnu	Vishnu Prabhakar	841
58.	Prakasa, Kshama	Kshama Prakasa	7560
59.	Parkash, Prem	Prem Parkash	11519

60.	Prakash, Indira Jai	Indira Jai Prakash	3430
61.	Prasad, Binod Mohan	Binod Mohan Prasad	10085
62.	Prasad, Braj Nandan	Braj Nandan Prasad	6997
63.	Prasad, Jagdish	Jagdish Prasad	9916
64.	Prasad, Janardan	Janardan Prasad	6998
65.	Prasad, Rajendra	Rajendra Prasad	10086
66.	Prasad, Ram	Ram Prasad	10087
67.	Prasad, Samta	Samta Prasad	2327
68.	Prasada, Kamala	Kamala Prasada	3906
69.	Prasada, Sucita Narayana	Sucita Narayana Prasada	7561
70.	Prasada, Visvanatha	Visvanatha Prasada	7650
71.	Rakesh, Pankaj	Pankaj Rakesh	10101
72.	Ram, Nandu	Nandu Ram	3489
73.	Ramani, Rasmi	Rasmi Ramani	846
74.	Ramani, Sarada	Sarada Ramani	847
75.	Ranjana, Sudhamsu	Sudhamsu Ranjana	7573
76.	Rawindara Rawi	Rawi, Rawindara	1218
77.	Sahaya, Prema	Prema Sahaya	7582
78.	Santosh, Dr.	Santosh	10145
79.	Satyarthi, Devendra	Devendra Satyarthi	860
80.	Satyawadi, Sudha	Sudha Satyawadi	578
81.	Sharan, Ishwar	Ishwar Sharan	3576
82.	Sharma, O.P., Dr.	Sharma, O.P.	7122
83.	Sharma, Suman, Dr.	Sharma, Suman	3581
84.	Shreshtha, Laxman	Laxman Shreshtha	7127
85.	Singh, Amar	Amar Singh	10188
86.	Singh, Baidyanath Prasad	Baidyanath Prasad Singh	6584
87.	Singh, Bansh Gopal	Bansh Gopal Singh	10189
88.	Singh, Bireshwar Prasad	Bireshwar Prasad Singh	7174
89.	Singh, Dinesh Kumar	Dinesh Kumar Singh	7131
90.	Singh, Harbans	Harbans Singh	594
91.	Singh, Hoshiar	Hoshiar Singh	6713
92.	Singh, Kuber	Kuber Singh	3561
93.	Singh, Kulwant	Kulwant Singh	10242
94.	Singh, Lal Babu	Lal Babu Singh	10193
95.	Singh, Prakash	Prakash Singh	3600
96.	Singh, Pritam	Pritam Singh	8261
97.	Singh, Raj Pal	Rajpal Singh	598

98.	Singh, Sarup	Sarup Singh	10190
99.	Singh, Shamser Bahadur	Shamser Bahadur Singh	7609
100.	Singh, Surendra	Surendra Singh	7134
101.	Singh, Swaran	Swaran Singh	600
102.	Singh, Tavleen	Tavleen Singh	3604
103.	Singh, Trilochan	Trilochan Singh	3501
104.	Singh, Vinod Kumar	Vinod Kumar Singh	318
104.	Singh, Vir	Vir Singh	9847
106.	Singh, Yogendra	Yogendra Singh	10226
107.	Sivadeva Susila	Susila, Sivadeva Simha	1236
108.	Snatak, Vijayendra	Vijayendra Snatak	870
109.	Suneel, Seema	Seema Suneel	10212
110.	Swarup, Ram	Ram Swarup	10214
111.	Vasudev, Aruna	Aruna Vasudev	6613
112.	Vijaya Lakshmi, Dr.	Vijaya Lakshmi	10254
113.	Yajan Veer	Dahiya, Yajan Veer	3725

The general error observed in rendering the above listed names from North India, is the blanket application of the mechanical rule "last part as the entry element" in respect of the entries except made at S. Nos. 1, 3, 5, 6, 7, 9, 11, 16, 20, 23, 24, 25, 26, 27, 30, 46, 47, 48, 52, 56, 57, 60, 73, 74, 76, 78, 79, 80, 82, 83, 84, 107, 108, 109, 111, 112 and 113. In fact, most of these names are simple personal names. Family name is not employed in any of these names. As per the prevailing traditions in North India, a personal name is generally broken into two or sometimes, in more than two parts, with each unit rendered as if it were an independent word. Hence, the entire name is the given name with the second and the subsequent component parts, if present, read always in the same sequence in which they appear in the name. The given name is the sole potent one in the absence of family name.

The entry word in respect of the names-of-persons consisting of only personal names, has to be generally the entire name as it stands. Yet, in some names, the choice has gone to the last word, for no apparent reason and preference of the authors having not been expressed as eastablished after verification.

Entry at S. No. 1 pertains to a Punjabi feminine writer who abandoned the usage of Kaur in her given name, and employs Pritam as her pen-name. Hence, the entry should go under her literary name. On the other hand, in the name listed at S. No. 6 includes his pen-name followed by his family name. Hence, the entry should be prepared under a set of two words, the pen-name and the surname.

The entry at S. No. 3 has been correctly prepared under the given name. But, the author has contracted his name as A. Chand in the publication, and hence, he has expressed his own preference. The entry should be made under Chand.

In the entries at S. Nos. 5, 7 and 113, the entry words have been wrongly chosen the personal names. In fact, Komal, Misra and Dahiya respectively are their family names. Therefore, all the entries be made under their family names. In respect of the name at S. No. 113, it is not known as to why the surname 'Dahiya' has not been included in the rendering?

In the names-of-persons at S. Nos. 9, 46, 57, 79, 80, 84, and 108, the last word is not the surname. In each name, it is an added appellation. It is to be preserved but in subordination to the personal name. In the name at S. Nos. 57, Prabhakar indicates that the bearer is holding the vernacular Bachelor's degree in Hindi. Similarly, in the name at S. No. 107, the suffix Snatak denotes that the bearer is a graduate from Gurukul.

The entries at S. Nos. 11, 16, 23, 24, 25, 26, 27, 47, 48, 52, 56, 78, 82, 83, and 112 include honorofic prefix titles which are superfluous. Hence, all of them be removed. In the name at S. No. 16, after the removal of the prefix Babu, the remaining is the personal name.

The name at S. No. 20 is of a Hindu saint. Narottam Giri is his personal name. He uses the prefix Swamy, which should be retained in an inverted order.

Entries at S. Nos. 30, 60, 73, 74, 109 and 111 pertain to female authors. The second part of the names is the name of the husband. Hence, the entries in all the names be made under their given names in the straight order followed by the epithet. In the name at S. No. 60, the name of the husband is Jai Prakash.

The name listed at S. No. 107 has been rendered under his personal name, where as his pen-name has been retained at the secondary position. It is also not known as to why his surname was dropped in the entry ? The correct entry be prepared under his pen-name. Similar is the case of the name-of-person at S. No. 76.

8.3 MUSLIM NAMES

Similarly, the following Muslim names-of-persons have been found to have been entered wrongly.

S.No.	Name in the list	Correct Entry	Reference
1.	Abbas, Sayyid Hasan	Hasan Abbas, Sayyid	8648
2.	Abdulla, Mohammed	Mohammed Abdulla	6769
3.	Abdulvahid, Qazi	Abdulvahid	8673
4.	Abdussattar, Qazi	Abdussattar	8590
5.	Abraham, Taisha	Taisha Abraham	6393
6.	Afrahim, Saghir	Saghir Afrahim	5136
7.	Ahmad, Ejaz	Ejaz Ahmad	3256
8.	Ahmad, Furqan	Furqan Ahmad	290
9.	Ahmad, Fuzail	Fuzail Ahmad	8593
10.	Ahmad, Mohiuddin	Mohiuddin Ahmad	494
11.	Ahmad, Qeyamuddin	Qeyamuddin Ahmad	6412
12.	Ahmad, Raziyah Fasih	Raziyah Fasih Ahmad	5138
13.	Ahmad, Saifuddin	Saifuddin Ahmad	11823
14.	Ahmad, S. Sami	Sami Ahmad, S.	6626
15.	Ahmad, Sayyid	Sayyid Ahmad	1510
16.	Ahmed, Fakhruddin Ali	Fakhruddin Ali Ahmed	11828
17.	Ahmed, Moudud	Moudud Ahmed	6413
18.	Ahmad, Saleem	Saleem Ahmad	2987
19.	Ahmed, Shamsuddin	Shamsuddin Ahmed	11779
20.	Akhtar, Rifat	Rifat Akhtar	8595
21.	Alam, Khursheed	Khursheed Alam	11781
22.	Alam, Muhammad Manzur	Manzur Alam, Muhammad	11782
23.	Alam, Qaiser Zoha	Qaiser Zoha Alam	292
24.	Ali, Asaf	Asaf Ali	7016
25.	Ali Cikmagluri, Asghar	Asghar Ali Chikmagluri	8596
26.	Ali, Mohamed	Mohamed Ali	5141
27.	Ali, Nurulain	Nurulain Ali	11783
28.	Ali, Rajah Ghazanfar	Rajah Ghazanfar Ali	8599
29.	Ali Sarangpurvale, Hasan	Hasan Ali Sarangpurvale	1513
30.	Ali, Sayyid	Sayyid Ali	8600
31.	Ali, Shah Muhammad Hidayat	Hidayat Ali, Shah Muhammad	5142

32.	Ali, Rashid	Rashid Ali	9723
33.	Ali, Sabir	Sabir Ali	293
34.	Ali, Sayyid Sadiq	Sadiq Ali, Sayyid	1515
35.	Anjum, Masih	Masih Anjum	8608
36.	Aqil, Muhammad	Muhammad Aqil	8597
37.	Ashraf, Ali	Ali Ashraf	6591
38.	Ashraf, Sayyid Daud	Daud Ashraf, Sayyid	8611
39.	Aslam, Muhammad Yaqub	Yaqub Aslam, Muhammad	5147
40.	Ayub, Harun	Harun Ayub	11789
41.	Ayuiba, Abu Sayida	Abu Sayida Ayuiba	3024
42.	Azam, Imam	Imam Azam	1576
43.	Baghdadi, Rafique	Rafique Baghdadi	9743
44.	Baqar, Agha Muhammad	Muhammad Baqar, Agha	8617
45.	Bari, Johurul	Johurul Bari	3032
46.	Bismillaha, Abdula	Abdula Bismillaha	3817
47.	Cand, Shaikh	Shaikh Cand	5154
48.	Fida Khalidi Dihlavi	Dihlavi, Fida Khalidi	11797
49.	Ghaffar, Qamar	Qamar Ghaffar	8592
50.	Ghaus, Zakirah	Zakirah Ghaus	8634
51.	Ghiyasuddin, Muhammad	Muhammad Ghiyasuddin	8590
52.	Habib, Irfan	Irfan Habib	3226
53.	Hadi, Nabi	Nabi Hadi	6704
54.	Hakim, Shabbir	Shabbir Hakim	11799
55.	Hamidullah, Muhammad	Muhammad Hamidullah	3227
56.	Hasan Khan, Rashid	Khan, Rashid Hasan	1529
57.	Hasan, Muhammad	Muhammad Hasan	8639
58.	Hasan, Mushirul	Mushirul Hasan	6727
59.	Hasan, Sayyid Faizan	Faizan Hasan, Sayyid	8640
60.	Hasan, Vazir	Vazir Hasan	5174
61.	Hifzurrahman, Muhammad	Muhammad Hifzurrahma	5175
62.	Husain Akbarpuri, Anvar	Anvar Husain Akbarpuri	8644
63.	Husain, Asfaq	Asfaq Husain	1571
64.	Husain, Muhammad Shahid	Shahid Husain, Muhammad	1536
65.	Husain, Sayyid Bakhshish	Bakhshish Husain, Sayyid	1537
66.	Husain, Sayyid Fida	Fida Husain, Sayyid	11800
67.	Husain, Sayyid Kamil	Kamil Husain, Sayyid	5189
68.	Husain, Sayyid Sajjad	Sajjad Husain, Sayyid	1538
69.	Hussain, Zakir	Zakir Hussain	2328

70.	Husena, Jabira	Jabira Husena	8645
71.	Ibrahim, Yusuf	Yusuf Ibrahim	1539
72.	Ilham, Sardar	Sardar Ilham	1541
73.	Imam, Mazhar	Mazhar Imam	1542
74.	Imam, Md. Ali	Ali Imam, Md.	1543
75.	Jauhar, Nazir	Nazir Jauhar	8647
76.	Javid, Sulaiman Athar	Athar Javid, Sulaiman	11801
77.	Kaifi, Habiba	Habiba Kaifi	11803
78.	Kamal, Farhat	Farhat Kamal	11802
79.	Khaliq, Anjum	Anjum Khaliq	8641
80.	Khaliq, Shakir	Shakir Khaliq	1555
81.	Khan, Abdulmaruf	Abdulmaruf Khan	8650
82.	Khan, Ahmadullah	Ahmadullah Khan	8651
83.	Khan, Em. Habib	Habib Khan, Em.	5204
84.	Khan, Muhammad Fazil	Fazil Khan, Muhammad	6822
85.	Khan, Rais	Rais Khan	9260
86.	Khan, Rashid	Rashid Khan, Ustad	9261
87.	Khan, Sultan	Sultan Khan	9260
88.	Khan, Tauhid	Tauhid Khan	8654
89.	Khan, Vahiduddin	Vahiduddin Khan	450
90.	Khan, Vilayat	Vilayat Khan	5741
91.	Khasim, Sek	Sek Khasim	5095
92.	Khatun, Rihanah	Rihanah Khatun	1552
93.	Khushtar Makranvi	Makranvi, Khushtar	1556
94.	Koshteh, M.H. Karim	Karim Koshteh, M.H.	6827
95.	Mahmood, Syed Tahir	Tahir Mahmood	9998
96.	Masud Husain Khan	Khan, Masud Husain	8665
97.	Masud Khan, Muhammad Athar	Khan, Muhammad Athar Masud	1564
98.	Matin, Ghiyas	Ghiyas Matin	1566
99.	Mohammad, Noor, Dr.	Noor Mohammad	415
100.	Muhammad Abdulvahid Khan	Abdulvahid Khan, Muhammad	8268
101.	Muhammad, Faiz	Faiz Muhammad	5192
102.	Muhammad, Shaikh Ghulam	Ghulam Muhammad, Shaikh	10955
103.	Muhiuddin, Mumin	Mumin Muhiuddin	8667
104.	Muiz, Abid	Abid Muiz	8668
105.	Mustafa, Seema	Seema Mustafa	6917
106.	Naimurrahman, Muhammad	Muhammad Naimurrahman	5195

107.	Nahid, Kishvar	Kishvar Nahid	8670
108.	Nami Ansari	Ansari, Nami	8671
109.	Nasim, Malikah	Malikah Nasim	1573
110.	Nayyar, Qiyam	Qiyam Nayyar	1574
111.	Parvez, Aslam	Aslem Parvez	8679
112.	Parvez, Shahid	Shahid Parvez	1580
113.	Peer, Mohammed	Mohammed Peer	3610
114.	Rafiq Ae. Es. Muhammad	Muhammad Rafiq, Ae. Es.	8685
115.	Rahman, Zillur	Zillur Rahman	11814
116.	Raza, Moosa	Moosa Raza	7051
117.	Saba Navidi, Alim	Navidi, Alim Saba	11816
118.	Sabir Arvi	Arvi, Sabir	1590
119.	Sadiq Naqvi	Naqvi, Sadiq	8688
120.	Sajid Siddiqi Lakhnavi	Siddiqi Lakhnavi, Sajid	8672
121.	Salim, Hamidah	Hamidah Salim	8691
122.	Salim, Vahiduddin	Vahiduddin Salim	5221
123.	Shafi, Muhammad, Mufti	Muhammad Shafi, Mufti	8715
124.	Shahin, Salma	Salma Shahin	8693
125.	Shakil, Faruq	Faruq Shakil	1600
126.	Shamim, Mubarak	Mubarak Shamim	8698
127.	Shuja, Asif	Asif Shuja	10180
128.	Suhail, Khalid	Khalid Suhail	8703
129.	Tanvir, Fatimah	Fatimah Tanvir	1608
130.	Ubaidurrahman, Muhammad	Muhammad Ubaidurrahman	5245
131.	Umar Ansari	Ansari, Umar	8706
132.	Umar, Mansur	Mansur Umar	1610
133.	Vahid, Sahba	Sahba Vahid	11826
134.	Vazir Hasan Dihlavi, Sayyid	Dihlavi, Sayyid Vazir Hasan	5248
135.	Yousuf, S.M. Anwar	Anwar Yousuf, S.M.	7256
136.	Zahir, Ali	Ali Zahir	1615
137.	Zahir, Sajjad	Sajjad Zahir	1616
138.	Zakir, Mohammad	Mohammad Zakir	6601

In rendering the Muslim names-of-persons listed above, again the general prescription 'last part as the entry word' has been employed rather mechanically. This has resulted in incorrect rendering of the names-of-persons in most of the names.

All the entries except at S. Nos. 1, 3, 4, 5, 12, 14, 22, 25, 29, 31, 34, 38, 39, 41, 43, 44, 48, 52, 56, 59, 62, 64, 65, 66, 67, 68, 74, 76, 77, 78, 79, 83, 84, 93, 94, 95, 96, 97, 99, 100, 102, 105, 108, 109, 114, 117, 118, 119, 120, 121, 123, 124, 129, 131, 133, 134 and 135 are personal name entries without any family name. Therefore, altering the natural sequence of the names is against the rule of the grammar.

The names listed at S. Nos. 3 and 4 include the Prefix, 'Qazi' denoting a religious position, which should be dropped.

S. Nos. 5, 12, 77, 78, 79, 105, 109, 121, 124, 129 and 133 pertain to female authors. The first part of these names is the personal name followed by the name of the husband or father. Hence, all the entries have to be prepared under the given names.

The names appearing at S. Nos. 22, 39, 64, 84, and 100 denote given names. As each name consists of three words and the first word is 'Muhammad' used as a part of the blessings, the entries have to be prepared under the remaining two words. The word 'Muhammad' has to be inverted. This has been despite some names terminating with 'Khan'.

In the S. No. 31, the name begins with 'Shah Muhammad'. Shah is the family name duly subordinated to the personal name, and Muhammad is used as the blessings. Hence, both the words be inverted.

The entry at S. No. 25 pertains to the name-of-person, beloging to the old Mysore region. The word Cikmagluri is used to convey that he hails from Chikmaglur. As it is an obvious place name, entry has to be avoided under it. Likewise, all the names at S. Nos. 29, 43 and 62 are terminating with place names, the entries have been prescribed in the other set of words. Yet, in the names at S. Nos. 48, and 134, the end part denotes the family name derived from the place Delhi. Hence, the entries have been prescribed under it as it has now become a recognised surname. On the other hand, the place name Lakhnavi appearing along with the surname Siddiqi at S. No. 120 has been retained in subordination to the surname.

The name listed at S. No. 41, consists of two parts. The first one is Abu Sayida which is the given name, and the other one is the name of her husband/father. Hence, the entry should be made in her name. In Indic names-of-persons, Arabic words carry Indian context.

The name at S. No. 44 begins with a prefix title 'Agha' and is followed by the given name. The title is required to be preserved as it has become the part of the name but only in the inverted order. Similar is the case of the names-of-persons at S. No. 76 and 102.

Name listed at S. No. 52 is of two parts. The first one is the personal name. The second part is the name of his father. Hence, the entry word should be the personal name, as indicated.

The names Sayyid Ahmed, Sayyid Ali, Shaikh Cand and Sek Khasim listed at S. Nos. 15, 30, 47 and 91 denote the personal names. Sayyid (or Shaikh/Sek) is generally employed as a prefix title, in the first part of many names. But, here it is the part of the names. Therefore, the entries have to be made under the straight sequence. Similar is the case with the name listed at S. No. 60, where Vazir is the part of the given name.

Similarly, entries at S. Nos. 1, 34, 38, 59, 65, 66, 67, 68, and 95 denote the personal names along with a prefix title Syed or its usual variant Sayyid. The title indicates that the person is a direct descendant of the family of Prophet Mohammad from Saudi Arabia. This title has by usage, become a part of the names-of- persons. Therefore, it is to be preserved but only in subordination to the personal name. On the other hand, the name at S. No. 134 includes the surname also. Hence, the prescribed entry has to be prepared under the surname. On similar lines, the abbreviation S. appearing as the prefix to the name at S. No. 14 looks a short form of Syed. The other two words are his personal name. Hence, the prescribed entry has been made under the given name with the initial S. inverted.

The names at S. Nos. 56, 96 and 97 consist of three or more parts, each ending with Khan. Hence, Khan is to be treated as the family name and the entries should have been prepared under it. Yet, in the names-of-persons listed at S. Nos. 81 to 90 barring 83 and 84, the word Khan has been used as the end part of the names. As all the names are of two words, Khan has been treated as the part of the given names. The entries in the names would be in the full form of the names. On the other hand, the name listed at S. No. 84, comprises three words, each ending with Khan, and the first word is Muhammed. Hence, Muhammad is to be inverted. The remaining two words have to be treated as personal name. The name at S. No. 83 begins with an initial Em. which appears to be the abbreviation of Mohammad. Hence, the treatment has to be similar.

All the names at S. No. 93, 108, 117, 118, 119, 120, 131 and 134 are terminating with the surnames under which the entries are to be prepared. However, the entry at S. No. 134 also contains the prefix Sayyid. The entry be made under the surname.

The names-of-persons at S.Nos. 94 and 114 are of 4 parts. The first two words have been converted into initials. The other two denote the personal name, under which the entries should be made.

The names at S. No. 99 denotes the personal name with a prefix Dr. The prefix be removed, and the entry be made under the personal name.

The name at S. No. 123 includes the prefix Mufti, and the remaining is the personal name. Similarly, the name-of-person at S. No. 135, comprises four parts. The first two words have beenn contracted into initials. The remaining two words denote the personal name. The entry should be made under this personal name.

8.4 EAST INDIAN NAMES

Incorrect renderings have been observed in a few Indic names-of- persons specially from the eastern parts of the country. These instances are described as under :

S.No.	Rendering in the List	Correct Entry	Reference
1.	Ahamada, Mainuddina	Mainuddina Ahamada	1053
2.	Ameda, Aphasara	Aphasara Ameda	6166
3.	Ameda, Sirajuddina	Sirajuddina Ameda	6167
4.	Ara-Rahamana, Masuda	Masuda Ara-Rahamana	6169
5.	Bala, Dhirena	Dhirena Bala	2911
6.	Bala, Prtha	Prtha Bala	2911
7.	Brahma, Trpti	Tripti Brahma	9643
8.	Bidyabinoda, Kshirodaprasada	Kshirodaprasada Bidyabinoda	9641
9.	Haka, Aminula	Aminula Haka	2946
10.	Haq, Hasan Azizul	Azizul Haq	6260
11.	Imadadula Haka Milana	Milana, Imadadula Haka	6263
12.	Isalama, Najarula	Najarula Isalama	6264
13.	Jabbara, Abadula	Abdula Jabbara	6266
14.	Majumadara, Sisira, Dr.	Majumadara, Sisira	2951

15.	Mostafa, Golam	Golam Mostafa	6906
16.	Piyasi, Kamal	Kamal Piyasi	535
17.	Rida, Abu	Abu Rida	6347
18.	Shankar, Daya	Daya Shankar	2340
19.	Shankar, Sangeeta	Sangeeta Shankar	9267
20.	Shastri, Ajay Mitra	Mitra Shastri, Ajay	7123
21.	Thrangu, Khenchen	Rinpoche, Khenchen Thrangu	7197
22.	Tulasi Kasyapa	Sharma Kasyapa, Tulasiram	4739

There are several reasons for preparing the above entries under incorrect word or word-groups, described as under:

The entries listed at S. Nos. 1, 2, 3, 5, 6, 7, 9, 12, 13, 15, 16, 17, 18 and 19 pertain to given name entries. Surname has not been used in any of the names. Therefore, altering the sequence of any name is not permissible.

Entry at S. No. 4 includes the name of the author's husband duly suffixed. Her personal name is Masuda Ara. The entry has to be prepared under her name.

The entry at S. No. 8 is the name-of-person without any surname. This author had flourished upto 1898. Strictly speaking, this name does not fall in the scope of this work, but included as an exception as he lived upto the end of the nineteenth century. At that time, many persons in Bengali speaking region were not employing surname. A name-of-person of that time had consisted of only the personal name. In the above name, the second part is the degree designation title and therefore, merely a qualifying epithet which does not deserve promotion as the main entry element.

The word Hasan occurring in the first part of the name at S. No. 10 reflects his family tradition, and Azizul Haq is the personal name. Hence the entry should go under the given name. The word Milana used as the last part of the name at S.No. 11 is the pen-name. The remaining two words denote the given name. The correct entry is to be prepared under his pen-name. The prefix Dr. in the name at S. No. 14 is required to be dropped.

The word Abu appearing in the name at S. No. 17 is the part of the given name. Indic names of Muslims do not always use these words with their true Arabic conditions.

The name appearing at S. No. 20 contains the surname Mitra. It also makes use of the degree title Shastri, which has been suffixed. The preference of the author is to treat it as an integral part of his name. It has become a case of a two-worded family name.

The name-of-person at S. No. 21 has the surname component 'Rinpoche'. Yet, it is not known why it was dropped at the time of rendering. It appears to be a Sikkimi name. Even if the family name is ignored, the entry ought to have been prepared under the personal name in the straight order. In this context, it is further stated that the word 'Rinpoche' is generally used as a prefix title. It means a reincarnated Lama. Yet, in this name, it is used as the suffix. Therefore, its status has been changed to some what to a family name.

The name listed at S. No. 22 is from Sikkim. He has used a combination of two caste names as his family name. The entry should be made under the set of the two caste names as indicated.

8.5 WEST INDIAN NAMES

S.No.	Rendered name in the List	Correct rendering	Reference
1.	Anand, Sudha Bhandari	Bhandari Anand, Sudha	9726
2.	Bala, Prakasa	Prakasa Bala	1007
3.	Bhatta, Diva Pandeya	Pandeya Bhatta, Diva	7274
4.	Borisagara, Ratilala	Ratilala Borisagara	7284
5.	Harsha, Ashok	Ashok Harsha	10425
6.	Hutheesing, Krishna Nehru	Nehru Hutheesing, Krishna	4291
7.	Hemacandra, Narayana	Narayana Hemacandra	10426
8.	Jagamohana, Sarala	Sarala Jagamohana	7600
9.	Jaising, Indira	Indira Jaising	6527
10.	Khilnani Saqi, Bhagvan	Saqi, Bhagvan Khilnani	1321
11.	Krshna, Divakara	Divakara Krshna	4430
12.	Kumaraappa, Jagadisacandra	Jagadisacandra Kumaraappa	4443
13.	Nanaji, Purushotama	Purushotama Nanaji	3762
14.	Naoroji, Dadabhai	Dadabhai Naoroji	10536
15.	Noronha, Leslie de	de Noronha, Leslie	10061
16.	Pagdi, Setumadhava Rao	Setumadhava Rao Pagdi	11350

17.	Pathakaji, Vyomesacandra Janardana	Pathaka, Vyomesacandra Janardana	10575
18.	Umaravadiya, Batubhai	Batubhai Umaravadiya	10659
19.	Yasavanta, Lokanatha	Lokanatha Yasavanta	8178

The entry no. 1 pertains to a feminine author, who does not use the name of her husband, but is making use of two family names, the first one belongs to her father and the second is of her husband. She is a Marathi and is married to a Punjabi person. Therefore, the entry has to go in both the surnames, as appearing in her name. It is a case of a double worded surname.

The name of the author at S. No. 2 is the personal name of a female. As is apparant from her name, she has discarded all the other attachments generally found in a name-of-person from the Western parts of the country. The entire is her given name. Hence, reversing the sequence is not justified.

In the entries at S. Nos. 4, 5, 7, 8, 9, 11, 12, 13, 14, 18 and 19 the sequence has been "Personal name-Father's or Husand's Name". Surname has not been used in any of the names. Hence, entries have to be prepared under the given names of the persons, and not under the name of the father or husband.

Name listed at S. No. 10 is a Sindhi. The name of his father is missing, and the pen-name is suffixed in the end. As a literary name if employed, becomes the most prominent component of a name, the entry should have gone under the "takhallus". In this respect, it is observed that there are two more similar entries in the list, and both have been prepared under their pen-names. Therefore consistency has been violated.

The name listed at S. No. 15 appears to be from Goa and belongs to a converted Christian group. The prefix 'de' is the part of her surname, and it is to be retained as such. However, it does not have a place value in the filing sequence.

S. No. 16 lists a Marathi author Setumadhava Rao Pagdi. This author spent major part of his life at Hyderabad. He earned his Telugu surname 'Pagdi' which means headgear. His another book is written under P. Setumadhava Rao. Hence the preference of the author is known. The entry should be made in his personal name.

In the rendering done at S. No. 17, the surname Pathakji has been retained as such. The termination ji of the family name is superfluous. Therefore it should be disregarded in the entry.

The name-of-person at S. No. 3 is having the two-worded surname in the end. It is however, not known why the entry was made under the personal names ?

At S. No. 6, the name of the sister of Jawaharlal Nehru has been listed. She has used two family names. The first one is of her father and the other is of her husband. She is married to a Marathi. The entry be prepared under the set of two family names.

8.6 SOUTH INDIAN NAMES

S.No.	Rendered name in the List	Recommended entry	Reference
1.	Abubakkar, Sara	Sara Abubakkar	10847
2.	Abdulaziz, Ji Zid Raziyah Begum	Raziyah Begum Abdulaziz Ji Zid	8624
3.	Ahamatu, Tasim	Tasim Ahamatu	5567
4.	Aikara, Jacob	Jacob Aikara	9720
5.	Aiyar, Mani Shankar	Mani Shankar Aiyar	9721
6.	Aladi, Aruna	Aruna Aladi	11568
7.	Alexander, Meena	Meena Alexander	2990
8.	Ali, B. Sheikh	Sheikh Ali, B.	8598
9.	Alunkal, Jon	Jon Alunkal	10963
10.	Anaikatta Perumal	Perumal, Anaikatta	11569
11.	Arampulickal, James	James Arampulickal	9734
12.	Arasanayagam, Jean	Jean Arasanayagam	6439
13.	Assayag, Jackie	Jackie Assayag	9735
14.	Avadhani, Ravi Yan	Ravi Yan Avadhani	8494
15.	Ayya, Dr. T.S.	Ayya, T.S.	6448
16.	Banni, Mallikarjuna	Mallikarjuna Banni	7674
17.	Basheer, Vaikom Muhammad	Muhammad Basheer, Vaikom	10972
18.	Belagere, Ravi	Ravi Belagere	10856
19.	Celly, Anu	Anu Celly	329
20.	Cenaiyin, Matavan	Matavan Cenaiyan	8322
21.	Cenni, Rajendra	Rajendra Cinni	900

22.	Chandy, Anna	Anna Chandy	6509
23.	Citamapalli Maruti	Maruti, Citamapalli	4286
24.	Cinnannatt, Rajan	Rajan Cinnannatt	7728
25.	Cinnatt, Vargis	Vargis Cinnatt	7729
26.	Das, Kamala	Kamala Das	4002
27.	Desikacaryulu, Tirumala Krsna	Krsna Desikacaryulu Tirumala	11710
28.	Devadas, Rajammal P.	Rajammal P. Devadas	6448
29.	Devadasan, Iris	Iris Devadasan	6564
30.	George, Annie	Annie George	7248
31.	Hegade, Divaspati	Divaspati Hegade	907
32.	Hegade, Gopalakrsna	Gopalakrsna Hegade	908
33.	Jackson, Monica	Monica Jackson	3297
34.	Jacob, George	George Jacob	6779
35.	James, Josef	Josef James	344
36.	Josaph, Sara	Sara Josaph	7737
37.	Kakkattil, Akbar	Akbar Kakkattil	7739
38.	Kamat, Mangalapura Narayana	Narayana Kamat, Mangalapura	7688
39.	Kanavalli, Sadananda	Sadananda Kanavalli	10928
40.	Kariyil, Anthony	Anthony Kariyil	3320
41.	Kattirimalaic, Caral	Caral Kattirimalaic	8374
42.	Kavunkal, Jacob	Jacob Kavunkal	9966
43.	Kepriyel, Matan	Matan Kepriyel	8377
44.	Kochuparampil, Xavier	Xavier Kochuparampil	6826
45.	Kottapalle, Naganatha	Naganatha Kottapalle	11277
46.	Kottoor, Gopi Krishnan	Gopal Krishnan Kottoor	9975
47.	Kottur, Rajarathinam Pillai	Rajarathinam Pillai Kottur	2350
48.	Kumar, K. Naresh	Naresh Kumar, K.	6837
49.	Kumarswamy, Jacintha S.	Jacintha S. Kumarswamy	456
50.	Kuntar, Mohan	Mohan Kuntar	10889
51.	Laxman, Kamala	Kamala Laxman	6847
52.	Lokasevanirata, Di. Kongadiyappa	Kongadiyappa Lokasevanirata, Di.	10892
53.	Mani, Ajit	Ajit Mani	6874
54.	Malasetti, Basavaraja	Basavaraja Malasetti	10944
55.	Mani, Sunil	Sunil Mani	6875
56.	Manokaran, Karuna	Karuna Manokaran	11635
57.	Maribasetti, Sasikaladevi Es.	Sasikaladevi Es. Maribasetti	10895
58.	Masali, Jivanna	Jivanna Masali	921

59.	Matthews, David	David Matthews	3009
60.	Matukkakkuli, Matyu	Matyu Matukkakhuli	10999
61.	Matyu, Ebraham	Ebraham Matyu	7747
62.	Mavinakuli, Jayaprakasa	Jayaprakasa	10898
63.	Menon, Anjolie Ela	Anjolie Ela Menon	6889
64.	Menon, Raghava R.	Raghava R. Menon	6890
65.	Menon, Vimala	Vimala Menon	7749
66.	Miyan, Mukammatu Arip	Arip Miyan, Mukammatu	8396
67.	Moorthy, Vasantha	Vasantha Moorthy	6905
68.	Munir, Muhammad	Muhammad Munir	978
69.	Murty, K. Satchidananda	Satchidananda Murty, K.	6576
70.	Naidu, M. Reddappa	Reddappa Naidu, M.	497
71.	Namboodiry, Udayan	Udayan Namboodiry	6922
72.	Nataracan, Centi	Centi Nataracan	5045
73.	Natarajan, Kanchana	Kanchana Natarajan	3418
74.	Nayak, Harogadde Manappa	Manappa Nayak, Harogadde	7697
75.	Nayar, Nancy Ann	Nancy Ann Nayar	3346
76.	Nayudu, Chandra	Chandra Nayudu	6939
77.	Nayyar Harish	Harish Nayyar	6632
78.	Nilamparan, Kautama	Kautama Nilamparan	5003
79.	Onakkur, Jorj	Jorj Onakkur	7753
80.	Pai, Sirisha	Sirisha Pai	8022
81.	Palattunkal, Joyikkutti	Joyikkutti Palattunkal	7754
82.	Parthasarathy, Indira	Indira Parthasarathy	5016
83.	Pasir, S. Muhammatu	Muhammatu Pasir, S.	5017
84.	Patmanapan, Nila	Nila Patmanapan	5019
85.	Pattakatav, Antani Es.	Antani Es. Pattakatav	11010
86.	Pattattanam, Srini	Srini Pattattanam	11011
87.	Perumthottam, Joseph	Joseph Perumttottam	6987
88.	Phillip, Mini	Mini Phillip	10079
89.	Philipp, Ceriyan	Ceriyan Philipp	11013
90.	Philipp, Sibu	Sibu Phillipp	7759
91.	Poruthur, Anthony	Anthony Poruthur	10083
92.	Prasad, Sheela	Sheela Prasad	7001
93.	Pulikkunnel, Josaph	Josaph Pulikkunnel	11014
94.	Puthiyedath, Jose	Jose Puthiyedath	100945
95.	Raghunathan, Sudha	Sudha Raghunathan	2312
96.	Raghuramayya, Mavuduri	Mavuduri Raghuramayya	8539
97.	Rahul, Ram	Ram Rahul	3482
98.	Rajendran, Cecil	Cecil Rajendran	3486

99.	Rajesvari, Dr.	Rajesvari	1465
100.	Rama Krishna, Rani	Rani Rama Krishna	3490
101.	Rama Rao, Saumya	Saumya Rama Rao	7030
102.	Ramachandran, Sudhir	Sudhir Ramachandran	6863
103.	Ramakrishnan, Prema	Prema Ramakrishnan	553
104.	Ramanamurti, Mutya Venkata	Venkata Ramanamurti, Mutya	5114
105.	Rangacarya, Kesva	Kesva Rangacarya	11557
106.	Rao, Bhanuji	Bhanuji Rao	8215
107.	Rao, Manju	Manju Rao	3504
108.	Rao Purnima	Purnima Rao	3440
109.	Rao, Ram Mohan	Ram Mohan Rao	3499
110.	Rao-Seshadri, Shreelata	Shreelata Rao-Seshadri	7042
111.	Reddy, A. Geeta	Geeta Reddy, A.	563
112.	Reddy, A. Ranga	Ranga Reddy, A.	6711
113.	Skariya, Josaph	Josaph Skariya	11007
114.	Seshadri, Vijayalakshmi	Vijayalakshmi Seshadri	7107
115.	Shiva, Vandana	Vandana Shiva	6478
116.	Sigihalli, Balanna	Balanna Sigihalli	10938
117.	Sobel, Prem	Prem Sobel	7144
118.	Stanislaus, M. Sebastian	Sebastian Stanislaus, M.	7159
119.	Talengala, Ramakrsna	Ramakrsna Talengala	3993
120.	Thomas, Sarah	Sarah Thomas	7785
121.	Tomas, Jorj	Jorj Tomas	7787
122.	Tottaykkat, Joys	Joys Tottaykkat	10977
123.	Tuppada, Basavesvara	Basavesesvara, Tuppada	10943
124.	Urs, Shrijay Devaraj	Devaraj Urs, Shrijay	3686
125.	Usman, Pasir	Pasir Usman	5068
126.	Valikara, Cennanna	Cennanna Valikara	10945
127.	Vanalli, Niranjana	Niranjana Vanalli	7712
128.	Vasudev, Aruna	Aruna Vasudev	6613
129.	Vatavukotu, Velayudhan	Velayudhan Vatavukotu	11039
130.	Vattanky, John	John Vattanky	10248
131.	Venkareddi, Madhu	Madhu Venkareddy	10947
132.	Verghese, Anila	Anila Verghese	3693
133.	Zachariah, Mathai	Mathai Zachariah	7257

The names-of-persons appearing at S. Nos. 3 and 68 are the personal names of Muslims from Tamilnadu and Kerala, with the usual prefixes such as the name of the father, etc., are missing. Hence, altering the sequence is not permissible. In the names at S. Nos. 48, 69, and

83 the initials have to be inverted, and the remaining two words in each denote the personal name. Similarly, the names-of-persons at S. Nos. 19, 97, 106, 109 and 125 denote personal names. Hence, reversing the order is not required. Likewise, the Telugu names-of-persons at S. Nos. 27 and 104 bear the sequence 'House Name - Given Name'. The entries should be made under the personal names.

The entry at S. No. 5 is of a Tamil personal name in which the name of his father does not figure in its present form. The ultimate last part of his name "Aiyer" is his surname which is subordinate to his personal name. The entry has to be prepared under his given name, without any change.

The name listed at S. No. 8 bear the given name Sheikh Ali. It is preceded by the initial B. denoting his village name. Except the initial, the entire is the personal name.

At S. No. 6, entry be made under the given name, and not under the house name. Similarly, in all the names listed at S. Nos. 4, 9, 10, 11, 12, 13, 16, 18, 20, 21, 23, 25, 37, 39, 40, 41, 42, 43, 44, 45, 46, 47, 50, 58, 60, 62, 79, 81, 85, 87, 91, 93, 94, 116, 119, 122, 123, 126, 127, 129 and 130, entries have been made under the house/village name. Since a house or village name in South India is found to be subordinate to the given name, all the entries need be made under the given name, as indicated. LIkewise, the name at S. No. 17 bears the sequence 'Village Name- Given Name'. The entry should be made under the given name.

The name listed at S. No. 14 is of a Telugu person. Here, the sequence is"Given Name - House Name - Surname'. The house name is being represented by the initial. The entry should be made under his personal name. Similarly, in the names at S. Nos. 15 and 99 the prefix Dr. is to be removed.

Names listed at S. Nos. 31, 32, 38, 63, 64, 65, 70, 71, 74, 75, 76, 77, 80, 111, 112, and 124 bear the caste name in the end. As a caste appellation in South India is subordinate to the given name, all the entries should have gone under the personal names. In this context, it further stated that in the name at S. No. 124 bear the father's name also. The sequence is 'Father's Name - Personal Name - Caste Name'.

Entries at S. No. 1, 2, 7, 28, 29, 30, 33, 36, 49, 51, 56, 57, 59, 72, 73, 78, 82, 84, 86, 88, 95, 96, 98, 100, 101, 103, 114, 115, 117, 120, 128, and 131 have been wrongly prepared under the name of husband/father. They should have been made under the personal names as corrected.

Similarly, in the names at S. Nos. 26, 67, 92, 107, and 108 only a part of the husband's or father's name has been suffixed. On the other hand, the entry at 110, includes the reverse order of the name of husband. All these entries should be made under the given name.

The names at S. Nos. 22, 24, 34, 35, 53, 54, 55, 59,-61, 89, 90, 102, 105, 113, 118, 121, 132 and 133 have been entered under the name of father. Corerct rendering has been indicated.

The name-of-person at S. No. 52 bears the sequence 'Given name-Initial - Surname'. Since, a family name is secondary in South India the entry should be prepared under the personal name. Likewise, the name at S. No. 66 is the personal name followed by the respectful suffix. The entry should have been made under his personal name. The suffix can be retained in subordination to the given name.

8.7 ANANLYSIS AND DISCUSSION

A critical examination of the Indic names-of-persons, identified from the Accessions List and tabulated as above, has revealed that about 6.1% entries have been prepared choosing the wrong word or word-groups as entry element. This has been despite the fact that all the cataloguers employed in the preparation of the Accessions List, are either natives of India or Pakistan. Had the bibliographers been from a European, North American or some other alien country, instances of inconsistencies could have been many more. The occurrance of such a considerable percentage of incorrect entries clearly brings out the fact that the indexers had not gone in detail into the naming practices of the cultures to which the authors belonged. If such an exercise had been carried out in ernst, the number of inconsistencies/errors could have been kept to a bare minimum. The guidelines suggested in this study at various points while discussing the naming practices among the cultural, religious and ethnic groups and the way they were subjected to non-indigeneous influences, could have ameliorated the difficulties encountered by the cataloguers in arriving at the right choice of entry words. This evaluation undoubtedly enhances the validity of the hypothesis of this study that"sociological frame-of-reference if brought to bear upon cataloguing of names, would yield better dividends by way of correctly analysing and entering the Indic names-of-persons'.

Chapter IX

CONCLUSIONS AND FINDINGS

9.1 GENERAL

The sociological investigation of the Indic names carried out as the first part of this research work, has revealed quite a number of complexities that are encountered in cataloguing. Based on this basic exercise, specific rules in modifications to AACR 2 have been prescribed and illustrated with relevant examples so as to bring more clarity. In addition, specific guidelines have been generated to help the cataloguers in handling Indic names-of-persons in a rational and appropriate manner.

9.2 MAIN FINDINGS

The main findings of the present research work, are enumerated below:

1. Indic names-of-persons can not be handled satisfactorily, with the few generalised rules of the AACR. Other existing codes of cataloguing including Classified Catalogue Code have not been of much help in this regard.

2. Structure of the Indic names-of-persons, to a large extent, varies with the linguistic background of the person.

3. Variation in the style of writing Indic names-of-persons demands separate rules of cataloguing. In general, these variations occur due to immigration to other linguistic regions or alien lands.

4. Terms such as family name and surname are quite ambiguous in the context of Indic names.

5. Religious minorities form a sub - set of the linguistic groups of a given region.

6. Tribal names-of-persons bear the basic pattern of naming prevailing in a linguistic region.

7. Personal names given to individuals are independent of the prevailing caste system. Thus, persons belonging to different castes, may have identical personal names.

8. Anglicisation and Western transformation of the Indic names-of-persons, pose specific problems. Similar is the case of Portuguese, French and Arabic influenced names. Hence, they need to be addressed differently by a cataloguing code.

9. Simplification and rationalisation of the Indic names-of-persons have brought in distortions. These processes show an upward trend in their occurrance mainly due to the availability of enhanced educational facilities.

10. Other sociological phenomena such as 'Westernization' and 'Sanskritization' have also complicated the scenario. Dropping, adding or changing the family names occurring on account of the operation of such phenomena affect the structure of the names in a baffling manner.

11. The evaluation of the rendering Indic names-of-persons, in the 'Accessions Lists' for 1995, has revealed that 6.1% entries were made wrongly.

9.3 GUIDELINES

The sociological investigation of the names-of-persons, from all parts of the country (excluding the North-East), including major minorities, and a few other small but important ethnic groups, has resulted in the formulation of specific guidelines, as detailed below :

1. Author's preference for rendering his or her name has received universal acceptance, even if it violates the basic rules of naming. In other words, if an author wants to be known by some part of his name which may be based on considerations other than the established norms, the cataloguer is to abide by such preference.

Names-of-persons disclosing only one word in full form and the remaining in initials are also covered by this guideline because the preference of the author is already known in such cases. Despite knowing the full name of the author from the book, or otherwise, the entry is still made under the word given in full.

2.An honorific title prefixed to an Indic name-of-person is generally to be excluded in cataloguing. However, there are three exceptions to it, and in all the situations, the prefix title has to be preserved, though in an inverted order, duly subordinated to the other parts of the name. The situations are described as under :

(i) A title bestowed by the British Government in India. It is equally valid for a Royal title of the British Government in London.

(ii) A title which has become part of the name. Such a a title is generally used for generations together, by all the family members. Among the Muslim names, there are a few prefixes recommended for retention. Among the Hindu names of North India, such prefixes occur rarely. In the names of the erstwhile rulers of the princely states and their immediate kin, names of well-known saints, etc. prefixes, if used, are to be preserved in inverted order.

(iii) A title in the name of the father or husband, as the case may be, where such a name forms an integral part of the name-of-person. In particular, names from South and West India include prefix titles in the name of father/husband.

3. If an author has used two different forms of his name in his publica tions, only one form has to be consistently chosen. The general choice should be the one which the person has acquired through literary fame. However, it can be a problem if the catalogue is an integrated one in which publications of several languages have been included. In such cases, the form most known to the users has to be chosen to bring all the works of an author together, under one form of his name. The other forms of his name not selected as the entry word(s) have to be connected by crossreferences (See reference).

4. If however, it becomes imperative to choose more than one form of the name of an author, they should be connected by See also cross-references.

5. If the name of an author has undergone a change, his latest known name is to be used. The other name if already entered and the new name are to be linked by suitable cross-reference.

6. Entry word(s) :

Broadly, Indic names-of-persons from different parts of the country, fall into the following categories :

(a) Names-of-persons possessing family name in the end: Entry word has to be the surname, and the other parts of the name such as the personal name and/or other component parts, have to be inverted. There is an exception to this, listed as under :

(i) A surname though used in the end part of a name is often found to be subordinate to the given name, as is generally the case in the southern parts of the country. Personal name together with the surname forms the entry element in such cases.

(b) Name-of-person having no family name, in the end part : The entry has to be under the personal name. Yet, there are exceptions, described as under :

(i) In a name-of-person without the family name, but with the second or a subsequent part having the given name (or a part) of the husband/ father, the natural choice for the entry is then limited to the personal name.

(ii) If the personal name is the last element of a name- of-person, and is artificially broken into two or more parts with the last part of it employed consistently as if it were a family name, the catalogue entry has to go under this part.

(iii) If the order of the components of a name-of-person, is altered in such a way that the house name, which normally comes in the beginning of a name, appears in the end, and holds the key to his identity, the entry has be prepared under it. Other wise, it is the personal name alone which qualifies for the entry word, even though the end part is the house name.

Generally, family names employed in the end part of the Indic names are single worded. However, there are a few double or more worded family names, existing in some families in some linguistic areas. Their broad description is given below :

(i) In some linguistic areas such as West Bengal, Orissa, Kashmir, and Goa, two or more worded compound surnames are in common use. Sometimes, there is no visible indicator to spot them easily. However, the coverage of such multi-worded family names, in different linguistic parts in this presentation, is helpful to identify them. Entry has to be made under the entire multi-worded family name.

(ii) A female author may employ, in rare instances, a set of two family names, the first denoting the surname of the father and the other representing that of the husband. Here again, there may or may not be any visible symbol, to identify them. The entry in a cataloguing system has to be made under the two words taken together.

(iii) A two worded family name in which one part denotes the caste of the bearer, and the other one may indicate profession, or some other feature. Here, both the words have to be treated as a single surname.

(iv) A double worded family name in which the first word, though irremovable, is merely an affectionate term. The entry has to be prepared under the other word. This has been found in usage in some of the names from Kashmir, where Kaul is used merely as an affectionate word. Yet, if Kaul alone is employed as the surname, the entry has to be made under it.

7. Suffixes

In some Indic names-of-persons, specific attachments may be suffixed. The suffix may generally denote one of the under- mentioned features :

(a) An Indian academic degree;

(b) A revered, esteemed or affectionate term;

(c) A holy or ecclesiastic order;

(d) A pen-name, literary name or poetic name, known in Urdu as takhallus. It may also include a similar appellation for non - writers, in exceptional instances.

(e) An explanatory epithet denoting specific status of the person.

If an Indian or vernacular academic degree designation is used in the end part of a name-of-person, its correct status is to be investigated. There are three possibilities, enumerated here :

(i) It is used as a surname, and the person is identified by it. The entry is to be prepared under the suffix.

(ii) It is used merely as an academic epithet. Hence, it is to be dropped at the time of cataloguing.

(iii) It is employed in combination with the family name. The surname along with the degree designation be considered as a case of a two worded family name. The entry is to be prepared under both the words taken together.

(b) If a revered, esteemed or affectionate title word is suffixed to an

Indic name-of-person, it is generally ignored, as it constitutes a superfluous appellation. Yet, it is recommended to be preserved if it appears in the father's or husband's name in those specific names- of-persons, where the practice to employ the name of the father or husband, as the case may be, in the names-of- persons is prevailing.

(c) If a holy order, or an ecclesiastic authority word is suffixed to a specific name-of-person, it is generally preserved, but in a subordinate position. In this respect, it may be observed that its placement in most of the names is after the given name. The same position has to be retained.

(d) If a pen-name or a similar designation is appended to a name-of-person, it generally acquires the most important role. If the person is identified by it, which is the case in most of such names, the main entry is to be made under it. This is despite usage of the surname or some other important component part in the name. If the pen- name is followed by a place name, the name of the place together with the word specifically used as the literary name constitutes the entry words.

(e) If an explanatory epithet has been suffixed to a name- of-person, and the person has not been identified by it, the same has to be preserved in subordination to the given name. If it is found to be superfluous, it can be removed.

8. Personal names

Depending upon the linguistic region, placement of the personal name can either be in the beginning, in the middle or in the end part of a name-of-person. In this context, it is observed that it generally remains fixed within a given linguistic area The present study would enable a cataloguer to identify the given name.

Given names can be single worded or multi-worded. In some parts of the country, if a personal name is complex, the general tendency is to break it into two parts. In rendering, both the parts appear as distinct words, though they are intelligible only when read together, in context. Similarly, in some other linguistic societies, a person is named by two names, generally known as the first name and the second name. However, both the names put in a definite sequence form the personal name. Hence, the order of the two names, need not be altered.

In Telugu and Kannada cultures, sometimes personal names can be multi-worded. However, the person is identified only by the last few words. The earlier words are called pre-substantive part. The present study would enable a cataloguer to spot the entry element in such a long -stringed name.

9.4 PAST STUDIES

Major findings and relevant recommendations of other scholars have been duly considered in this thesis. Their details are given below:

Ranganathan's endeavour has initially been in analysing the problems connected with the Indic names-of-persons. He was fortunate to get the Unesco Project on Asian Names, sanctioned. However, the outcome and the findings of the Project, have not been of help to a cataloguer. The so called Statistical Principle has been more of an over-simplification rather than a device that provides pragmatic solutions. Further, his background of Mathematics perhaps made him believe that Indic names-of-persons could be put to a stringent logic, in the selection of the entry words, in cataloguing. This has resulted in his recommending unique prescriptions which are inconsistant with the prevailing traditions. Probably, it was because of this reason that the Statistical Principle was never accepted by the cataloguing world.

Another major prescription of Ranganathan, calling for disclosure of contents of the name of the author on the verso of the title- page failed to ellicit a favourable response from the writers. National Standards promulgated within the country have gone unheeded by the authors as well as the book trade.

Yet, another unique prescription of Ranganathan called as the "Recall Value" calls for the entry to be prepared under that part of the name by which library readers would be able to recall the author. Though, valid for South Indian names, where in the recall value is concentrated in the given names, its validity could not be extended to names from other regions. Even this pescription is not applicable universally to all South Indian names and did not find favour among the cataloguers.

Sengupta together with IASLIC and IFLA, had made great efforts in resolving the issues. However, they viewed most of the problems from a distance and they were successful in tackling the problems only at the theoretical plane. Though, the resolutions of the IASLIC and IFLA were excellent contributions in providing a better frame-of-reference, no acceptable solutions were provided. In addition, the prescriptions in respect of several linguistic regions were not consistent with the established social practices.

The results of this research work are the outcome of the in-depth study of the sociology of naming practices in each linguistic area. Though, this sociological aspect in a strict sense, is not a part of the cataloguing subject, nevertheless it helps the formulation of prescriptions and guidelines, which provide the required frame-of-reference in understanding and deciding the entry elements for Indic names of authors.

9.5 CONTRIBUTION OF THIS WORK

Indic names-of-persons have been studied in this research work with a view to analyse the grammatical sequence of the words as prevailing in usage. The following elements have been identified while covering the significant religious communities, among different linguistic regions.

1. Removable words;

2. Essential but impotent attachments;

3. Entry elements.

The present research work has provided an opportunity to delve into such a diverse field, at a much deeper sociological level and based on it, to formulate elaborate cataloguing rules, supplementing those in AACR 2. With suitable modifications, they can equally be adopted in other cataloguing codes, if so desired. The present work would go a long way in facilitating the systematic treatment of the Indic names by the cataloguers, bibliographers and indexers.

9.6 VALIDATING THE HYPOTHESIS

The evaluation of the Indic names-of-persons as rendered in the 'Accessions List' has revealed that about 6.1% entries were made under the wrong word or word-groups. These mistakes would not have occurred had the sociological frame-of-reference of the Indic names was taken into consideration by the indexers. Redoing the exercise in the light of the sociological investigations, carried out has resulted in the reduction of the wrong entries to a negligible level. Hence, the hypothesis framed for the study, has been substantially validated in quantitative measure.

Further, the different rules formulated for cataloguing, the guidelines, the findings and recommendations in this research study, would enable a cataloguer to enter most of the Indic names in a cataloguing system with little difficulty. Hence the hypothesis which provided the direction for the work proceeding to its culmination, has also been substantially validated, in qualitative terms.

9.7 LIMITATIONS OF THE WORK

India is a complex and vast country having a large number of cultural entities, each with several religious followings. Fragmentation of these religious and linguistic groups in sects and sub-sects, regions and zones have further compounded the problem and though every effort is made in this work to cover as many groups as possible, many such groups are not included on account of their small numbers, and restricted exposure. In addition, aspects such as the following are kept outside the purview of this study, with a suggestion that they can be taken up as subjects for further study/research :

(a) Phonetic variation in the words employed as parts of the names.

(b) Pseudonyms.

(c) Tribal communities from all the parts of the country. In the present work, though some Tribal groups have been included, it has been felt that their coverage is not adequate.

(d) Specific communities living on the sea-shores and other areas, having regular interactions with the foreigners.

(e) Problems arising out of migration to another cultural belt, have not been fully investigated.

(f) Influence of alien culture in the colonial pockets of the country, needs a more detailed study.

(g) Religious minority groups present in various linguistic regions, forming an insignificant proportion of their population, can be a potential subject of further research.

In addition to the problem areas described above, there are some situations in which the cataloguer can not take correct decisions in rendering all the names-of-persons. Such names pertain to Karnataka, Kerala and Tamilnadu. In Karnataka, the name of the village if occurring in a name belonging to the Marathi dominant area, is the surname under which the catalogue entry is to be made, where as in the other parts of the state, it is a secondary part of the name. Similarly, in Karnataka, Kerala and Tamilnadu, in such names bearing the name of father, problem exists in knowing which part denotes the personal name. As the source of obtaining the given name and the name of the father is the same, and the father's name can either be suffixed or prefixed, it can cause confusion. In this context, it is added that in most of the names, the placement of the parts can help in spotting each part correctly, as well as in understanding whether the place name is used as the family name or not. Yet, if the placement of the component parts of a name is altered, and the author does not provide any such indications, it can result in loss of clarity. The problem of identifying the masculine component part in a feminine name-of-person is not there. Here the cataloguer is advised to make cross-reference entry in case of any doubtfusituation.

The outcome of the present research work on the 'Treatment of the Indic Names in AACR 2 - A study' is presented to the cataloguing world, with the hope that the same will be a useful tool in properly indexing the names of Indic writers. The work, it is believed, has succeeded in a fair measure, in providing a better understanding of the prevailing structures of the Indic names-of- persons, and the relative arrangement of the parts of such names. The objectives of this study would have been achieved to the satisfaction of the author if the work helps the cataloguers in resolving the conflicts encountered in deciding the entry elements for a variety of Indic authors.

Appendix A

Glossary Of Terms

Acharya:-Teacher. It is also a vernacular degree meaning Master of Arts.

Amil:-A name given in erstwhile Sindh to educated members of the Lohana community, a Hindu caste consisting of principally of bankers, clerks andminor officials.

Amir:- High noble.

Anglicisation:- The process of converting specific words used in the names-of- persons into their English form so as to suit the tongue of the former British rulers.

Atak:-Gujarati surname.

Auxiliary:-A common noun, used as the middle part of a name. It has to be read in the context of the word preceding it.

Babu:- Respectable and honourable prefix title often used for an educared person. In West Bengal, it denotes a gentleman. Also, a clerk.

Bahadur:- Literally, brave or warrier. A title used by both Hindus and Muslims, often bestowed by the erstwhile British Government in India, added to other titles, it increases their honour but alone, it designates an inferior ruler.

Bauda:- Slave of the court (A person in the Emperor's service).

Begum:- The feminine of 'Nawab'. Now employed as a respectable suffix in feminine names of the Muslims. At times, it is also used as a prefix to a married Muslim female.

Bhil:- A tribe in Madhya Pradesh.

Bibi:- A feminine auxiliary employed by the married Muslims. Also a prefix used in Punjabi female names.

Biswas:- Village accountant. This term is mostly used in West Bengal.

Chaturvedi:- Knowing all the four Vedas of Hindus. Its short form is Chobey.

Chaudhury:- Land-lord. It is also used as a prefix by the persons of martial castes.

Daroga:- Suprintendent (in Police).

Darwesh:- Mystic, member of sufic order, whence English "dervish".

Dastur:- Parsee priest. It is used as a prefix as well as a suffix.

Desai:- Revenue officer, similar to a Dy. Collector.

Deshmukh:- Maratha title of a hereditary official in charge of a group of villages.

Family Name:- A word or word-group consisting of proper noun or sometimes by common noun, reflecting the caste status or some other background of the bearer, used as the end part of the names.

Faqir:- Needy, destitute; conventionally applied with reference to self.

Ghazi:- Victorious in war against infidels; title generally adopted by rulers after success in such a war.

Given Name:- The name given to a person, generally at the time of his birth. It is also known as personal name, and is equivalent to a christian name in the Western countries.

Gotra:- A clan to which a Hindu family belongs, through genealogical relationship.

Gulam:- Slave. It is used as an auxiliary in Muslim and Hindu names.

Hajji:- One who has performed the pilgrimage to Mecca (Haj).

Hakim:- Unani medical doctor.

Hakkim:- Ruler; jagirdar, holder of a territorial charge.

Hazrat:-(Venerable, honourable) presence; used as a prefix to the name of Emperor, saint, etc.

Inamdar:- Receiver of a gift, particularly granted free of revennue.

Intiperu:- Telugu house name used as the first part of a name. It is found subordinate to the personal name.

Ism:- The given name of a Muslim. It is also known as Alam.

Jagirdar:- Receiver of a jagir assigned by a ruler to land lord on spe-cial terms.

Jamindar:- Landlord. Also used for a farmer.

Kalam:- Big; senior, yogi.

Kamtarin:- Lowliest, most humble.

Katib:- Scribe, writer.

Kazi:- Muslim judicial person. Also performs marriages.

Khatun:- Feminine of Khan. It is a suffix in a Muslim feminine name, used as an auxiliary.

Khitab:- A distinguished title of honour, generally bestowed by a ruler.

Kotwal:- Chief police official of a town.

Kulkarni:- Village accountant. The term is mostly used in Karnataka.

Kunyah:- Literally means patronymic, and sometimes indicates descent. It normally consists of Abu Ibn, Umm, bin or bint, etc.

Lala:- Honourable prefix title used for a merchant.

Laqab:- An honorific or descriptive epithet, sometimes a nick-name, often a title.

Maharaja:- King.

Maharani:- Queen.

Mansabdar:- Holder of rank (mansab) in the Mughul service.

Matriliny:- The system under which the office, property and the family name of the mother's brother is passed on to the next generation.

Maulvi:- A learned Muslim.

Misl:- Denoting different Sikh jathas or groups which became powerful in Punjab after the last invasion of Ahmed Shah Abdali in 1769 and which divided the entire territory of Punjab among themselves.

Mukhi:- Chief.

Munshi:- Title for a post of clerk.

Mu'azzin:- Person giving call to Muslim prayer.

Mulla:- Muslim theologian or scholar.

Naik or Nayak:- Community head.

Name-of-person:- Full name of the person used in offical files and other documents.

Nasab:- Pedgree, a list of the ancestors, immediately following the given name or ism. Each personal name is denoting the given name of the father, grand father and so on. A connecting word such as ibn, or bin (son of) or bint (daughter of) is employed to separate the two personal names.

Nawab:- Deputy; mode of address for a noble (of Excellancy, Highness).

Nisbat:- A distributive adjective indicating the place of birth, origin or dwelling place, sect, tribe, family occupation, trade, or profession of the owner.

Nizam:- Governer during the Mughul period. It had been used for the ruler of the former Hyderabad state.

Padshah:- King or Emperor.

Pagadi:- Headgear.

Pandit:- A prefix employed by the persons belonging to Brahmin caste. Also, it refers to a learned person.

Patil:- An equivalent of Patel generally used in Maharashtra and North Karnataka.

Patel:- Village headman.

Pathak:- Full command over at least in one Veda. Another version is that it denotes a person performing puja once a day.

Patriliny:- The system under which the office, property and the surname of the person is passed through the male line, from father to son.

Patwari:- Village accountant.

Pir:- Mystic (sufic) guide/Muslim saint.

Pradhan:- Village chief. The term is generally used in Orissa.

Pramukh:- Chief.

Prefix title:- A word of respect. It may denote the caste, profession or social status of the person. At times, it may also be a conferred title of honour.

Pujari:- One who offers Puja, Priest.

Qalandar:- Member of a sect of ecstatic mystics among Muslims.

Raja:- Ruler; a title given by Mughal emperors usually to Hindu nobles.

Rajamata:- Mother of the ruler.

Sadhu:- Hindu ascetic.

Sadr:- Judge.

Sahukar:- Money lender, Merchant.

Sanskritization:- A social process in which a lower caste persons move higher. In the names-of-persons, persons belonging to the lower castes are making use of the higher caste family names.

Sardar:- Brave. It is a generic prefix for a male Sikh name. Its feminine is Sardarni.

Shastri:- Vernacular degree means Bachelor of Arts. Also, used as a surname by Brahmins in south India.

Shaikh:- Head of (Arab) tribe; Chief, elder, religious devine, complimentary epithet for Indian Muslim (also Shaikhzada).

Sudra:- The fouth division of the Hindus who were recognised to do all the service work for the upper castes.

Suffix:- A respectable and honourable word. It may also denote a vernacular academic degree.

Sufi:- Muslim mystic.

Surname:- Synonymous to family name.

Swamy:- A revered title prefixed to the names of Hindu saints.

Takhallus:- It is the literary name under which a poet or a writer acquires prominence in public. It is known in Hindi as 'upnam'.

Talukdar:- Officer incharge of a district (in Hyderabad State) or collector of today.

Tarafdar:- Ruler; governer of a territory (taraf).

Tarwad:- Malayalam house name used as a prefix to the given name. It is subordinate to the given name.

Trivedi:- Having full knowledge of at least three Vedas. Its other forms are Tiwari and Tripathi.

Upnam:- An equivalent of pen-name, used by the Hindi authors.

Urf:- Denotes the nick-name of the person. In some names, it has been used as the takhallus or the literary name. In others, is is only an added name.

Ustad:- Teacher, master-painter or singer, etc.

Vaidya:- A Hindu Ayurvedic medical doctor.

Vaisya:- The third main division of the Hindus who were in involved in trading and business.

Veethuperu:- Malayalam family name, generally used as the first part of a name-of-person.

Vidya-vachaspati:- Doctor of Philosophy.

Wazir:- Minister; in the Mughul empire, the principal minister who also controlled finance.

Westernization:- A social process under which higher caste persons abandon the usage of family names.

Zat:- Rank; expressed in numerals, that indicated the holder's personal pay and status in the Mughul hierarchy.

Appendix B

Bibliography

Abdul Huq, A.M. 1974 Cataloguing Bengali names. ***Herald of Library Science***. Vol. 13 (3-4) : pp. 224 - 9.

Abdul Huq, A.M. 1976a Names as catalog entries. pp. 1 - 16. ***In*** Encyclopedia of Library and Information Science (ed. by Allan Kent). Vol. 19. Marcel Dekker, New York.

Abdul Huq, A.M. 1976b? An unpublished study at the St. John's Uni versity. p. 2. ***Quoted in*** 'Names as catalog entries' (by A.M. Abdul Huq). In Encyclopedia of Library and Information Science (ed. by Allen Kent). Vol. 19. Marcel Dekker, New York.

Abdul Huq, A.M. 1979 Problems and prospects in the organization of Bengali materials. ***Libri***. Vol. 29 (1): pp. 51-63.

Accessions List : South Asia 1995 The Library of Congress Accessions List: South Asia including cumulative index 1995. 4 V. The LIbrary of Congrss Office, New Delhi.

Ali Houissa 1993 Structure and rendering of Arabic proper names for bibliographic purposes. pp. 351 -66. ***In*** Encyclopedia of Library and Information Science (ed. by Allen Kent). Vol. 52. Marcel Dekker, New York.

American Library Association 1988 Anglo - American Cataloguing Rules 2nd rev. ed. Chicago, American Library Association. pp. 384-6.

Anantha Krishna Iyer, L.K. 1912. The tribes and castes of Cochin. Vol. 3. Reprinted by Cosmo Pub., Delhi, 1981. p. 455.

Atkinson, Edwin T. 1882 The Himalayan gazetteer. Vol.3 Pt. 1. Reprinted by Cosmo Pub., Delhi, 1973. pp. 268-76.

Avram, Henriette D., et. al. 1967 Fields of information on Library of Congress catalog cards : Analysis of a random sample, 1950-1964. Library *Quarterly.* Vol. 37 (2) : pp. 180 - 92.

Badiur Rahman, Abul Fazl Mohammad 1970 Problems in descriptive cataloguing in Pakistan. *Eastern Librarian.* Vol. 4(4) : pp. 277-85.

Balasubramanyan, S. 1961 Rendering of South Indian names appearing on the title pages of works in Roman alphabet: An outline of the problems involved with some suggestions for discussion. pp. 72-9. *In* Indic names including proceedings of the Seminar on the Rendering of Indic Names (IASLIC Special Publication no.2). IASLIC, Calcutta.

Basham, A.L. 1967 The wonder that was India. Reprinted by Rupa and Co., New Delhi, 1995. p. 152.

Belsare, V.B. 1960 Maharashtrian names- their nature and problem in cataloging. *IASLIC Bulletin.* Vol. 5(2) : p. 74 -7.

Bendall, Cecil 1887 Letter to the editor on the choice of the entry element of the Indic names-of-person. *Indian Antiquary: A Journal of Oriental Research.* Vol. 16 : pp. 312-3. (Reprinted by Swati Publications, Delhi in 1984).

Bendall, Cecil 1893 Preface to the Supplement to the Catalogue of San skrit, Pali and Prakrit books. British Museum, London. pp. v- vi. *Quoted in* Ranganathan, S.R. and Sivaraman, K.M. Rendering of Hindu names in headings: Function vs position. *Modern Librarian*. Vol. 10 (2) : 1940 : p. 69. (Original not seen).

Bhattacharyya, G. 1969 Cataloguing research in India. *Library Science with a slant to Documentation.* Vol. 6 (4) : pp. 307 - 86.

Bhattacharyya, G. 1973 A critique of the "General Principles" in AACR. *Library Science with a slant to Documentation.* Vol. 10 (3): pp.393-427.

Biswas, Subhodh Kumar 1993 Velip. pp. 201-8. *In* Goa (People of India. Vol. 21) (ed. by K.S. Singh). Popular Prakashan and Anthropological Survey of India, Mumbai.

Blumhardt, J.F. 1886 Catalogue of Bengali printed books in the Library of the British Museum. British Museum, London. pp. ix, 150.

Blumhardt, J.F. 1889 Preface to the Catalogue of Hindustani printed books in the Library of the British Museum. British Museum, London. pp. v - vi.

[Book review] 1887 Book notices : Catalogue of Bengali printed books in the Library of the British Museum; by J.F. Blumhardt. ***Indian Antiquary: A Journal of Oriental Research***. Vol. 16 : pp. 227-8. (Reprinted by Swati Pub., Delhi, 1984).

Bulsara, Jal F. 1969 The Parsis. ***Illustrated Weekly of India***. Vol. 90 (35): pp. 9 - 11.

Census of India 1981 National Informatics Centre terminal at Hyderabad. (Unpublished).

Census of India 1991 1995 Paper 1 of 1995 (Series 1 : India). Controller of Publications, Delhi. pp. xii-xxi; 55.

Chand, Mahendra Pratap 1971 Muslim names and their rendering in cataloguing. ***Indian Librarian***. Vol. 26(2) : pp. 95-9.

Chopra, S.K. 1971a Khatris of North India. ***Illustrated Weekly of India***. Vol. 92(14) : pp. 6 - 11.

Chopra, S.K. 1971b Stories behind Khatri names. ***Illustrated Weekly of India***. Vol. 92 (14) : p. 13.

Dave, Shanti Lal 1977 Problems in rendering of Indic names. Master's degree in Library Science dissertation submitted in Panjab University, Chandigarh. (Unpublished).

Dayal, Chandravati 1971 The Kayasthas. ***Illustrated Weekly of India***. Vol. 92 (24) : pp. 6-9.

Dhongde, R.V. 1994 Personal names in Marathi. pp. 86-107. In the book of Indian names (ed. by Raja Ram Mehrotra). Rupa and Co., New Delhi.

Dogra, R.C. 1973 Cataloguing Urdu names. ***International Library Review***. Vol. 5 (3): pp. 351 - 77.

Dogra, R.C. 1976 Notes on Hindi names. ***International Library Review***. Vol. 8(3) : pp. 327 - 47.

Fazal Elahi, et. al. 1961 Cataloguing of Oriental names. ***Quarterly Jour nal of the Pakistan Library Association.*** Vol. 2 (1) : pp. 5-16.

Gauba, Gopi 1969a Sindhis. ***Illustrated Weekly of India***. Vol. 90 (41) : pp. 9 - 13.

Gauba, Gopi 1969b What's in a [Sindhi] name ? ***Illustrated Weekly of India***. Vol. 90 (41) : p. 13.

Ghatak, Sanchita 1993a Bhutia. pp. 23 - 31. ***In*** Sikkim (People of India. Vol. 39.). Seagll Books and Anthropological Survey of India, Calcutta.

Ghatak, Sanchita 1993b Damai. pp. 57-62. ***In*** Sikkim (People of India. Vol. 39) (ed. by K.S. Singh). Seagull Books and Anthropological Survey of India, Calcutta.

Ghatak, Sanchita 1993c Lepcha. pp. 89 - 103. ***In*** Sikkim (People of India. Vol. 39) (ed. by K.S. Singh). Seagull Books and Anthropological Survey of India, Calcutta.

Ghosal, Samit 1993a Chhettri. pp. 50 - 62. ***In*** Sikkim (People of India. Vol. 39) (ed. by K.S. Singh). Seagull Books and Anthropological Survey of India, Calcutta.

Ghosal, Samit 1993b Limbu. pp. 104 - 11. ***In*** Sikkim (People of India. Vol. 39) (ed. by. K.S. Singh). Seagull Books and Anthropological Survey of India, Calcutta.

Gill, M.S. 1969 What is in a Sardarji's name ?. ***Illustrated Weekly of India***. Vol. 90 (47) : p. 51.

Girja Kumar and Krishan Kumar 1982 Theory of cataloguing. 4th ed. Vikas Pub., New Delhi. pp. 237-51.

Goil, N.K. 1969 Choice of heading and problems in rendering the Indian Hindu names of personal authors. ***Library Herald***. Vol. 11 (1-2) : pp. 112-21.

Gopala Sarana 1994 Forward. pp. 7-10. In Marriage and kinship among Muslims in South India (by C.G. Hussain Khan). Rawat Pub., Jaipur.

Gupta, A.S.N. 1993 Mana intiperla loni rahasyam. (The secracy of sur names). ***Swathi.*** Vol. 37(9) : p. 20. (In Telugu)

Gupta, Kamleshwar Nath, and Mohammed Haroon 1986 Application of Ranganathan's Canons of Cataloguing to Indian Muslim names. pp. 363 - 81. ***In*** Ranganathan's philosophy, assessment, impact and relevance (ed. by T.S. Rajagopalan). Vikas, Delhi.

Gupta, S.K. et. al. 1975 Indic names and computers. ***Annals of Library Science and Documentation.*** Vol. 22 (2) : pp. 78 - 86.

Haas, Ernst 1876 Preface to the "Catalogue of Sanskrit and Pali Books." British Museum, London. pp. iii- vii. ***Quoted in*** Ranganathan, S.R. and Sivaraman, K.M. Rendering of Hindu names in heading : Function vs position. ***Modern Librarian.*** Vol. 10 (2) : 1940: pp. 66-7. (Original not seen)

Hingwe, K.S. 1961 Standardization of Maharashtrian surnames. pp. 63-71. ***In*** Indic names including proceedings of the Seminar on the Rendering of Indic Names. (IASLIC Special Publications. no. 2) IASLIC, Calcutta.

Howarth, Lyne C., comp. 1994 AACR 2 : Decisions rule interpretations. 6th ed. Ontario, Canadian Library Association. Chapter 22 pp. 40-1.

Hussain Khan, C.G. 1994 Marriage and kinship among Muslims in South India. Jaipur, Rawat Publications. pp. 38-41.

IASLIC 1959 Announcement of holding the Third National IASLIC Conference on Indic Names during 23 - 25 January, 1960, at Calcutta. ***IASLIC Bulletin***. Vol. 4(4) : pp. 125 - 6.

IASLIC 1960 Symposium on the Rendering of Indic Names for the International Cataloguing Code. (Chairman: S.K. Mookerjee). Summary. ***IASLIC Bulletin***. Vol. 5 (1) : pp. 33 - 4.

IASLIC 1961a Indic names including proceedings of the Seminar on the Rendering of Indic Names, Calcutta, Dec. 30, 1960 - Jan. 1, 1961. (IASLIC Special Publications. no. 2). IASLIC, Calcutta. pp. 9 - 21.

IASLIC 1961b Schedule of anglicized Maharastrian surnames. pp. 151-61. ***In*** Indic names including proceedings of the Seminar on the Rendering of Indic Names. (IASLIC Special Publicatrion. no. 2). IASLIC, Calcutta.

IASLIC 1961c Seminar on Indic Names. Resolutions. pp. 22-3. ***In*** Indic names including proceedings of the Seminar on the Rendering of indic Names (IASLIC Special Publications. no. 2). IASLIC, Calcutta.

IASLIC 1961d Variant Romanised spellings of entry words (last names) of Hindu personal names (with suggested standardized forms) : As passed in the Special Committee meeting on 16.04. 61. pp. 122 - 50. ***In*** Indic names including proceedings of the Seminar on the Rendering of Indic Names (IASLIC Special Publications. no. 2). IASLIC, Calcutta.

Ibbetson, Denzil 1916 Panjab castes : Races, castes and tribes of the people of Panjab. Reprinted by Cosmo Pub., New Delhi. 1981. pp. 118-26; 208; 247-53.

Indian Library Association 1963 [Review article] : IFLA, International Conference on Cataloguing Principles. ***Journal*** (Indian Library Association). Vol. 5 (1-3) : pp. 12-9.

IFLA 1963 International Conference on Cataloguing Principles, Paris,

Oct. 9-18, 1961. Report. Reprinted by Clive Bingley, London, 1969. pp. 1-119.

INFA 1972; 1982; and 1992. India's who's who 1972, 1982, and 1992. Infa Pub., New Delhi.

IS : 790 - 1987 Indian standard : Guidelines for preliminary pages of a book (First revision). Bureau of Indian Standards, New Delhi.

Jain, Mahendra Raja 1969 A critical study of the rules for entry of Hindi names in major existing codes. ***Libri***. Vol. 19 (1) : pp. 17 - 51.

Jain, Mahendra Raja 1972 Hindi names. Libri. Vol. 22 (3) : pp. 200 - 26.

Jain, Mahendra Raja 1982 Further notes on Hindi names. ***Herald of Library Science***. Vol. 21 (1-2) : pp. 15-30.

Jamil Ahmed and Sengupta, B. 1961 Muslim names in India. pp. 94 - 102. ***In*** Indic names including proceedings of the Seminar on the Rendering of Indic Names. (IASLIC Special Publication. no. 2). IASLIC, Calcutta.

Jayaraman, R. 1989 Towards a sociological understanding of Hindu personal names and surnames. ***Journal of Library and Information Science.*** Vol. 14 (2): pp. 115 - 27.

Justin, A. 1994 Nicobarese. pp. 131 - 55. ***In*** Andaman and Nicobar Islands (People of India. Vol. 12) (ed. by K.S. Singh). Affiliated East-West Press and Anthropological Survey of India, Chennai.

Kalb, Bernard 1962 In an Asian name. ***New York Times Magazine,*** Jan 7: pp. 41, 43.

Kanga, Bachi M. 1969 Ear plug, ear plug, here cometh the Parsi! ***Illustrated Weekly of India***. Vol. 90 (35) : pp. 18 - 9.

Karnow, Stanley 1966 The Asian name game. ***Saturday Review***, May 7: p. 84.

Kaul, R.K. 1970 Kashmiri names. ***Herald of Library Science***. Vol. 9 (4): pp. 294 - 308.

Kaul, R.K. 1980 Indic names (A documentation list). Seemant Prakashan, Delhi. pp. 15-32; 69-104.

Kaula, P.N. 1962 International Conference on Cataloguing Principles. ***Herald of Library Science.*** Vol. 1(1) : pp. 32-4.

Kaula, P.N. 1977 Cataloguing of books in Urdu language. ***Herald of Library Science***. Vol. 16 (1) : pp. 25 - 31.

Kaushik, Devendra Kumar 1986 Indic names in AACR II. M.S. dissertation submitted to the Florida State Universsity, Tallahassee (USA).(Unpublished)

Kesavan, B.S. 1961 Resume of the address of the President of the Semi nar on Indic Names. p. 7. *In* Indic names including proceedings of the Seminar on the Rendering of Indic Names. (IASLIC Special Publication. no. 2). IASLIC, Calcutta.

Ketkar, Shridhar Venkatesh 1924 Aadnave. pp. 86-8. *In* Maharashtrian giankosh. Vol. 7. Maharashtrian Giankoshmandal Ltd., Nagpur. (In Marathi).

Khan, Mazhar Bari 1969 From the cataloguer's point of view : A short note on Hindu Bengali names. ***Eastern Librarian***. Vol. 3 (3) : pp. 49-51.

Khan, Muzaffar A. 1994 Nomenclature of Kashmiri. pp. 3 - 13. *In* the book of Indian names (ed. by Raja Ram Mehrotra). Rupa and Co., New Delhi.

Koul, Anand 1924 Kashmiri Pandits. Reprinted by Utpal Pub, Delhi, 1991. p. 20.

Koul, Onkar N. 1994 Surnames and nick names in Kashmiri. pp. 14-22. *In* the book of Indian names (ed. by Raja Ram Mehrotra). Rupa and Co., New Delhi.

Krishan Kumar 1993 Cataloguing. Har-Anand, New Delhi. pp. 209-23.

Lakshmi, G.R. 1996 Mughal. pp. 485-9. *In* Delhi (People of India. Vol. 20) (ed. by K.S. Singh). Manohar Pub. and Anthropological Survey of India, Delhi.

Lambert, Claire M. 1969 Library provision for Indian and Pakistani communities in Britain. ***Journal of Librarianship.*** Vol. 1 (1) pp. 41-61.

Madhuri Devi, Th. 1993 Study of the peculiarities of the names of the North-East region of India for cataloguing. Ph.D. thesis submitted to the Manipur University. (Unpublished).

Mangla, Pramod B. 1966 Punjabi names : An analysis and their render ing. ***Herald of Library Science.*** Vol. 5 (2): pp. 121-9.

Mehrotra, R.R. 1979 Name change in Hindi : Some sociocultural dimensions. ***Anthropological Linguistics.*** Vol. 21 (4) : pp. 205 -10.

Mehrotra, R.R. 1982 Personal names in Hindi. pp. 816 - 8. *In*

Proceedings of the 13th International Congress of Linguists, Tokyo, 1982. Proceedings Publishing Committee, Tokya, 1983.

Mehrotra, Raja Ram, ed. 1994 The book of Indian names. Rupa and Co., New Delhi.

Mishra, Mannilal 1949 Kankubja vanshavali. Srikrishna Pustakalaya, Mumbai. p. 12. (In Hindi).

Mistry, P. J. 1994 Personal names: Their structure, variation and grammar in Gujarati. pp. 63 - 85. ***In*** the book of Indian names (ed. by Raja Ram Mehrotra). Rupa and Co., New Delhi.

Mitra, Subodh 1961 Address to the IASLIC Seminar on Indic Names.p. 6. ***In*** Indic names including proceedings of the Seminar on the Rendering of Indic Names. (IASLIC Special Publications. no. 2). IASLIC, Calcutta.

Mittal, R.L. and Gupta, Shamsher 1966 Dictionary catalogue : A practi cal manual. Metropolitan Book, Delhi. pp. 80-113.

Mohammed Haroon 1984 Cataloguing of Indian Muslim names. Indian Bibliographies Bureau, Delhi. pp. 7-34.

Mookerjee, B.P. and Neogi, Dipika 1994 Paris principles : Some questions answered. ***Eastern Librarian.*** Vol. 19(1-2) : pp. 15- 26.

Mookerjee, S. 1959 Bengalee surnames. ***Annals of Library Science and Documentation.*** Vol. 6(3) : pp. 81-91.

Moquitul Hasan, Sayyid 1961 A note on the system of transliteration for Arabic, Persian and Urdu words. ***IASLIC Bulletin.*** Vol. 6(1) : pp. 46-8.

Mrigeppa, A. 1994 Personal names of Karnataka. pp. 161-70. ***In*** the book of Indian names (ed. by Raja Ram Mehrotra). Rupa and Co., New Delhi.

Mukerjee, S. 1957 Problems of surnames in India. ***ISI Convention Papers,*** Chennai. Doc DB 6 : pp. 1 - 4. (Unpublished).

Naidu, T.S. 1994 Maraikayar. pp. 261-4. In Pondicherry (People of India. Vol. 36) (ed. by K.S. Singh). Affiliated East-West Press and Anthropological Survey of India, Chennai.

Nanda, B. and Datta, N. 1975-79 Cataloguing problems and their solu tions: A survey of Delhi University Library practices. ***Library Herald.*** Vol. 17 (1-4) : pp. 181-95.

Nasreen Akhtar 1989 Indexing Asian names. ***Indexer***. Vol. 16 (3) : p.156-8.

Notes and News 1952 Unesco Project on Asian Names. ***Bulletin*** (Indian Library Association). Vol. 2(3) : p. B231.

Pachouri, Priti 1996 Musalman Rajput. pp. 496-501. ***In*** Delhi (People of India. Vol. 20) (ed. by K.S. Singh). Manohar Pub. and Anthropological Survey of India, Delhi.

Pal, A.C. and Das, B.N. 1988 About transliteration : Some problems on Indic names. (Unpublished).

Parthasarathy, S. 1959 Persian names. ***Annals of Library Science and Documentation***. Vol. 6(2): pp. 63 - 4.

Parthasarathy, Vengal 1997 The name of the game. ***Hindu*** - Saturday supplement: Young World. May 31, 1997: p. I.

Patil, Vimla [Prabhakar] 1970 a Common surnames [of Saraswats]. ***Il lustrated Weekly of India.*** Vol. 91(25): p. 8.

Patil, Vimla [Prabhakar] 1970b Saraswats. ***Illustrated Weekly of India.*** Vol. 91(25) : pp. 6-12.

Patnaik, B.N. 1994 Some observations on the personal names in Oriya. pp. 118-30. ***In*** the book of Indian names (ed. by Raja Ram Mehrotra). Rupa and Co., New Delhi.

Pearson, J.D. 1966 Oriental and Asian bibliography : An introduction with some reference to Africa. Cross Lockwood and Sons, London. pp. 231-2.

Pearson, J.D. 1978 Languages of Asia, with special reference to the Islamic world. Indexer. Vol. 11 (2) : pp. 63-7

Periera, Braganca 1940 Etnographia da India Portuguesa. pp. 247- 65. Chapter II. Tr. into English. ***In*** Goa (People of India. Vol. 21) ed. by K.S. Singh). Popular Prakashan and Anthroplogical Survey of India, Mumbai.

Piggott, Mary 1990 The classifier's way through AACR 2 : From document receipt to document retrieval. The Library Association, London. pp. 86-7.

Poindron, Paul 1961 Preparation for the International Conference on the Principles of Cataloguing, Paris, 1961. Tr. and abr. from French by Richard H. Shoemaker. ***Library Resources and Technical Services.*** Vol. 5 (3) : pp. 225-37.

Puranik, K.D. and Phadnis, S.P. 1957 Where are you in the list - chaos in the arangement of names. ***ISI Convention Papers,*** Chennai: Doc. DB 2 : pp. 1 - 8. (Unpublished).

Puranik, K.D. and Phadnis, S.P. 1958-59 Chaos in the arrangement of Indian names. ***Library Herald***. Vol. 1(2) : pp. 78-85.

Raghunath, S. 1996 The game of changing names. ***Deccan Chronicle*** (Hyderabad) Sept. 13 : p. 16.

Rait, S.K. 1981 Cataloguing and transliteration of Indic literature. South Asia ***Library Group Newsletter*** (17) : Jan : pp. 7-9.

Rait, S.K. 1983a Cataloguing Punjabi Muslim names in British public libraries. ***International Library Review***. Vol. 15 (1) : pp. 105-13.

Rait, S.K. 1983b Indic languages provision in British public libraries. ***Library Association Records***. Vol. 85 (1) : pp. 21, 23.

Rait, S.K. 1984 Asian languages services in Bradford libraries. ***Commu nity Services Group Newsletter*** (6) : May : pp. 5-7.

Rajasekharan Nair, N. 1994 Personal names in Malayalam. pp. 171-80. ***In*** the book of Indian names (ed. by Raja Ram Mehrotra).Rupa and Co., New Delhi.

Randhawa, Indira 1969 Caste system amongst the Sikhs. ***Illustrated Weekly of India***. Vol. 90(47) : pp. 27.

Ranganathan, S.R. 1938 Theory of library catalogue. (Madras Library Association. Publication Series no.7). Madras Library Association, Chennai. pp. 287; 295-7.

Ranganathan, S.R. 1950 Library catalogue : Fundamentals and procedure. (Madras Library Association. Publication Series no. 15). Madras Library Association, Chennai. pp. 72-8.

Ranganathan, S.R. 1952 Bibliographical and documentation services : Some first steps in Asia. ***Annals*** (Indian Library Association). Vol 2(5) : pp. 109 - 36.

Ranganathan, S.R. 1953a. Asian names. ***Annals*** (Indian Library Associa -tion). Vol. 3 (2) : pp. 45-54.

Ranganathan, S.R. 1953b International catalogue code : Its scopeand the first steps. ***Annals*** (Indian Library Association). Vol.3 (3) : pp. 141 -58.

Ranganathan, S.R. 1953c Standardization of rules for rendering of Asian names in bibliographical and catalogue entries. ***Bibliographical Newsletter*** (Unesco Library Division). Vol. 2 : pp. 9 - 11.

Ranganathan, S.R. 1954a Authorial homonym and synonym. ***Annals of Library Science and Documentation***. Vol. 1 (3) : pp. 174-84.

Ranganathan, S.R. 1954b Standard practice for specifying author's name (personal author). ***ISI Bulletin***. Vol. 9 (4) : pp. 120-5.

Ranganathan, S.R. 1954c Tow for author-heading. ***Libri***. Vol. 5 (2): pp. 122-41.

Ranganathan, S.R. 1955a Headings and canons : A comparative study of five catalogue codes. S.Viswanatha, Chennai. pp. 156-7.

Ranganathan, S.R. 1955b Third International Congress of Libraries and Documentation Centres. ***ISI Bulletin***. Vol. 7 (6) : pp. 181-2.

Ranganathan, S.R. 1957a Preliminary pages of a book - need for an international standard. ***ISI Bulletin***. Vol 9 (2) : pp. 72-3.

Ranganathan, S.R. 1957b Standard for author-statement on the title-leaf of a book - what, why, and how ? ***ISI Convention Papers***, Chennài, Doc. DA 2 : p. 1-4. (Unpublished).

Ranganathan, S.R. 1959a International catalogue code. ***Annals of Library Science and Documentation***. Vol. 6 (1) : pp. 13-20.

Ranganathan, S.R. 1959b Name of person. ***Annals of Library Science and Documentation***. Vol. 6(3) : pp. 77-80.

Ranganathan, S.R. 1960 Name of person heading : Recommendations or the International Conference on Cataloguing, 1961(Cataloguing problem 2). ***Annals of Library Science and Documention***. Vol. 7 (2) : pp. 33 -46.

Ranganathan, S.R. 1961 International Conference on Cataloguing 1961. ***Annals of Library Science and Documentation***. Vol. 8 (1) : pp. 19-25.

Ranganathan, S.R. 1962a International Conference on Cataloguing Principles, Paris, 9th - 18th October 1961 and its findings. ***Annals of Library Science and Documentatin***. Vol. 9 (1) : pp. 15-38.

Ranganathan, S.R. 1962b Name-of-person heading for books of tomorrow. ***Herald of Library Science***. Vol. 1(3) : pp. 103-9.

Ranganathan, S. R. 1964 Classified catalogue code with additional rules for dictionary catalogue code. 5th ed. Asia Pubishing House, Mumbai. pp. 205-45.

Ranganathan, S.R. 1969a Name-of-Person heading for books of tomorrow. ***Herald of Library Science***. Vol. 8 (1) : pp. 20-5.

Ranganathan, S.R. 1969b Recall value and entry word in heading. ***Library Science with a slant to Documentation***. Vol 6 (4) : pp. 289-306.

Ranganathan, S.R. 1971 Simplified rules for the cataloguing of books of tomorrow in a service library. ***Library Science with a slant to Documentation***. Vol. 8(2) : pp. 161-71.

Ranganathan, S.R. and Sivaraman, K.M. 1940 Rendering of Hindu names in headings : Function vs position. ***Modern Librarian***. Vol. 10 (2): pp. 63-75.

Rangra, V.K. 1977 Name pattern of Indian musicians and choice of entry element. ***Library Science with a slant to Documentation***. Vol. 14 (3-4) : pp. 124-8.

Ranjit Daniels, R.J. 1996 The vanishing aborigines of the Andaman and Nicobar islands. ***Current Science***. Vol 70 (9): pp. 775-6.

Rao, K.R. 1961 Indic family names, caste names or surnames. pp. 80-2. ***In*** Indic names including proceedings of the Seminar on the Rendering of Indic Names (IASLIC Special Publications. no. 2). IASLIC, Calcutta.

Rao, K.R. 1993a Catholic carpenter/Thopvoi. pp. 16-22. ***In*** Goa (People of India. Vol. 21) (ed. by K.S. Singh). Popular Prakashan and Anthroplogical Survey of India, Mumbai.

Rao, K.R 1993b. Catholic Kharvi. pp. 29 - 35. ***In*** Goa (People of India. Vol. 21) (ed. by K.S. Singh). Popular Prakashan and Anthropological Survey of India, Mumbai.

Rao, K.R., 1993c Catholic Mandool/Dhobi. pp. 36-41. ***In*** Goa (People of India. Vol. 21) (ed by K.S. Singh). Popular Prakashan and Anthropological Survey of India, Mumbai.

Rifaquat Ali, S. 1970a Kashmir Pandits. ***Illustrated Weekly of India***. Vol. 91 (14) : pp. 6 - 11.

Rifaquat Ali, S. 1970b Their [Kashmiri Pandits] surnames. ***Illustrated Weekly of India***. Vol. 91 (14) : p. 8.

Saha, J. et. al., comp. 1961 Indic names and catalogue code : An annotated bibliography. pp. 103 - 15. ***In*** Indic names including proceedings of the Seminar on the Indic names (IASLIC Special Pubications. no. 2). IASLIC, Calcutta.

Saif-ul-Islam, K.M. 1980 Cataloguing Bengali Muslim names : Problems and possible solutions. ***Unesco Journal of Information Science, Librarianship and Archives Administration***. Vol. 2 (1) : pp. 35-41.

Sankhyan, A.R. 1996 Introduction. pp. 1-22. ***In*** Himachal Pradesh (People of India. Vol. 24) (ed. by K.S. Singh). Manohar Pub. and Anthropological Survey of India Manohar, New Delhi.

Sarkar, D.C. 1963 Rendering of Indic names of person for catalogue entry and shelf arrangement : A neglected aspect. ***IASLIC Bulletin***. Vol. 8 (3) : p. 116 - 25.

Sarkar, J.K. 1994 Locals. pp. 95-105. ***In*** Andaman and Nicobar (People of India. Vol. 12) (ed. by K.S. Singh). Affiliated East- West Press and Anthrological Survey of India, Chennai.

Saxena, Indira 1971 Their [Kayasthas] surnames. ***Illustrated Weekly of India***. Vol. 92 (24) : p. 9.

Saxena, R.S. 1952 U.P. names in cataloguing. ***Annals*** (Indian Library Association). Vol. 2 (5) : pp. 137 - 9.

Sen, T. 1961 Inaugural address to the IASLIC Seminar on Indic names. pp. 3-5. ***In*** Indic names including proceedings on the Seminar on the Rendering of Indic Names (IASLIC. Special Publications. no. 2). IASLIC, Calcutta.

Senapati, Nilamani and Sahu, Nabin, ed. 1968 Orissa gazetteer : Balangir. Orissa Government Press, Cuttack. p. 99.

Sengupta, Benoyendra 1952 Asiatic personal author's names and the problem of their standardisation. ***Indian Librarian***. Vol. 7(2) : pp. 39 - 47.

Sengupta, Benoyendra 1958 Rendering of Indic names in catalogue en -tries. ***Indian Librarian***. Vol. 13 (3) : pp. 93-106.

Sengupta, Binoyendra 1959a Certain suggestions and rules for rendering Indic names in catalogue entries. ***Indian Librarian***. Vol. 13(4) : pp. 133-9.

Sengupta, Benoyendra 1959b Indic names in westernised form : Problems and suggested solutions. ***IASLIC Bulletin***. Vol. 4 (2) : p. 57-63.

Sengupta, Benoyendra 1959c Indic names of person in works in Roman alphabets - problems of their standardization. ***IASLIC Bulletin***. Vol. 4 (4) : pp. 127-54.

Sengupta, Benoyendra 1959d Rendering of Hindu and Muslim names in catalogue entries. ***Indian Librarian***. Vol. 14 (2): pp. 57-63.

Sengupta, Benoyendra 1960a The scope and outline of the working papers for the Seminar on Indic Names. ***IASLIC Bulletin***. Vol. 5 (3): pp. 117-23.

Sengupta, Benoy[endra] 1960b Towards a national cataloguing code for India. ***Journal*** (Indian Library Association). Vol. 2(4) : pp. 7-12.

Sengupta, Benoyendra 1961 Rendering of Indic names of person in catalogue entries. pp. 33-62. ***In*** Indic names including proceedings of the Seminar on the Rendering of Indic Names (IASLIC Special Publications no. 2). IASLIC, Calcutta.

Sengupta, Benoyendra 1963 Rendering of Indic names-of-person in catalogue entries. pp. 255-65. ***In*** International Conference on Cataloguing Principles organised by IFLA, Paris, Oct. 9-18, 1961. Reprinted by Clive Bingley, London, 1969.

Sengupta, Benoyendra 1968 Review article : Anglo - American Cataloguing Rules. ***Indian Librarian***. Vol. 23(1) : pp. 61-4.

Sengupta, Benoyendra 1974a Cataloguing : Its theory and practice. 3rd ed. Calcutta, World Press. pp. 271-86.

Sengupta, Benoyendra 1974b Indic names; a background study. pp. 377-92. ***In*** Cataloguing : Its theory and practice. 3rd ed. (by Benoyendra Sengupta). World Press, Calcutta.

Server Hossain 1980-81 Cataloguing problems in Bangladesh. ***Library Herald***. Vol. 19 (3-4): pp. 130 - 3

Sharify, Nasser 1960 Cataloguing of Persian works - Iranian personal names : their characteristics and usage. ***Unesco Bulletin for Libraries***. Vol. 14 : pp. 205-9; 232.

Sharma, C.D. 1973 Classified Catalogue Code in theory and Practice. Metropolitan Book, Delhi. pp. 20-30.

Shashi, S.S. 1971 Himachal - nature's peaceful paradise. Indian School Supply Department, Delhi. pp. 131-2

Shashi, S.S. 1995 Tribes of Andhra Pradesh. Anmol Pub., New Delhi. p.207.

Shirodkar, P.P., et. al. 1993 Introduction. pp. xix - xxviii. ***In*** Goa (People of India. Vol. 21) (ed. by K.S. Singh). Popular Prakashan and Anthropological Survey of India, Mumbai.

Shukla, C.P. 1961a Cataloguing problems of Indic names (A commentary on the resolutions of the Seminar on Indic Names). pp. 24 - 32. ***In*** Indic names including proceedings of the Seminar on the Rendering of Indic Names (IASLIC Special Publications. no. 2). IASLIC, Calcutta.

Shukla, C.P. 1961b Resume of the speech by the Director of the of the Seminar on Indic Names. p. 8. ***In*** Indic names including proceedings of the Seminar on the Rendering of the Indic Names (IASLIC Special Publications no. 2). IASLIC, Calcutta.

Singh, K.S., ed. 1993a Goa. (People of India. Vol 21). Popular Prakashan and Anthropological Survey of India, Mumbai. pp. vii - xi.

Singh, K.S., ed. 1993b Lakshadweep. (People of India. Vol. 28). Affiliated East - West Press and Anthropological Survey of India, Chennai, pp. xiii - xxii; 1-62.

Singh, K.S., ed. 1993c Sikkim. (People of India. Vol. 39). Seagull Books and Anthropological Survey of India, Calcutta. pp. 1- 22.

Singh, K.S. ed. 1994a Andaman and Nicobar Islands. (People of India. Vol. 12). Affiliated East - West Press and Anthropological Survey of India, Chennai. pp. 1-29.

Singh, K.S. ed. 1994b Dadra and Nagar Haveli. (People of India. Vol. 18). Popular Prakashan and Anthropological Survey of India, Mumbai.

Singh, K.S. ed. 1994c Daman and Diu. (People of India. Vol. 19). Popular Prakashan and Anthroplogical Survey of India, Mumbai.pp. 1-19.

Singh, K.S., ed. 1994d Pondicherry. (People of India. Vol. 36). Affiliated East-West Press and Anthropological Survey of India, Chennai. pp 1-69.

Singh, K.S., ed. 1994e Scheduled castes. (People of India. National Series. II). Oxford University Press and Anthropological Survey of India, New Delhi. pp. 1-14; 329.

Singh, K.S., ed. 1994f Scheduled tribes. (People of India. National Series. Vol. III). Oxford University Press and Anthropological Survey of India, New Delhi. p. 339.

Singh, K.S. ed. 1996a Communities, segments, synonyms, surnames and titles. (People of India. National Series. Vol. VIII). Oxford University Press and Anthropological Survry of India, New Delhi. pp. 1-34; 1369; 1412; 1558.

Singh, K. S., ed. 1996b. Delhi (People of India. Vol. 20). Manohar Pub. and Anthropological Survey of India, Delhi. pp. xiii - xxvi.

Singh, K.S. ed. 1996c Himachal Pradesh. (People of India. Vol. 24). Manohar Pub. and Anthropological Survey of India, Delhi.

Sinha, N.K. 1994a Khoja. pp. 93-8. ***In*** Daman and Diu. (People of India. Vol. 18) (ed. by K.S. Singh). Popular Prakashan and Anthropological Survey of India, Mumbai.

Sinha, N.K. 1994b Momin. pp. 145-9. ***In*** Daman and Diu (People of India. Vol. 18 (ed. by K.S. Singh). Popular Prakashan and Anthropological Survey of India, Mumbai.

Sinha, N.K. 1994c Parsi. pp. 93-7. ***In*** Dadara and Nagar Haveli (People of India. Vol. 18). Popular Prakashan and Anthropological Survey of India, Mumbai.

Sinha, N.K. 1994d Siddi. pp. 168-73. ***In*** Daman and Diu (People of India. Vol 18) (ed. by K.S. Singh). Popular Prakashan and Anthropological Survey of India, Mumbai.

Sircar, Arjya 1994 Personal names in Bengali : A selective indexing. pp. 108-17. ***In*** the book of Indian names (ed. by Raja Ram Mehrotra). Rupa and Co., New Delhi.

Sivaraman, K.M. 1940 Standards in cataloguing. (Memoirs, Madras Li -brary Association, 1940). Madras Library Association, Chennai. pp. 98 - 112.

Sjoberg, Andree F. 1994 Telugu personal names : A structural analysis. pp. 147-60. *In* the book of Indian names (ed. by Raja Ram Mehrotra). Rupa and Co., New Delhi.

Smith, Elsdon C. 1950 The story of our names. Harper & Brothers, New York. pp. 157-9.

Soni, Ramgopal 1992 Marathi aadnave. Manohar Katha Prakashan, Nagpur. pp. 5-9 + 1-172 (In Marathi).

Sreedhara Menon, A. 1979 A social and cultural history of Kerala. Ster -ling, New Delhi. pp. 103-4.

Srinivas, M.N. 1966 Social change in modern India. Reprinted by Orient Longman, Hyderabad, 1992. pp. 1-88.

Srinivasachar, S. 1970a Ayyangars. ***Illustrated Weekly of India***. Vol.91(37): pp. 8-14.

Srinivasachar, S. 1970b Ayyangar names. ***Illustrated Weekly of India***. Vol. 91(37) : p. 15.

Srivastava, Anurag and Rajaraman, V. 1991 Computer recognition of Sanskrit-based Indian names. ***IEEE Transations on Systems, Man and Cybernetics***. Vol. 21 (1) : pp. 287 - 90.

Subhadra Krishnamurthy 1983 Oh, those South Indian names. ***Reader's Digest***. Vol. 123(738): Oct. 1983: pp. 150-1.

Subba Rao, C.V. 1961a Cataloguing Andhra authors : A study. pp. 83-93. ***In*** Indic names including proceedings of the Seminar on the Rendering of Indic Names.(IASLIC Special Publications. no. 2). IASLIC, Calcutta.

Subba Rao, C.V. 1961b A conspectus of international and national catalogue codes and Indian anthroponyms. ***IASLIC Bulletin***. Vol. 6(1) : pp. 34 - 45.

Subbakrishna 1994 Coorgi. pp. 59-63. ***In*** Andaman and Nicobar Islands (People of India. Vol. 12) (ed. by K.S. Singh). Affiliated East - West Press and Anthropological Survey of India, Madras.

Supner, D.N. 1993a Muslim (sunni). pp., 167-70. ***In*** Goa (People of India. Vol. 21) (ed by K.S. Singh). Popular Prakashan and Anthropological Survey of India, Mumbai.

Supner, D.N. 1993b Saraswat Brahmin. pp. 185-9. ***In*** Goa (People of India. Vol. 21) (ed. by K.S. Singh). Popular Prakashan and Anthropological Survey of India, Mumbai.

Tandan, V.K. 1993a Manikfan. pp. 83-90. ***In*** Lakshadweep (People of India. Vol. 28) (ed by K.S. Singh). Affiliated East-West Press and Anthropological Survey of India, Chennai.

Tandan, V.K. 1993b Raveri. pp. 104 -10. ***In*** Lakshadweep (People of India. Vol. 28) (ed. by K.S. Singh). Affiliated East-West Press and Anthropological Survey of India, Chennai.

Tandan, V.K. 1993c Thakru. pp. 97-103. ***In*** Lakshadweep (People of India. Vol. 28) (ed. K.S. Singh). Affiliated East-West Press and Anthropological Survey of India, Chennai.

Tandan, V.K. 1993d Thakrufan. pp. 91-6. *In* Lakshadweep (People of India. Vol. 28) (ed. by K.S. Singh). Affiliated East-West Press and Anthropological Survey of India, Chennai.

Trivadi, V.D. 1970b What's in a Ayyer name except milege ? ***Illustrated Weekly of India***. Vol. 91(4) : p. 13.

Uppal, Om Prakash 1975 Modern Hindu names. ***Herald of Library Science***, Vol. 14 (1) p. 94 - 8.

Viswanathan, C.G. 1965 Cataloguing : Theory and practice. Asia Pub., Mumbai. pp. 177-90.